Seminars in Alcohol and Drug Misuse

£12.50

College Seminars Series

Series Editors

Professor Hugh Freeman, Honorary Professor, University of Salford, and Honorary Consultant Psychiatrist, Salford Health Authority

Dr Ian Pullen, Consultant Psychiatrist, Royal Edinburgh Hospital

Dr George Stein, Consultant Psychiatrist, Farnborough Hospital, and King's College Hospital

Professor Greg Wilkinson, Editor, *British Journal of Psychiatry*, and Professor of Psychiatry, The London Hospital Medical College

Other books in the series

Seminars in Child and Adolescent Psychiatry. Edited by Dora Black & David Cottrell

Seminars in Basic Neurosciences. Edited by Gethin Morgan & Stuart Butler

Seminars in Psychology and Social Sciences. Edited by Digby Tantam & Max Birchwood

Seminars in Psychiatric Genetics. By Peter McGuffin, Michael J. Owen, Michael C. O'Donovan, Anita Thapar & Irving I. Gottesman

Forthcoming titles

Seminars in the Psychiatry of Learning Disabilities. Edited by Oliver Russell

Seminars in Adult Psychiatry. Edited by George Stein & Greg Wilkinson

Seminars in Forensic Psychiatry. Edited by Derek Chiswick & Rosemarie Cope

Seminars in Psychiatry for the Elderly. Edited by Brice Pitt & Mohsen Naguib

Seminars in Psychopharmacology. Edited by David King

The chain of habit

"But, in attempting to subtract the vinous potation by little and little, a difficulty arises which every one conversant with the subject must have observed. As soon as the limited portion of the liquor is swallowed, an agreeable glow is experienced; and by it so grateful a feeling is conveyed to the mind, which in an instant connects the chain of habit, that is our duty to break. This glow and feeling are associated in the patient's mind with all those pleasurable sensations he has been accustomed to receive from his former bumper. He therefore reasons with himself that he finds much relief; and as he is aware that the effect of the present dose will only be of short duration, he must take another to prolong his reverie, and ward off some intruding care."

The extract above is taken from Thomas Trotter's MD thesis on *The Nature of Inebriety*, submitted in 1788 to Edinburgh University; the frontispiece of the thesis is displayed overleaf (courtesy of Edinburgh University Library). Originally published in 1804, *An Essay, Medical, Philosophical and Chemical on Drunkenness and its effects on the Human Body* is available as a 1988 Routledge edition.

DISSERTATIO MEDICA

INAUGURALIS,

QUÆDAM DE

Ebrietate, ejufque Effectibus in Corpus Humanum complectens,

QUAM,

ANNUENTE SUMMO NUMINE,

Ex Auctoritate Reverendi admodum Viri,

D. GULIELMI ROBERTSON, S. S. T. P.

ACADEMIÆ EDINBURGENÆ Praefecti;

NEC NON

Ampliffimi SENATUS ACADEMICI confenfu,
Et nobiliffimae FACULTATIS MEDICÆ decreto,

PRO GRADU DOCTORIS,

SUMMISQUE IN MEDICINA HONORIBUS AC PRIVILEGIIS
RITE ET LEGITIME CONSEQUENDIS;

Eruditorum examini fubjicit

THOMAS TROTTER,

SCOTO-BRITANNUS,

Claffis Regiae Chirurgus,
Soc. Reg. Med. Edin. S.
Soc. Phyf. Americ. Soc. Honor.

———————*Dulce periculum eft,*
O Lenæe ! feque Deum
Cingentem viridi tempora pampino. HOR.

Ad diem 12. Septembris, hora locoque folitis.

EDINBURGI:

Apud BALFOUR et SMELLIE,
Academiae Typographos.

M,DCC,LXXXVIII.

Seminars in
Alcohol and Drug Misuse

Edited by
Jonathan Chick & Roch Cantwell

GASKELL

British Library Cataloguing in Publication Data

Seminars in Alcohol and Drug Misuse
(College Seminars Series)
  I. Chick, Jonathan II. Cantwell, Roch
  III. Series
  616.86

ISBN 0-902241-70-2

Distributed in North America
by American Psychiatric Press, Inc.
ISBN 0-88048-6333

Gaskell is an imprint of the Royal College of Psychiatrists,
17 Belgrave Square, London SW1X 8PG
(The Royal College of Psychiatrists is a registered charity, number 228636)

The views presented in this book do not necessarily reflect those of the Royal College of Psychiatrists, and the publishers are not responsible for any error of omission or fact. College Seminars are produced by the Publications Department of the College; they should in no way be construed as providing a syllabus or other material for any College examination.

Phototypeset by Dobbie Typesetting Limited, Tavistock, Devon
Printed by Bell & Bain Ltd, Glasgow

Contents

Contributors

Dr Roch Cantwell, Lecturer, Department of Psychiatry, University Hospital, Queen's Medical Centre, Nottingham NG7 2UH

Dr Jonathan Chick, Consultant Psychiatrist, Royal Edinburgh Hospital, 35 Morningside Park, Edinburgh EH10 5HD and Part-time Senior Lecturer, Department of Psychiatry, Edinburgh University

Dr Christopher Cook, Consultant Psychiatrist, Princess Alexandra Hospital, RAF Wroughton, Swindon, Wiltshire SN4 0QJ

Dr Timothy G. Dinan, Professor of Psychological Medicine, St Bartholomew's Hospital, London EC1A 7BE

Dr Michael Farrell, Consultant Psychiatrist, The Maudsley Hospital, Denmark Hill, London SE5 8AZ

Dr J. Spencer Madden, Consultant Psychiatrist, Mersey Regional Alcoholism and Drug Dependence Service, Countess of Chester Hospital, Liverpool Road, Chester CH2 1 BQ

Dr John Marks, Life Fellow, Girton College, Cambridge CB3 0JG

Dr Karen O'Flynn, Research Registrar, Department of Psychiatry, St James's Hospital, James's Street, P.O. Box 580, Dublin 8, Ireland

Dr Bruce Ritson. Consultant Psychiatrist, Alcohol Problems Clinic, Royal Edinburgh Hospital, Edinburgh EH10 5HD and Part-time Senior Lecturer, Department of Psychiatry, Edinburgh University

Professor Bill Saunders, Associate Professor, School of Psychology, Curtin University of Technology, Perth, Western Australia

Dr John Strang, Consultant Psychiatrist, Drug Dependence Clinical Research and Treatment Unit, Maudsley Hospital, Denmark Hill, London SE5 8AZ

Dr Sujata Unnithan, Senior Registrar, Maudsley Hospital and National Addiction Centre, Denmark Hill, London SE5 8AF

Foreword
Series Editors

The publication of *College Seminars*, a series of textbooks covering the breadth of psychiatry, represents a new venture for the Royal College of Psychiatrists. At the same time, it is very much in line with the College's established role in education and in setting professional standards.

College Seminars are intended to help junior doctors during their training years. We hope that trainees will find these books useful, on the ward as well as in preparation for the MRCPsych examination. Separate volumes will cover clinical psychiatry, each of its subspecialities, and also the relevant non-clinical academic disciplines of psychology and sociology.

College Seminars will also make a contribution to the continuing medical education of established clinicians.

Psychiatry is concerned primarily with people, and to a lesser extent with disease processes and pathology. The core of the subject is rich in ideas and schools of thought, and no single approach or solution can embrace the variety of problems a psychiatrist meets. For this reason, we have endeavoured to adopt an eclectic approach to practical management throughout the series.

The College can draw on the collective wisdom of many individuals in clinical and academic psychiatry. More than a hundred people have contributed to this series; this reflects how diverse and complex psychiatry has become.

Frequent new editions of books appearing in the series are envisaged, which should allow *College Seminars* to be responsive to readers' suggestions and needs.

Hugh Freeman
Ian Pullen
George Stein
Greg Wilkinson

Preface

Patients misusing alcohol and drugs form a substantial proportion of the patients seen in emergency and liaison psychiatry. Primary care health workers often seek psychiatric advice and assistance on how to help such patients and there is a continuing need for in-patient and/or specialist psychiatric care for some. All psychiatrists should know how to take a drug and alcohol history, and make it part of their routine practice. The psychiatric complications of alcohol and drug misuse must be recognised and treated confidently. We hope this book will help psychiatrists in training to understand what they hear, and to know how to offer help.

Epidemiology provides much aetiological understanding. However, it also has great importance for prevention, which more often depends on public health measures than modifying individual psychology, genes or biochemistry. For this reason, it seemed appropriate to present epidemiology with prevention. Some aetiological aspects have been less researched for drug misuse than alcohol misuse, for example, genetics. This is in part because drug misuse as a psychiatric disorder is a newer phenomenon, and even now presents less often to clinicians than alcohol misuse. Therefore in a book such as this, the amount of evidence to be discussed on alcohol is, for some topics, greater than for drugs.

Chapter 10, on medical aspects of alcohol and drug misuse, is mainly canonical rather than discursive. The aim has been to meet the needs of practising psychiatrists (refreshing and updating their undergraduate knowledge), not those of the physician, specialist, or researcher.

Grateful thanks for their advice are due to Dr Ray Brettle, Dr Shay Griffin, Dr Niall Finlayson, Dr Anne Tait, Dr Hugh Gurling, Dr M. Waters, Dr N. Hill, and the publisher's advisors who commented on the first draft.

Dr Jonathan Chick
Dr Roch Cantwell
February 1994

1 Dependence: concepts and definitions
Jonathan Chick and Roch Cantwell

---

*Definitions of dependence and misuse ● Elements of dependence ●
Degrees and dimensions ● Advantages and limitations of the
dependence concept*

Thirty years ago epidemiology, conducting surveys in the general population
of drinking and its hazards, dissected out what had been a rather conglomerate
concept, alcoholism. Since the term was coined by Magnus Huss in 1865
alcoholism had become weighed down with denigratory stereotypes and its
definition had remained fluid. Epidemiologists recommended that the amount
of drinking was to be assessed separately from the social, mental and physical
problems caused by the drinking (acute problems from heavy sessional intake
and cumulative problems from regular use). These in turn, were to be
distinguished from dependence – certain patterns of use, symptoms, and
attitudes capturing the relapsing, repetitive nature of some people's drug use
despite the risk or actual experience of harm. This approach has been applied
to substance misuse generally (Fig. 1.1). It is encapsulated in the latest
International Classification of Diseases (ICD-10; World Health Organization,
1992) and the *Diagnostic and Statistical Manual of Mental Disorders*, the
current edition of which is DSM-III-R (American Psychiatric Association, 1987)
with DSM-IV just published (American Psychiatric Association, 1994). These
two classifications are the most widely accepted internationally and are
important for international communication about advances in the subject.
However, in everyday life other definitions are used.

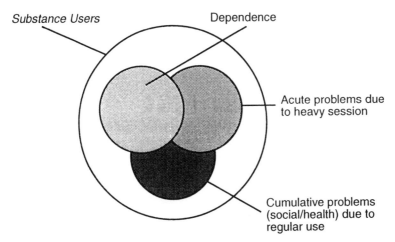

Fig. 1.1 Figurative relation of substance use to problems and dependence.

A workplace policy might for example read: "Employees with a substance misuse problem are those whose regular use, or intermittent use, of a substance repeatedly interferes with their ability to work, their relationships with colleagues or clients, or their job performance".

ICD-10 and DSM-III-R have converged in their definitions of psychotropic substance use disorders. ICD-10 is the more clearly influenced in its definition of dependence by the elements proposed as epitomising alcohol dependence by Edwards & Gross (1976). Table 1.1 shows the closeness of the two systems in their definitions for 'harmful use' (ICD-10) and 'abuse' (DSM-III-R), and demonstrates overlaps as well as some differences in their criteria for 'dependence'.

Table 1.1   Comparison of ICD-10 and DSM-III-R diagnostic criteria for psychoactive substance use disorder

	ICD-10	DSM-III-R
Substance misuse	Harmful use	Psychoactive substance abuse

	Substance misuse is responsible for causing actual damage to the mental or physical health of the user
	
	Acute intoxication or 'hangover' is not in itself sufficient (No duration specified)
	
	Not diagnosed if dependence syndrome present
		(1) A maladaptive pattern of substance use indicated by at least one of the following:
		   (a) continued use despite knowledge of having a persistent or recurrent social, occupational psychological or physical problem that is caused or exacerbated, or
		   (b) recurrent use in situations in which use is physically hazardous (e.g. driving while intoxicated)
		(2) Some symptoms of the disturbance have persisted for at least 1 month, or have occurred repeatedly over a longer period of time
		(3) Never met the criteria for alcohol dependence

Dependence	Dependence syndrome	Dependence
Criterion duration	Three or more of (a) to (f) have been experienced or exhibited at some time during the previous 12 months:	At least three of the following have persisted for at least one month, or have occurred repeatedly over a longer period of time:

(*continued*)

Table 1.1 (*continued*)

Dependence	Dependence syndrome	Dependence
Compulsion	(a) A strong desire or sense of compulsion to take the substance	
Impaired control	(b) Difficulties controlling substance-taking behaviour in terms of its onset, termination or levels of use	(1) Substance often taken in larger amounts or over longer period than the person intended (2) Persistent desire or one or more unsuccessful efforts to cut down or control substance use
Withdrawal	(c) A physiological withdrawal state;	(8) Characteristic withdrawal symptoms
Relief use	Substance use to relieve or avoid withdrawal symptoms	(9) Substance often taken to relieve or avoid withdrawal symptoms (may not apply to cannabis, hallucinogens or phencyclidine)
Tolerance	(d) Evidence of tolerance such that increased doses are required in order to achieve effects originally produced by lower doses	(7) Marked tolerance: need for markedly increased amounts of substance (i.e. at least 50% increase) in order to achieve intoxication or desired effect or markedly diminished effect with continued use of the same amount
Salience	(e) Progressive neglect of alternative pleasures or interests because of substance use, increased amount of time necessary to obtain or take the substance or to recover from its effects (f) Persisting with substance despite clear evidence of overtly harmful consequences. Narrowing of the personal repertoire of patterns of psychoactive substance use has also been described as a characteristic feature	(3) A great deal of time spent in activities necessary to get the substance, taking the substance or recovering from its effects (4) Frequent intoxications or withdrawal symptoms when expected to fulfil major role obligations, or when substance use is physically hazardous (5) Important social occupational or recreational activities given up or reduced because of substance use (6) Continued substance use despite knowledge of having a persistent or recurrent problem caused or exacerbated by the use

DSM-III-R has been shown by Cottler *et al* (1991) to be a slightly broader definition of dependence than ICD-10: some of the patients whose responses to the substance abuse module of the Composite International Diagnostic Interview (CIDI) placed them in DSM-III-R 'dependence', are placed by ICD-10 in 'harmful use'. This is mainly because DSM-III-R dependence allows some 'points' for problem items. When ICD-10 'dependence' and 'abuse' (harmful use) were combined, the instruments performed similarly although 11% of individuals were included as having a substance use disorder by one classification but not by the other. This study was conducted in several cultures and languages.

Proposed elements of dependence

This introductory chapter gives a description of the phenomena and conceptual pitfalls of the elements of dependence. Patterns of dependent use specific to various substances will be described in later chapters, together with the specific withdrawal symptoms. Table 1.2 sketches out the pattern of association between the common psychotropic agents and related harm and dependence. 'Psychological dependence' is a widely used term, covering the feelings of desire (craving) and compulsion, and the repetitiveness and intrusiveness of some drinking/drug using. The term 'physical' or 'chemical'

Table 1.2 Psychotropic substances: aspects of dependence and harm

Type	Dependence			Harm to health	
	'Psycho- logical dependence'	With- drawal syndrome	Toler- ance	Acute	Cumulative
Opiates	+++	+++	++	+/−	−
Cocaine	+++	?	?	+	+
Cannabis	+++	?	?	−	+
Amphetamines	+++	?+	++	+	++
Hallucinogens	++	?	+	+	?
Solvents	+	?	+	++	++
Barbiturates	++	++	++	+/−	?
Ethanol	++	++	++	+	++
Benzodiazepines	+	+	+/−	−	?
Tobacco	++	++	+	+/−	+++
Caffeine	+	+	+	?	?

?, still under investigation; −, no association; +/−, under certain circumstances or only in high dose; +, weak association; ++, moderate association; +++, strong association.

Regulation: Opiates to hallucinogens - International convention; Solvents to tobacco - Local control (variable). The restrictiveness of conventions/controls is not related to extent of health harm, and is influenced by social and market pressures.

dependence is used when discontinuing the drug results in a withdrawal syndrome. However, as there is ample evidence for psychological factors in the emergence of withdrawal symptoms and for a neuropharmacological substrate to drug-seeking behaviour, the use of these terms is at best a convenient shorthand.

Tolerance

We can envisage that the brain adapts to compensate for the presence of certain types of drug. However, not everyone, for example, who drinks alcohol regularly and 'can hold his drink' develops withdrawal symptoms if he stops. Research with animals also makes it clear that tolerance can be dissociated from the tendency to discontinuance (withdrawal) symptoms. In particular, intermittent presentation of the drug is less likely to lead to withdrawal symptoms than continuous administration. There may be more than one kind of nerve cell adaptation. To compensate for a depressant drug, for example, a nerve cell might maintain normal activity by becoming more excitable, which would result in a withdrawal syndrome, whereas another form of adaptation might be to decrease the potency of the drug by an opposing force, which would not lead to withdrawal hyperexcitability.

Practically speaking, however, tolerance for a drug greatly outside normal is an indicator that withdrawal symptoms will probably occur following discontinuation – for example, the patient who walks into the clinic straight and steady without slurring his words and whose breathalyser reading indicates a blood alcohol concentration (BAC) of 250 mg% (i.e. a very high tolerance) is very likely to be tremulous after 10 hours with no more alcohol, when his BAC will have fallen to about 100 mg%, and be vomiting and very sweaty 10 hours after that.

Regular benzodiazepine use is only rarely followed by tolerance with a tendency to increase the dose, although psychological dependence characterised by a sense of needing the drug and withdrawal symptoms, does occur. This is one of the important differences between benzodiazepines and barbiturates (see Table 1.2).

DSM-III-R, under 'tolerance', has kept in an item from older descriptions of alcoholism which is very complex: diminished tolerance. This represents several phenomena. The report by a drinker, or his relatives, is that now a mere fraction of the prodigious quantities previously consumed causes him to stagger and fall down. A breath test for BAC reveals that his small morning drink is actually on top of a considerable level accumulated over days of constant drinking and this has simply tipped the balance into visible intoxication. Or perhaps there has been a recent period of 3–4 weeks abstinence during which his tolerance reverted to normal but the drinking that he resumes is the quantity he was always in the habit of taking. In some older patients, brain damage means that neuroadaptation like other mental functions is curtailed and a true loss of behavioural tolerance occurs. It is only in very marked liver disease that reduced capacity to metabolise alcohol is the basis for diminished tolerance.

Reinstatement after abstinence

This concept, which neither definition attempts to include but was well described by Edwards & Gross (1976), touches on the nub of addictions – the repetitiveness of the behaviour despite accumulating harm. Withdrawal symptoms from the commonly abused substances subside in a few days once the patient abstains (although there is debate especially for benzodiazepines about whether there are some symptoms that go on for weeks – see Chapter 4). But once the drug is again taken (the 'priming dose'), patients describe and clinicians see a sometimes surprisingly rapid reinstatement of the original pattern of daily use of increasing doses with withdrawal symptoms and use for relief.

It is difficult in the clinical situation to disentangle the role that pre-laid plans, or expectations, play in this. "I might as well be hung for a sheep as a lamb", perhaps helps the patient justify restarting his old habit after taking the first dose, or the oversimplified version of the belief that some pick up in the folk-lore of addictions – "you cannot stop after taking the first one" (see Chapter 8: the abstinence violation effect).

Experimentally in humans this has been taken only a little further. Studies have been made of the response after a recently detoxified alcoholic is given a substantial dose of alcohol in the laboratory. Those whose dependence was scored as severe rather than moderate had a higher pulse rate increase, more tremor, more self-reported wish to drink, and drank faster when alcohol was presented. This effect was more than when a placebo drink was consumed which deceived the patient into thinking he was being given alcohol (summarised by Edwards, 1986).

A model of reinstatement of physical dependence after abstinence has also been demonstrated in mice and rats – the tendency to withdrawal phenomena is more easily evoked in animals who have previously already been made physically dependent (Goldstein, 1979; Tang & Falk, 1983). But this phenomenon is not only a matter of re-evoking withdrawal symptoms. Lever-pressing by rats to self-administer rewarding drugs will be extinguished if the drug ceases to be delivered. The lever-pressing can be re-initiated by giving the rat just one 'free' injection. It is as if the priming dose triggers memory (Jaffe, 1989).

Box 1.1   Possible explanations of reinstatement after abstinence

Abstinence violation effect
Carry-over of propensity to withdrawal symptoms
Priming dose triggers memory

Compulsion

From Table 1.1 it can be seen that DSM–III–R has omitted items reflecting 'compulsion'. Compulsion, like 'craving', has long been a difficult concept for the clinician or researcher to operationalise, other than in questions such as "do you get a strong urge to use?". Neither system has included craving, a word used in descriptions of addictions since at least the 18th century. Research in animals on drugs as reinforcers, especially of the role of the dopaminergic neurones in the ventral-tegmental area of the brain stem, shows that one element of addiction in humans – the repetitive, inflexible drug-seeking behaviour with the feeling of 'urge' or longing which addicts describe, is probably distinct from withdrawal-induced craving (Jaffe, 1989). Some of this is, however, captured in the 'salience' items in the definitions, which can be seen as a way of operationalising craving.

Salience

Obtaining and consuming the drug/drink begins to take up more time and resources. Other activities are relegated – hobbies, family outings, even work. Its importance begins to override other considerations, with accumulative harm. As others comment on damage that is resulting, rationalisations and deceits develop, or there is angry rebuttal.

Narrowing of repertoire

Narrowing of repertoire, as described by Edwards & Gross (1976), has proved difficult for clinicians and researchers to epitomise in a few questions of the type that patients can reliably answer. It has to do with the tendency that some patients describe of changing from drinking in many varied situations to settling into a routine of drinking a certain amount in a fixed setting, perhaps sticking to one beverage. Obviously, as part of increasing intake, users move from weekends only to weekdays as well. Rather than narrowing their repertoire, many drinkers and other drug users, as their consumption increases and their habit appears to deepen, actually widen their source of supply and sites of consumption, varying the amount depending on what they can obtain. There are almost certainly cultural snags with the concept of narrowing of repertoire as a hallmark of dependence. Take northeast England, for example, where for men 93% of all alcohol consumption is accounted for by beer drunk in pubs and clubs in what can only be described as a ritualised way (Wilson, 1980). Here, a narrowed drinking style is the cultural norm not the exception. Nevertheless 'narrowing' remains (often ill-understood by students) as a symptom of dependence in many textbooks and in ICD-10, if not in DSM–III–R. The dependence syndrome elements have perhaps become more ossified than their authors had intended, despite their prudent use of the term 'provisional' in their seminal paper (Edwards & Gross, 1976).

Impaired control

Once called 'loss' of control, this is a concept that causes confusion. There are times, especially in drinkers, when on a given occasion more drug is consumed than intended, perhaps leading to greater intoxication than intended. However, many patients say that the idea of setting a limit, or intending to get drunk or not to get drunk, does not occur to them. They go for a drink, leaving what will happen open. On the other hand, some users describe knowingly drinking to oblivion, as in these words by Charles Lamb who "lifted up the veil of his weakness" in *The Essays of Elia* (1823):

> "In my stage of habit, in the stage which I have reached, to stop short of that measure which is sufficient to draw on torpor and sleep, the benumbing apoplectic sleep of the drunkard, is to have taken none at all."

Loss of control on single occasions (ending up more intoxicated with the drug than intended) should not be confused with the issue of whether or not a patient who tries to cut down or stop using the substance is repeatedly unsuccessful. DSM-III-R distinguishes these. Students of the social history of the concept of dependence suggest that the existential experience of 'losing control' over drink or drugs or over one's life only emerged in the late 18th century. This was the time of the Enlightenment, and the rise in the middle classes of ideas of social worth, self-control – for example time-keeping in the new industrial work environment – and of the individual's consciousness. Before then, whether or not people 'controlled' themselves, it is said, was less an issue (Room, 1989).

Degrees and dimensions

Historically, psychiatry has been wary of classifications in terms of dimensions of severity, preferring categories in which the implication is that individuals placed within a category are relatively homogeneous. However, DSM-III-R, for substance disorders, takes a stride across this divide by recommending the following criteria for severity of psychoactive substance dependence:

(1) Mild: Few, if any, symptoms in excess of those required to make the diagnosis, and the symptoms result in no more than mild impairment in occupational functioning or in usual social activities or relationships with others.
(2) Moderate: Symptoms or functional impairment between 'mild' and 'severe'.
(3) Severe: Many symptoms in excess of those required to make the diagnosis, and the symptoms markedly interfere with occupational functioning or with social activities or with relationships with others.

(4) In partial remission: During the past six months, some use of the substance and some symptoms of dependence.

(5) In full remission: During the past six months, either no use of the substance, or use of the substance and no symptoms of dependence.

Severity of dependence can be measured by the Severity of Opiate Dependence Questionnaire – SODQ (Sutherland *et al*, 1987) and the Severity of Alcohol Dependence Questionnaire – SADQ (Stockwell *et al*, 1983). The Addiction Severity Index (McLellan *et al*, 1980), increasingly used in the international literature, is a structured interview permitting a rating of severity of dependence on a range of substances as well as a scale measuring problems and social supports.

The dependence concept in clinical practice: advantages and limitations

The clinician is faced with the problems caused by use of psychotropic substances, not their use *per se* – problems such as complaints about the users' behaviour, or harm to their mental or physical health. Debates about definitions of dependence may seem irrelevant to the needs of a clinical team deciding, for example, what help to offer a family where the husband regularly has drunken arguments, or the opiate user where the Court has requested psychiatric advice after yet another housebreaking conviction.

Some psychiatrists in British substance disorder teams have eschewed the centrality of the concept for their clinical work. Without getting embroiled in epistemology, the following points lay out the pros and cons for the clinician. There are clinical and experimental validations of the concept (see Edwards, 1986), which cannot all be covered here, but some examples will be quoted.

Box 1.2 The dependence concept in clinical practice

Moves problem away from moral plane	+ +
Focuses treatment onto the drug/drink habit	+ +
Helps patients construct plan of action	+ / −
Predicts outcome	+
Indicates need for more intensive treatment	+
Indicates necessity for abstinence	+

Warning: Motivational dialogue is initially more important than slavishly checking for dependence symptoms, if intervention is to be brief.

---

1. The dependence concept is morally neutral

Offering the diagnosis of dependence helps the patient and relatives move away from the moral plane, so that treatment facilities can be used. The varying ways that patients are helped, or help themselves, by seeing their problem as an illness are discussed shortly (p. 14).

Objectors would agree that for some patients disabled by shame, to regard their state as 'illness' can help their recovery. But being seen as dependent or having dependency symptoms, is not a prerequisite for using social/behavioural or pharmacological approaches, not even to joining Alcoholics Anonymous (AA) or Narcotics Anonymous (NA). Patients diagnosed as alcohol misusers appear to make as much use of AA as those diagnosed alcohol dependent (using DSM-III-R criteria), at least in California (Shuckit *et al*, 1985). In that study, dependence symptoms did not seem to be a prerequisite for using the AA type of illness self-view. Further, as Glatt, who revitalised treatment for addictions in Britain in the 1950s, observed to Thorley (1985): "I do not believe that alcoholics attending AA meetings in future are likely to stand up and say 'My name is so-and-so and I have the alcohol dependence syndrome'!"

2. The dependence concept helps patients make sense of their plight

People in turmoil are helped by having a framework to peg their experiences on, a gestalt which has some inner cohesion. They feel less confused. They see more easily a plan of action. But to diagnose 'alcoholism', or 'drug addiction', which over the years have developed disparaging stereotypes, often gets patient and physician into a fruitless argument. 'Dependence', it can be argued, does not.

Objectors say they find that the dependence syndrome rarely helps patients make sense of their condition, or helps the clinician communicate with them. Rather, it is argued, patients need to understand how their problems have developed so that they can see what needs to change. Then, to the extent that their problems are drug or alcohol-related, they must decide whether they wish to change their habits and, if so, work out how to facilitate that change (see Fig. 1.2). Certainly, some of their drug/alcohol use has become part of the chain of habit, and this is recognised, but those clinicians prefer to "not complicate semantics for the patient by substituting the word dependence for a good English word, habit".

3. Dependence presages decline

In community samples, those drinkers classified as dependent because they admit withdrawal symptoms, relief drinking or impaired control, tend to be slightly more likely to carry on accumulating problems in future than those

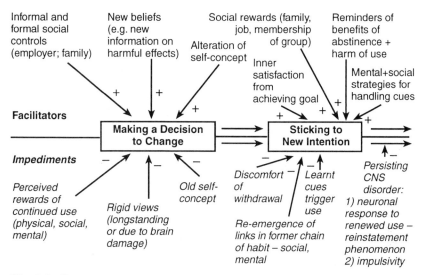

Fig. 1.2 Factors influencing substance use and recovery portrayed as facilitators and impediments to change.

classified as misusers, and are less likely to have shaken off all their alcohol problems when the sample is reinterviewed some years later. This has been shown in the United States and in Sweden.

However, follow-up studies of alcohol/drug abusers treated at clinics tend not to show a simple relationship in which severe dependence predicts worse outcome. In some studies it polarises outcome: some of the most severely dependent turn out to be the success stories, while others have the poorest outcome. This may be because some severe cases pursue abstinence with a dedication commensurate to the pain they have suffered: they are prepared to take radical steps.

Objectors would say that the link between dependence and outcome in clinic samples is simply not clear enough to be useful to clinicians. Shuckit *et al* (1985) in the study just cited examined a wide range of social, psychological and drinking outcome measures one year after treatment. When those who had been diagnosed alcohol dependent were compared to those who only met alcohol misuse criteria (i.e. no withdrawal symptoms, not definite increased tolerance) the only differences found after a year were that the dependent group, as originally, drank more heavily on days when they drank and continued to be prone to morning shakes. These authors suggested returning to using an old rough and ready diagnosis of alcoholism, with a case-note record about whether or not substantial tolerance or withdrawal symptoms were present. But it must be added that, in keeping with having been heavier consumers, dependent patients originally reported more health damage. It is possible that, if the follow-up had been continued for longer, accumulated dose-related health damage might have been significantly worse in the dependent group (see also Babor *et al*, 1987).

4. Severity of dependence may indicate treatment needs

The beginnings of research into brief versus more intensive treatments suggested that severely dependent patients tended to do better if allocated to the more intensive option. However, reviewing this finding, Edwards (1986) regarded it as "very tentative and in need of confirmation".

However, it may well be that dependence only indicates what treatment is needed, in so far as assessing the degree of physical dependence permits an estimate of whether and in what dose medication or management should be provided to get the patient through withdrawal symptoms. When brief advice, without even detoxification, is compared to more intensive treatment, it is not surprising that physically dependent patients do better with more intensive help, since they will have needed medication, or in-patient care, to detoxify before commencing reorganising their lives.

Presently, in studies published from drug and alcohol clinics, the measures which have proved most powerful in predicting which type of treatment following detoxification is best for which type of patient have been measures of severity of psychiatric symptoms and social problems, and personality type, not severity of dependence (Institute of Medicine, 1990; Chick, 1992).

5. Dependence makes future safe use of the substance very improbable

It is sometimes said that it is highly unlikely that people who have been severely dependent on a substance can resume use and prevent it escalating, with the return of problems. They reinstate the syndrome, while those who have not been dependent may sometimes succeed at becoming 'social users'. It is widely accepted, for example, that cigarette smokers are best advised to try to stop completely rather than attempt to cut down. For alcohol, the Rand study of 758 men treated at a range of United States agencies (Polich *et al*, 1981), found that men who were drinking without problems 4 years later, and had managed that for at least the 6 months leading up to that point, tended to be those who had never had symptoms of dependence (and who were younger).

A Canadian study found that clients who perceived themselves as alcoholic (which correlated with scoring on a measure of dependence more highly than not seeing oneself that way) were likely to say that they thought that cutting down to a few drinks a day was not possible.

Other research, in the alcohol field at least, has not borne out the theory that level of dependence is the key to identifying those who have to abstain to overcome their problem. Studies at clinics where drinkers with problems are offered a choice of goals – abstinence or 'controlled' drinking – have found that dependence is not the best predictor of which patients will successfully be able to resume problem-free drinking. Better predictors turn out to be whether the goal matches the patient's choice; or whether the patient has in the past been the type who once he starts drinking goes on a spree, or does not stop until he is drunk or runs out of drink or money to buy more. When a long-term follow-up of previous patients of a Swedish clinic was conducted, personality type (whether or not impulsive) and social stability were found to be the important predictors of future controlled drinking (Nordstrom & Berglund, 1987). Madden (1979) had anticipated this and other evidence which would accumulate during the 1980s (reviewed by Chick, 1992) when he surmised that "clinicians had too readily grasped at severity of dependence as the key to the complex task of deciding which patients can safely resume drinking". These issues are far from resolved. The implications for therapy of alcohol disorders are discussed in Chapter 7.

6. Successful treatment focuses on the dependence

It can be said that dependence on the drug (whatever its aetiology in a given subject) is self-perpetuating and eclipses both its causes and its results. To understand this dictates the correct approach: the determined assault on the consumption of that drug. The success of AA and NA bears witness to this statement. Indeed, it is argued that in treating those dependent on drugs or alcohol, to allow that the drug use is a symptom of the main problem (as dynamic psychotherapy, for example, might imply), will increase denial of the role of the drug and thus help to perpetuate its use.

The counter argument goes as follows. There is a risk that, in focusing on the dependence syndrome, it will be inferred that it is only the drinking or drug use, that is the problem. This could well result in overlooking the social or psychological difficulties that are intertwined and are in fact often the patient's presenting complaints. And as well as the presenting complaint, it is extremely important that other possible domains of problems arising from alcohol and drug use are covered in assessing the patient, since facing these honestly (e.g. legal problems, trouble in the marriage or at work) is often a key to recovery. Only with an understanding of the real cost to them of their drug use, will patients be motivated to do anything about it. Then, and only then, are they ready for action on their use of the drug.

7. It is important that other disciplines and the public understand dependence

Dependence is more than just habit, and it carries risks. Particularly with a socially acceptable drug like alcohol it is vital that we convey to society the meaning of dependence. It has been necessary to expose this fact for the benzodiazepines too.

However, if over-emphasised, the dependence concept may actually hamper attempts to improve management of substance disorders in other disciplines such as social work, nursing, or general medicine, if it focuses attention on collecting symptoms of dependence to make a diagnosis, instead of commencing the dialogue with patients about their perceptions of their use of the drug and the rewards and harm that result. Giving advice empathically or starting counselling should be the aim, and there, dialogue is at the core. In primary care especially it can be unproductive for a doctor slavishly to go through a check list of dependence symptoms.

Alcohol problems in liver clinics and other general hospital departments are associated much less with dependence as measured by the usual instruments than among patients in psychiatric and addictions clinics. Work with the large numbers of cases in general medicine departments is associated much less with dependence as measured by the usual instruments than among patients in psychiatric and addictions clinic. Work with the large numbers of cases in general medicine would be restricted if too much emphasis was placed on looking for dependence.

Is dependence on a psychotropic substance a disease?

In North America, surveys show that the public and those treating substance misusers (though not researchers with doctorates) are mostly comfortable with the disease appellation. In the UK, while a majority of the lay public are happy to use the term disease, it is less commonly used in the treatment field. Workers whose concept of disease does not embrace addictions feel that their clients and patients do not need to be seen as ill to be shown compassion and given help. In the UK there have not been the medical insurance implications as in many Western countries where payment for treatment requires the illness denomination.

In the chapters following this, there will be ample opportunity to show that biological factors are important in dependence: neurophysiological function, neuronal chemistry, and genetics. Some individuals are probably protected from developing dependence on a drug because of their constitutional intolerance to it – this has been demonstrated for ethanol – and perhaps others are constitutionally predisposed because they are susceptible to the euphoric effects of the drug.

The sight of withdrawal symptoms may change a wife away from the view that her alcoholic husband is just self-indulgent and hedonistic, so that she sees him at that point as ill. However, it is also clear that psychological, social, and sometimes moral forces are at work in an individual's recovery from addiction and often no medical intervention is necessary. It is perhaps paradoxical that Alcoholics Anonymous and Narcotics Anonymous, who do encourage the belief in illness, proceed for most affiliates entirely by social methods.

The semantics of this debate (since clearly it may hang on how 'disease' is defined), and the logic, have been dealt with elsewhere (Reznek, 1987; Chick, 1993). From a purely practical viewpoint, there seem to be graduated levels to which patients are helped by calling their problem a disease. At the extreme, some will accept it completely: "I am like a diabetic. I have developed (or have always had) a life-long life-threatening illness to do with the way I metabolise this drug. Like the diabetic I must follow a daily regime, and I must order my life sensibly avoiding the drug completely." This is not saying that he has an illness which means he cannot resist the drug. The recovering patient still takes responsibility for avoiding the drug, getting advice and following it. This is different from using illness, as occasionally happens, as an excuse, as if he is a passive victim. Less rigidly, another will believe "I have shown again and again that if I start to use this substance, it ends up causing me and others harm. I do not know why this is – a failing in me, or something about my chemistry? – but it makes sense to me to avoid this completely." While at the other, the 'moral', end of the spectrum a patient may say "I am the sort of person who is not strong enough to use this substance sensibly. Therefore I will try not to use it at all." This person may hopefully still be prepared to use the available help to assist in that endeavour of will.

Conclusion

Without question, it is central in helping patients with drug and alcohol problems to make a wide-ranging analysis of what prevents them (1) seeing the need to do something about this, and (2) succeeding in their efforts to do so. The elements of the dependence concept described above help us to understand some of this. It is convenient for clinicians to use a shorthand, 'degree of dependence', to convey to the patient and perhaps to colleagues the nature of the struggle (if struggle there will be) for the individual, and perhaps his family and his therapist too, in preventing the problems recurring or worsening. Fig. 1.2 is a simple working model which shows some of the types of facilitators and impediments to change which drug and alcohol abusers often meet. These are expanded upon in the following chapters.

The history of psychiatry shows the dangers of premature reification of syndromes. As Edwards (1986) put it, the most we can say for the present is that the dependence syndrome formulation "is beginning to look like a useful idea."

Recommended reading

Royal College of Psychiatrists (1986) *Alcohol, Our Favourite Drug*. London: Tavistock.
—— (1987) *Drug Scenes*. London: Gaskell.

Ludwig, A. M. (1986) *Understanding the Alcoholic's Mind: the Nature of Craving and How to Control It.* Oxford: Oxford University Press.

Edwards, G. & Lader, M. (1990) (eds) *The Nature of Drug Dependence.* Oxford: Oxford University Press.

References

American Psychiatric Association (1987) *Diagnostic and Statistical Manual of Mental Disorders* (3rd edn, revised) (DSM–III–R). Washington, DC: American Psychiatric Association.

—— (1994) *Diagnostic and Statistical Manual of Mental Disorders* (4th edn) (DSM–IV). Washington, DC: American Psychiatric Association.

Babor, T., Cooney, N. & Lauerman, R. (1987) The dependence syndrome concept as a psychological theory of relapse behaviour: an empirical evaluation of alcoholic and opiate addicts. *British Journal of Addiction,* **82**, 393–405.

Chick, J. (1992) Emerging treatment concepts. In *Annual Review of Addictions Research and Treatment, Volume 2* (eds J. Langenbucher, B. McCrady & P. Nathan), pp. 297–312. New York: Pergamon Press.

—— (1993) Alcohol dependence – An illness with a treatment? *Addiction,* **88**, 1481–1492.

Cottler, L. B., Robins, L. N., Grant, B. F., *et al* (1991) The CIDI-core substance abuse and dependence questions – cross-cultural and nosological issues. *British Journal of Psychiatry,* **159**, 653–658.

Edwards, G. & Gross, M. M. (1976) Alcohol dependence: provisional description of a clinical syndrome. *British Medical Journal,* **1**, 1058–1061.

—— (1986) The alcohol dependence syndrome: a concept as stimulus to enquiry. *British Journal of Addiction,* **81**, 171–183.

Goldstein, D. (1979) Some promising fields of inquiry into biomedical alcohol research. *Journal of Studies on Alcohol,* (suppl. 8), 204–215.

Institute of Medicine (1990) *Broadening the Base of Treatment for Alcoholism.* New York: Wiley.

Jaffe, J. H. (1989) Addictions: what does biology have to tell? *International Review of Psychiatry,* **1**, 51–61.

Madden, J. S. (1979) 'Commentary on Shaw'. *British Journal of Addiction,* **74**, 349–352.

McLellan, A. T., Luborsky, L., Woody, G. E., *et al* (1980) An improved diagnostic evaluation instrument for substance abuse patients: The Addiction Severity Index. *Journal of Nervous and Mental Disease,* **168**, 26–33.

Nordstrom, G. & Berglund, M. (1987) A prospective study of successful long-term adjustment in alcohol dependence – social drinking versus abstinence. *Journal of Studies on Alcohol,* **48**, 95–103.

Polich, J. M., Armor, D. J. & Braisker H. B. (1981) *The Course of Alcoholism.* New York: Wiley.

Reznek, L. (1987) *The Nature of Disease.* London: Routledge & Kegan Paul.

Room, R. (1989) Drugs, consciousness and self-control: popular and medical conceptions. *International Review of Psychiatry,* **1**, 63–70.

Shuckit, M. A., Zisook, S. & Mortola, J. (1985) Clinical implications of DSM-III diagnoses of alcohol abuse and alcohol dependence. *American Journal of Psychiatry,* **142**, 1403–1408.

Stockwell, T., Hodgson, R. & Rankin, H. (1982) Alcohol dependence, beliefs and the priming effects. *British Journal of Addiction*, **20**, 513–522.

——, Murphy, D. & Hodgson, R. (1983) The Severity of Alcohol Dependence Questionnaire: its use, reliability and validity. *British Journal of Addiction*, **78**, 145–156.

Sutherland, G., Edwards, G., Taylor, C. *et al* (1987) The measurement of opiate dependence. *British Journal of Addiction*, **81**, 485–494.

Tang, M. & Falk, J. L. (1983) Production of physical dependence on ethanol by a short drinking episode each day. *Pharmacology, Biochemistry and Behaviour*, **19**, 53–55.

Thorley, A. (1985) The limitations of the alcohol dependence syndrome in multidisciplinary service development. In *The Misuse of Alcohol: Crucial Issues in Dependence, Treatment and Prevention* (eds N. Heather, I. Robertson & P. Davies), pp. 72–94. London: Croom Helm.

Wilson, P. (1980) *Drinking in England and Wales*. London: HMSO.

World Health Organization (1992) *The ICD-10 Classification of Mental and Behavioural Disorders: Clinical Descriptions and Diagnostic Guidelines*. Geneva: W.H.O.

2 Illicit drug use: aetiology, epidemiology and prevention

Michael Farrell & John Strang

Changing patterns of use ● *Aetiology of drug use* ● *Epidemiology of drug use* ● *Epidemiology of inhaled substance use* ● *Drugs and HIV epidemiology* ● *Drugs and crime* ● *Prevention of illicit drug use*

Changing patterns of use

The pattern of drug problems in a community is influenced by events world-wide. Drug production is affected by factors such as climate and soil in the growing areas and by international changes, for example in economic and cultural links between producer and consumer countries (Stimson, 1987). It appears that the saturation of the North American cocaine market has resulted in South American producers diversifying into opiate production. The transit route of drugs through different countries varies. Opiates produced in southeast Asia may pass through Africa or eastern Europe on route to Europe and similarly South American cocaine may pass through Africa or Spain on route to Europe. Transit countries experience spillage of drugs with the evolution of problems around such drug availability – Spain is a recent example. Despite the determined efforts of enforcement agencies to interrupt supply there is a considerable range of illegal drugs available in many countries. The producer countries have responded to criticism by insisting that the consumer countries adopt strategies to reduce the demand for these drugs, thereby placing responsibility jointly with the producers and the consumers.

Patterns of use, as with use of legal psychoactive substances, are influenced by cost and availability. Cost may be a determining factor at the experimental and recreational phase of use but heroin and cocaine are relatively price inelastic for dependent drug users, i.e. increased price does not substantially alter demand (Wagstaff, 1989).

The pattern of drug use has changed over the past three decades in the UK. Until the early 1960s there were few opiate addicts in the UK, informally estimated at approximately 600. The advent of the 1960's 'counterculture' focused attention on cannabis and psychedelic drug use as symbols of alternative living (Stevens, 1989). Despite public attention and concern the actual level of the drug problem appeared to remain minimal. There was a major increase in cannabis consumption through the '60s and '70s. In the late '70s and early '80s there was a sharp rise in the availability of heroin in a smoking form and 'Chasing the Dragon' spread rapidly through sections of the young population. Notifications to the Home Office Addicts Index rose from just 2000 in 1981 to over 20 000 in 1991 (Home Office, 1992*b*).

18

In the late 1980s there were seizures of large quantities of cocaine and it was viewed that Europe had become the focus of cocaine traffickers because of the saturation of the American market. Grim predictions of an American style cocaine epidemic in the UK are to date unfounded (Kleber, 1991) but increased numbers of cocaine/crack users are presenting to services with primary cocaine problems. The late 1980s and early 1990s saw the growth of a new music and drug culture with the drug 'ecstasy' (MDMA-3,4, methylene dioxymethamphetamine) being consumed by large numbers of young people at 'Acid House' and 'Rave' parties (Farrell, 1989). Such young people were more likely to be experimental drug users and the pharmacological properties of MDMA seem to be such that it rapidly produces tolerance but is unlikely to induce dependence. The explanation for the limited dependence-inducing potential of MDMA and other drugs of similar chemical structure may relate to the much reduced effect from repeated use and the need for significant gaps between episodes of use if the full subjective effects are to be experienced (see also Chapter 3).

Injecting and other forms of amphetamine use remains one of the least described patterns of drug use in the UK. The population of amphetamine injectors may have increased in the past decade and is exposed to a high level of human immunodeficiency virus (HIV) risk-taking behaviour (Klee *et al*, 1992). It is likely that amphetamines rather than cocaine will be one of the thornier problems for drug services in the 1990s. Multiple substance problems including alcohol problems are likely to make substantial demands on services. The final chapter of drug misuse for the 1990s is the misuse of prescribed pharmaceutical agents such as the benzodiazepine temazepam and the opiate buprenorphine. The injecting of benzodiazepines has presented a new range of problems both medical and social (Strang *et al*, 1992). Temazepam injecting has caused limb ischaemia resulting in amputations and is linked with high levels of HIV risk-taking behaviour.

Taking anabolic steroids is a minority activity among sports enthusiasts and body builders. However such drugs may be associated with injecting and sharing and have been associated with steroid induced psychosis with reports of homicides.

Aetiology of drug use

Drug use may be experimental, recreational or compulsive. The factors which antecede the first drug use, experimental or recreational, have been widely researched (e.g. Jessor & Jessor, 1976; Huba *et al*, 1979). However, the factors which facilitate continued drug use are perhaps the most important, but the least understood. If experimental drug use is part of normal adolescence and often harmless, then the progress to regular drug use becomes the critical factor.

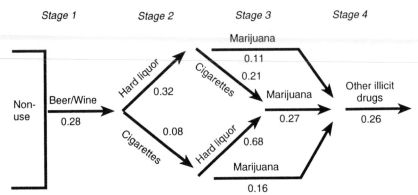

Fig. 2.1 Probabilities of progression through four stages of substance abuse in a group of teenage high school students (from Kandel, 1975).

Explanatory models

In the sequencing of drug initiation and drug use, Kandel (1975) argued that in North America there are four stages. Beer or wine tend to be the first substances used, followed by tobacco and spirits, then marijuana and finally other illegal substances. Use of 'hard drugs' was preceded by use of 'soft drugs' (Fig. 2.1). Parental models play a part in shaping alcohol consumption while peer factors influence initiation to marijuana. A family history of substance use, poor family relationships and unconventional social attitudes interact with individual personal susceptibility, stage of development, and the level of drug exposure at a given stage of development.

Taking risks, to a limited extent a normal feature of adolescence, is for socially and emotionally deprived children a way of offsetting their psychological and social deficits and achieving personal goals. This is the essence of the thesis of Jessor & Jessor (1977) (based on social learning theory; Bandura, 1977) called 'problem behaviour theory'. Substance use is one type of risk-taking.

The 'disturbed personality' model (e.g. Khantzian, 1985) holds that the individual factors contributing to drug use relate to coping with intra- and inter-personal difficulties. Deviant behaviour in childhood (aggressiveness, truancy, stealing) is a predictor of drug use in early adult life shown, for example, in US black communities by Robins & Murphy (1967). Temperamental traits such as impulsiveness and sensation-seeking have been implicated, though have emerged more clearly in some of the studies of the childhood predictors of alcohol misuse (see Chapter 6). As with other behavioural disorders of adolescence, problems from drug use are related to illegitimacy and family break-up.

The 'social-cultural' model focuses on environmental factors: drug availability, selling pressures, and peer pressure (Bachman *et al*, 1984), and material and cultural social deprivation. In the 1960s and 70s drug use appeared evenly spread across social classes in the UK and North America, with a slight bias towards young people from professional families. Since then, a strong link between drug use and social deprivation has been seen (Plant *et al*, 1985; Parker *et al*, 1987; Wilson, 1987). A fruitful research question will be why some children from these extremely impoverished, high-risk zones do not become drug users.

Aetiology of drug dependence

In understanding the evolution from experimental drug use to continued use to dependence, conditioning and learning theory has stimulated research, and influenced treatment approaches, for two decades (Wikler, 1965; Bandura, 1977; Marlatt, 1985). Biological properties of the drugs involved, especially their powerful rewarding effects (the 'high' which the drug user seeks), are also recognised (Bozarth, 1990), but no unified, accepted explanation of dependence on drugs and relapse has yet emerged.

Animals readily learn to self-administer through a previously implanted catheter opiates, stimulants such as cocaine and amphetamine, nicotine, barbiturates, some benzodiazepines, and alcohol. These drugs are therefore defined as rewarding, or reinforcing. The reward effect of stimulants is mediated by the mesocortical and mesolimbic dopamine system, (Bozarth, 1990) and this may be important for other drugs too. It has been demonstrated that the pharmacology of reward is different from the pharmacology of withdrawal (Bozarth & Wise, 1983).

Behavioural pharmacology has shown that drug-seeking behaviour should not only be seen as avoidance of withdrawal symptoms but also as seeking after reward (Fig. 2.2). Cocaine, for example, is a drug with modest withdrawal symptoms but a powerful reward effect. After periods of abstinence, or extinction of drug-seeking behaviour by substituting diminishing rewards, 'relapse' to drug-seeking behaviour in the animal can be facilitated by a few priming doses of the drug. Stimuli associated with the drug, for example the

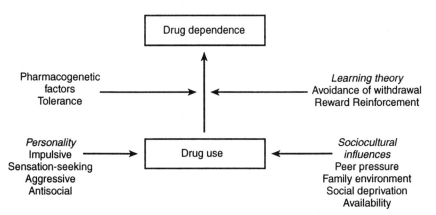

Fig. 2.2 Factors in the development of drug use and dependence.

physical or social environment or the equipment for taking the drug, can help to trigger drug-seeking behaviour. These processes seem to be important in human drug users as well as in the animal models. It is thought that sometimes conditioning results in these cues triggering withdrawal symptoms.

Natural history: the Vietnam veterans

The progression of drug use to continued use to dependence has been seen as a 'career' rather than, to use the biomedical concept, an evolving of a 'natural history'. 'Career' (Hughes, 1959) perhaps implies a more varied development than 'natural history', with choices towards or away from drug use, with the environment having an influence (Strang *et al*, 1990). It is believed that only few cannabis users develop a serious drug problem. United States data suggest that while many have experimented with cocaine only a proportion progress to compulsive use (Kozel & Adams, 1985).

Natural cessation patterns, as well as certain aetiological questions, were illuminated by the follow-up in 1972-74 of US soldiers who, three years before, had left the Vietnam war (Robins, 1993).

First, although the fear of war was a contributing factor in initial use for some (8% gave this as a reason, while 'to feel high' was the commonest reason), the importance of availability was emphasised. Heroin and opium were cheap and plentiful, and 45% of Army enlisted men tried these at least once. As many as 20% claimed they had felt 'strung out' or 'addicted' to narcotics while in Vietnam, and the researchers confirmed that for almost all this meant regular use with classic withdrawal symptoms. Even though warned that the discharge medical examination would include a urine screen, almost 11% of enlisted men tested positive for opiates at discharge from the Army.

Second, it was shown that the sequence of drug use seen in the US general population adolescent (Fig. 2.1) was not fixed. In Vietnam, young men were regularly using opiates before using alcohol or even tobacco.

Third, a history of previous deviant behaviour, and thus perhaps of personality or temperamental factors, still showed through, despite the influence of availability and stress of war. Truanting, drunkenness, fighting, arrest and school expulsion were pre-Army characteristics which predicted drug use in Vietnam.

Fourth, only 5% of those addicted in Vietnam remained addicted on return. Very few had treatment: 6% of those positive on departure, and 14% of those positive on departure who continued to use after return. Those who did enter treatment had relapse rates as high as other, civilian, addicts in treatment. Robins concluded that drug users who appear for treatment have problems that will not be solved just by getting them off drugs.

Fifth, readdiction was rare. Although nearly half the men addicted in Vietnam tried narcotics again after return, only 6% returned to regular use, with signs of physical dependence and withdrawal. Neither personality, social factors, war experience, IQ, past psychiatric care, nor pattern of use distinguished these men from those who used heroin again but did not get readdicted. Robins speculates that a biological factor may contribute to the predisposition for addiction to be reinstated.

Epidemiology of drug use

The illicit nature of much of the behaviour has made it difficult to ascertain information on the range of drug use within the general population. There is a lack of studies with precise case definitions and descriptive terminology.

There is a need for a national framework for the collection of data on illicit drug use. There is also a need for standardised methods of information gathering to improve cross-national comparison of drug problems. In the United States information is collected on drug use in the General Household Survey and also as part of the Epidemiological Catchment Area survey of mental health (Regier *et al*, 1990). Such surveys give some indication of the prevalence of use of a range of drugs but under-reporting is likely. However annual or biannual studies will still provide important data on underlying trends if a consistent methodology is used. In the UK the Wellcome survey of sexual behaviour (Johnson *et al*, 1992) included questions on injecting drug use and reported that for the population aged under 45 the proportion reporting ever injecting was 1.0% for men and 0.5% for women. The highest rates were amongst those living in London with 2.1% of men and 0.8% of women ever injecting. Applying these figures to the general population of England and Wales gives an estimate of 100 000 injecting in the past five years and 175 000 ever injecting.

As well as household surveys a number of countries also conduct regular school based surveys (Johnson *et al*, 1986, 1988). In the UK a number of small scale school studies have been conducted (Plant *et al*, 1985; Swadi, 1988; Health Education Authority, 1992).

These two types of study can provide useful data on the numbers of people who have ever used specific drugs, as an indication of life time use, and the number who have used in the last month as an indication of regular use. Thus it should be possible to have a reasonable estimate of the frequency and quantity of use of the commoner drugs in the general population. However, the use of drugs such as heroin or others where the prevalence is 1% or less requires a large sample to provide useable data. In both the school and the adult population careful attention needs to be paid to sampling bias. For example, in school based studies failure to include truanters, and in the general household survey failure to take account of particular institutions such as prisons, may result in significant underestimates for problematic drug use.

There is also difficulty in confining the issue to illicit drug use as in many countries the misuse of prescribed or pharmaceutical agents may also present substantial problems, as in the injecting of benzodiazepines and buprenorphine (Sakol *et al*, 1989; Strang *et al*, 1992).

Any such national prevalence studies need to be complemented by local prevalence studies allowing for the marked geographical variations. For purposes of service planning there is a need to have some estimate of local prevalence and pattern of drug use. To date there are no proper national household or general population surveys of drug misuse in the UK. For this reason there is no overall framework to put any local picture into context. In the UK most data is gathered from those who make contact with the treatment services. It is estimated that one-fifth to one-third of problem drug users make contact with treatment services. There is no good data to indicate that the population using the service is demographically different from those not using it. Indeed some of the US studies comparing in treatment and out of treatment samples of heroin and cocaine users indicate similar levels of problems for both cohorts (Rounsaville & Kleber, 1985; Carroll & Rounsaville, 1992).

Home Office Addicts Index

The Home Office Addicts Index, in the UK, is the main national data source. It provides information only on those who have presented to doctors and have been identified as dependent on controlled drugs. The doctor is required to record the addict's name, sex, mode of drug use and type of drug prescribed. Males outnumber females by 3 to 1 and approximately half of new notifications are aged between 21 and 29; the remainder are split approximately evenly above and below this age band.

Regional Drug Misuse Database

In the UK where populations are divided up into regions a data gathering system has been developed with the aim of ascertaining the level of service use by drug misusers. While the Home Office Addicts Index has been completed only by doctors the regional drug misuse database form will be completed by any general or specialist worker having contact with a drug misuser. The Regional Drug Misuse Database (Department of Health, 1994) codes a contact's initials and date of birth, drugs used and route of use.

General practitioner and pharmacy surveys

In the UK there have been some occasional national surveys such as the survey of 10% of general practitioners in 1986 seeking information on their extent of contact with opiate misusers, and the national survey of pharmacists enquiring into the extent of contact with injectors in 1989. An estimated 6–9000 opiate addicts already see their general practitioner every month (not necessarily seeking care directly related to their misuse of drugs); and an estimated

20 000 injectors seek to purchase needles and syringes from community pharmacists every month.

Information on admission rates to general hospitals, use of accident and emergency departments and use of obstetric and gynaecology services has to date been extremely difficult to access and quantify. They are however important sources of information which will give useful data on the health burden of this population but will also if matched to other sources give some indication of the proportions of users who are not in contact with other services. The feasibility of collecting such information may improve in an information technology era.

Enforcement data

Data on arrests, cautioning and convictions are clearly related to the level of police activity, but they can also provide some information on both national and local drug scene activity. Approximately 80% of police activity occurs around cannabis. Regional information on police arrests is available in the Home Office reports but more detailed information should be available from local police forces. Enforcement data (Home Office 1992*a*) in the UK shows that arrests for the possession of amphetamine exceeded arrests for possession of heroin, indicating a substantial population of amphetamine users. Both arrests and seizures of cocaine suggest an increase in the use of cocaine in the general population in the UK.

Information from probation services will also provide data on groups of problem drug users who may not overlap into the treatment services.

Studies of hidden populations

A range of methods has evolved due to the difficulties inherent in studying illicit behaviour. These involve specific outreach methods to estimate local patterns of drug use, for example, the 'snowball' study technique among particular populations such as injecting amphetamine users, drug using sex workers (prostitutes), prison populations and ethnic minority groups. The snowball technique involves making contact with a group of individuals and encouraging them to introduce interviewers to acquaintances involved in the behaviour of interest, who might otherwise be difficult to access.

Interviewers may be full-time researchers or use may be made of 'indigenous' interviewers, who through past or present behaviour, usually drug using, are acquainted with and acceptable to drug users. As well as gathering quantitative information, studies have attempted to gather qualitative information, using ethnographic study frameworks to provide data on patterns of drug use and specific social processes influencing the range of risk-taking behaviour.

An example of useful ethnographic work is the study of the history and evolution of steroid misuse in sport. Through detailed interviews with competitive sports people of differing generations it has been possible to build up a picture of this secretive world. Similar studies of activities such as drug dealing and drug dealers would be valuable.

Local geographical studies

To better identify patterns of local use, researchers have attempted to talk to drug users out of contact with treatment services as well as the more visible treatment populations. Attempts have been made to use these data to estimate the extent of health care needs in a community, and have indicated that the true extent of opiate misuse in a community was approximately five times greater than the figure recorded in the Home Office Addicts Index (Hartnoll *et al*, 1985).

Recently Frischer (1992) conducted a local drug use prevalence study in Glasgow. He ascertained identifier data for all people using the multiplicity of services which have contact with drug users including police and probation, courts, drug services, general hospitals etc. Using capture-recapture methods, developed for estimating deer population, he estimated that Glasgow had approximately 9000 drug users. The majority of those identified in the study had not been reported to the Addicts Index, exemplifying the need for cautious interpretation of Addicts Index data. As data collection improves throughout the UK drug services it would be interesting to see this method applied in a number of localities that could be used to extrapolate to a larger scale. While there have been no national studies numerous local surveys have been conducted in the UK. Some of these studies were conducted in the mid '80s and charted the rapid spread of heroin through many northern English housing estates. Pearson (1987) noted the marked local variation, with some localities experiencing high levels of availability and use of heroin while adjacent localities remained virtually drug free.

Box 2.1   Sources of epidemiological data in the UK

National general population data
  none in UK to compare with General Household Survey (US)

National referred population data
  Home Office Addicts Index
  Regional Drug Misuse Database
  general practitioner and pharmacy surveys

Local general population and student surveys

Indirect measures
  enforcement data

Epidemiology of inhaled substance use

Surveys in UK secondary schools during the 1980s found rates of 'ever sniffing' volatile solvents or gases varying from 1–10%, but reducing to a mean of

3.6% for 'ever intoxicated'. Current regular users amounted to 0.5-1% (Chadwick *et al*, 1989).

Girls admit to sniffing as often as boys, but most of the deaths (149 in the UK in 1990) are in boys. Currently deaths due to solvents are stable, but deaths due to butane and aerosols are rising. It occurs in most cultures, and is under-reported. In Japan, the number of secondary school students prepared to admit to solvent inhalation (around 1%) has been shown to be less than the number with toluene metabolites in urine indicating recent use (Wada & Fukui, 1993).

As with other adolescent drug experimentation, inhaled substance use is associated with spending more time with the peer group than with the family, family disruption including single-parent and broken families, delinquency and poor school adaptation. Concern about the increase in solvent abuse in intact families in Japan led to a study which found that, in intact families, the absence of the father at the evening meal was also a correlate of child solvent abuse, drawing attention to the social changes occurring in that culture (Wada & Fukui, 1993).

In some developing countries, inhalation of petrol is a serious health problem, especially because of its lead content.

The products used (see Chapter 3 for details) are cheap and in common use. In the UK the 1985 Supply of Intoxicating Substances Act made it an offence to sell, or offer for sale, substances to people under age 18 if the vendor knows or has reasonable grounds for believing that those substances are likely to be inhaled to achieve intoxication (Gossop, 1993). Prosecutions are rare.

Drugs and HIV epidemiology

The advent of HIV has even further emphasised the importance of having good epidemiological data on the prevalence of injecting and non-injecting drug users in the community. There is major regional variation in the prevalence of HIV among injecting drug users in the UK and Europe. Anonymised HIV saliva sampling has been conducted on a range of people in contact with services and some out of contact samples. There is considerable risk of sampling bias in these studies. The proportion of drug injectors estimated to be infected in the UK is 1-5%, Italy is 30-80%, Spain 40-60% and France up to 58% compared to Holland at 30% and Germany at 20% (World Health Organization, 1991). Most available figures are based on those who have been tested and may not be representative of the total population of drug injectors.

In Europe and the US injecting drug users form the second largest group of reported cases of AIDS, making up 27.5% and 29% of cases respectively. Early on in the HIV epidemic there was a focus on the role of contaminated injecting equipment in HIV transmission. Only recently, as the levels of HIV seroprevalence have appeared to stabilise among injecting drug users, has there been renewed emphasis on the role of sexual transmission. The risk to non-injecting drug users appears an important factor in the dynamics of HIV transmission in the community (see Chapter 10).

To date there is no satisfactory explanation for the regional variation in HIV prevalence in injecting drug users. It is probably best explained by the point in time of original introduction of HIV into the population of each country, in relation to knowledge and perceived risk of HIV. The two frequently identified factors in rapid spread appear to be (1) lack of AIDS awareness and (2) opportunities for efficient mixing of the drug injecting population (des Jarlais, 1992).

In Europe after the initial dramatic epidemic recent figures suggest an apparent levelling off in the first half of 1990 in the number of newly diagnosed AIDS cases. In the UK the exact epidemiology of HIV among drug users is poorly defined. Available information can be used to extrapolate best guesses (Glanz *et al*, 1986, 1990). There is a need for more careful sampling frames with corrections for selection bias, better instruments for the measure of HIV risk-taking behaviour, prospective longitudinal cohort studies to calculate the HIV sero-incidence (HIV sero-conversion rates) as a measure of ongoing HIV transmission, and better use of HIV surrogate markers such as hepatitis B and C.

Drugs and crime

Delinquency and drug use are linked but the nature of this link is unclear – frequently their evolution is intertwined. Longitudinal studies have identified a robust group of risk factors that precede the onset of drug use and delinquency (Farrington & Hawkins, 1991). Overall the evidence suggests that multiple risk factors, such as environmental, psychological (Elliott *et al*, 1984), family problems and family substance problems and previous physical or sexual abuse (Dembo *et al*, 1989) are implicated in the aetiology of both drug use and non-drug use delinquency. However the extent to which delinquency leads to drug use or vice versa and to which both are related to family and environmental factors is complex.

Studies by Chicago sociologists in the 1930s showed an association between drug use and crime (Hughes, 1971). Inner city areas with high levels of drug use had associated high levels of criminality and vice versa. Studies of drug using populations report high levels of criminal activity of the acquisitive variety. In the UK it is estimated that between 3 and 13% of household burglaries, between 8 and 30% of thefts from the person and between 0.08% and 11% of shoplifting offences may have been committed by dependent drug users (Mott, 1986).

Studies of prison populations find high levels of problem drug users with reports ranging from 30% in Europe up to 50% in some American studies (Farrell & Strang, 1991). American studies also report on the high level of drugs detected in the urine of arrested offenders. In the late 1980s cocaine was detected in over 70% of arrestees in Washington but has recently been reported as declining.

These studies cannot show whether drug use causes crime or whether crime is exacerbated by drug use. The extent of the relationship is important in attempting to calculate the likely effect of an expanded treatment system on overall criminality. To date studies would suggest that treatment exerts a modest but significant effect in reducing levels of criminal activity (Gerstein & Harwood, 1990).

Prevention of illicit drug use

'Supply-side strategies' comprise efforts to restrict the production of illicit drugs, their movement across and within countries, and their promotion and sale. Draconian efforts to limit the supply of drugs, by political and even military interference in countries where coca and opium grow, and police and customs activity, cannot be said to have prevented a rise of illicit drug use in North America or Western Europe in the 1980s and '90s.

'Demand-side strategies' aim to reduce a consumer population's demand for and use of drugs. Again, their efficacy in prevention of drug misuse has been hard to demonstrate. Dorn & Murji (1992) summarise these strategies, as described in the English language literature as follows:

(1) providing information to individuals aimed to influence their decision about whether or not to take drugs
(2) education attempting to remedy supposed deficits in moral values or living skills
(3) bolstering anti-drugs norms, so that there is more peer resistance to pressure to use drugs
(4) law enforcement against users, especially at the point of purchase.

At a wider level, prevention may require reduction of unemployment and opportunities for material wealth, adventure and excitement. There is also a 'traditional' societal approach emerging in Western countries – that restoring the family values of the two-parent family, particularly the father's role, may in a liberal society be necessary to increase compliance with the society's standards.

If it is accepted that some drug use is inevitable, then it is legitimate to take secondary prevention measures i.e. to promote methods to reduce harm from that activity (see Chapter 3). The sharing of needles has been targeted as an activity to discourage. The "kebab skewer" poster in England showed a large needle passing through four separate forearms and carried the message "Don't share". Another poster exploited the double entendre of "It only takes one prick to give you AIDS". Such messages are applicable to individual users and can be publicised at a local or national level, with the aim of persuading injecting users to reduce injecting and sharing.

A composite strategy will be multidimensional, aiming

(1) to delay the age of experimental drug use
(2) to reduce the number of experimental users who go on to regular use
(3) to increase the number of users who give up
(4) to modify the behaviour of regular users to minimise the harm they incur.

This entails a range of agencies, targeting a variety of groups, with suitably tailored techniques.

References

Bachman, J. G., O'Malley, P. M. & Johnson, E. D. (1984) Drug use among young adults: the impact of role status and social environment. *Journal of Personality and Social Psychology*, **47**, 629-645.

Bandura, A. (1977) Self-efficacy: toward a unifying theory of behavioural change. *Psychological Review*, **84**, 191-215.

Bozarth, M. A. & Wise, R. A. (1983) Neural substrates of opiate reinforcement. *Progress in Neuro-Psychopharmacology and Biological Psychiatry*, **7**, 569-575.

Bozarth, M. (1990) Drug addiction as a psychobiological process. In *Addictions Controversies* (ed. D. M. Warburton). Reading: Harwood Academic.

Carroll, K. & Rounsaville, B. (1992) Contrast of treatment seeking and untreated cocaine abusers. *Archives of General Psychiatry*, **49**, 464-471.

Chadwick, O., Anderson, H. R., Bland, M., *et al* (1989) Neuropsychological consequences of volatile substance abuse: a population based study of secondary school pupils. *British Medical Journal*, **298**, 1679-1684.

Dembo, R., Williams, L., La Voie, L., *et al* (1989) Physical abuse, sexual victimization and illicit drug use: replication of a structural analysis among a new sample of high risk youths. *Violence and Victims*, **4**, 121-138.

Department of Health (1994) *Drug Misuse Statistics*. Statistical Bulletin 3/94. ISBN 185839-1997.

des Jarlais, D. (1992) The first and second decades of AIDS among injecting drug users. *British Journal of Addiction*, **87**, 347-353.

Dorn, N. & Murji, K. (1992) *Drug Prevention: a Review of the English Language Literature*. SDD Research Monograph 5. London: Institute for the Study of Drug Dependence.

Elliott, D. S., Huizinga, D. & Ageton, S. S. (1984) *Explaining Delinquency and Drug Use*. Beverly Hills: Sage.

Farrell, M. (1989) Ecstasy and the oxygen of publicity. *British Journal of Addiction*, **84**, 943.

———— & Strang, J. (1991) Drugs, HIV and prisons; time to rethink current policy. *British Medical Journal*, **302**, 1477-1478.

Farrington, D. P. & Hawkins, J. D. (1991) Predicting participation, early onset and later persistence in officially recorded offending. *Criminal Behaviour and Mental Health*, **1**, 1-33.

Frischer, M. (1992) Estimating prevalence of injecting drug use in Glasgow. *British Journal of Addiction*, **87**, 235-243.

Gerstein, D. R. & Harwood, H. J. (eds) (1990) *Treating Drug Problems, Vol. 1*. A study of the evolution, effectiveness and financing of public and private drug treatment systems. Washington: National Academy Press.

Glanz, A., *et al* (1986) Findings of national survey on the role of general practitioners in the treatment of opiate misuse: extent of contact with opiate misusers. *British Medical Journal*, **293**, 106-107.

——, *et al* (1990) Prevention of AIDS among drug misusers: the role of the high street pharmacy. London Institute of Psychiatry, Addiction Research Unit.

Gossop, M. (1993) Volatile substances and the law. *Addiction*, **88**, 311-314.

Hartnoll, R., Lewis, R., Mitcheson, M., *et al* (1985) Estimating the prevalence of opioid dependence. *Lancet, i*, 203-205.

Health Education Authority (1992) *Tomorrows Young Adults; 9-15 year olds Look at Alcohol, Drugs, Exercise and Smoking*. London: Health Education Authority.

Home Office (1992*a*) *Statistics on the Misuse of Drugs: Seizures and Offenders Dealt with, United Kingdom 1991*. London: HMSO.

—— (1992*b*) *Statistics of the Misuse of Drugs: Addicts Notified, United Kingdom 1991*. Home Office Statistical Bulletin. London: HMSO.

Huba, G. J., Wingard, J. A. & Bentler, P. M. (1979) Beginning adolescent drug use: peer and adult interaction patterns. *Journal of Consulting and Clinical Psychology*, **47**, 265-276.

Hughes, E. C. (1959) The study of occupations. In *The Sociological Eye: Selected Papers*, pp. 283-297, 1984. New Brunswick NJ: Transaction Books.

—— (1971) *The Sociological Eye*. Chicago: Aldine.

Jessor, R. & Jessor, S. L. (1977) *Problem Behaviour and Psychosocial Development: a Longitudinal Study of Youth*. New York: Academic Press.

Johnson, A., Wadsworth, J., Wellings, K., *et al* (1992) Sexual lifestyle and HIV risk. *Nature*, **360**, 410-412.

Johnson, L. D., O'Malley, P. M. & O'Malley, P. (1988) Illicit drug use, smoking and drinking by America's high school students and young adults: 1975-1985. *NIDA Monograph*. Rockville MD: National Institute on Drug Abuse.

——, —— & Bachman, J. G. (1986) Drug use among American high school students, college students and other young adults: National trends through 1985. Rockville MD: National Institute on Drug Abuse.

Kandel, D. (1975) Stages in adolescent involvement in drug use. *Science*, **190**, 912-914.

——, Davies, M., Karus, D., *et al* (1986) The consequences in young adulthood of adolescent drug involvement. *Archives of General Psychiatry*, **43**, 746-754.

Khantzian, E. J. (1985) The self-education hypothesis of addictive disorders: focus on heroin and cocaine dependence. *American Journal of Psychiatry*, **142**, 1259-1264.

Kleber, H. D. (1991) Epidemic cocaine abuse: America's present, Britain's future? *British Journal of Addiction*, **83**, 1359-1371.

Klee, H. (1992) A new target for behavioural research–amphetamine misuse. *British Journal of Addiction*, **87**, 439-446.

Kozel, N. & Adams, E. (eds) (1985) Cocaine use in America: epidemiologic and clinical perspectives. *NIDA Monograph 61*. Rockville, MD: National Institute on Drug Abuse.

Marlatt, G. A. & Gordon, J. R. (1985) *Relapse Prevention: Maintenance Strategies in Addictive Behaviour Change*. New York: Guilford Press.

Mott, J. (1986) *British Crime Survey*. London: Home Office.

Parker, H., Newcombe, R. & Bakx, K. (1987) The new heroin users: prevalence and characteristics in Wirral, Merseyside. *British Journal of Addiction*, **82**, 147–157.

Pearson, G. (1987) *The New Heroin Users*. Oxford: Blackwell.

Plant, M., Peck, D. & Samuel, E. (1985) *Alcohol, Drugs and School-Leavers*. London: Tavistock.

Regier, D., Myers, J. K., Kramer, M., *et al* (1984) The Epidemiological Catchment Area Program. *Archives of General Psychiatry*, **41**, 934–941.

——, Farmer, M. E., *et al* (1990) Comorbidity of mental disorders with alcohol and other drug abuse: results from the Epidemiological Catchment Area (EA) Study. *Journal of the American Medical Association*, **264**, 2511–2518.

Robins, L. N. & Murphy, G. E. (1967) Drug use in a normal population of young negro men. *American Journal of Public Health*, **57**, 1580–1596.

—— (1993) Vietnam veterans' rapid recovery from heroin addiction: a fluke or normal expectation. *Addiction*, **88**, 1041–1054.

Rounsaville, B. & Kleber, H. D. (1985) Untreated opiate addicts: how do they differ from those seeking treatment? *Archives of General Psychiatry*, **42**, 1072–1077.

Sakol, M., Stark, C. & Sykes, R (1989) Buprenorphine and temazepam abuse by drug takers in Glasgow – an increase. *British Journal of Addiction*, **84**, 439–441.

Stevens, J. (1989) *Storming Heaven: LSD and the American Dream*. London: Paladin.

Stimson, G. V. (1987) The war on heroin: British policy and the international trade in illicit drugs. In *A Land Fit for Heroin* (eds N. Dorn & N. South). London: Macmillan Education.

Strang, J. Gossop, M. & Stimson, G. (1990) Career versus natural history of drug dependence. In *Substance Misuse and Dependence* (eds H. Ghodse & D. Maxwell).

——, Farrell, M. & Sievwright, N. (1992) The misuse of benzodiazepines. In *Benzodiazepine Dependence* (ed. C. Hallstrom). Oxford: Oxford University Press.

Swadi, H. (1988) Drug and substance use among 3333 London adolescents. *British Journal of Addiction*, **83**, 935–942.

Tarter, R. E., McBride, H., Buonpane, N., *et al* (1977) Differentiation of alcoholics: childhood history and drinking pattern. *Archives of General Psychiatry*, **34**, 761–768.

Wada, K. & Fukui, S. (1993) Prevalence of volatile solvent inhalation among junior high school students in Japan and background lifestyle of users. *Addiction*, **88**, 89–100.

Wagstaff, A. (1989) Economic aspects of illicit drug markets and drug enforcement policies. *British Journal of Addiction*, **84**, 1173–1182.

Wilker, L. (1965) Conditioning factors in opiate addiction and relapse. In *Narcotics* (eds D. I. Willner & G. G. Kassenbaum), pp. 85–100. New York: McGraw Hill.

Wilson, W. J. (1987) *The Truly Disadvantaged: The Inner City, The Underclass, and Public Policy*. Chicago: University of Chicago Press.

World Health Organization (1991) *AIDS among Drug Abusers in Europe: Review of Recent Developments*. EUR/ICP/GPA 049. Geneva: World Health Organization.

3 Illicit drug use: clinical features and treatment

John Strang & Michael Farrell

---

*Health care needs of different cases ● Principles of assessment ●
Principles of treatment ● Specific syndromes and treatment
options ● Conclusions*

Health care needs of different cases

Treatment as a response requires a condition to be treated. What is it that
defines the individual as a suitable case for treatment? The Management
Executive of the National Health Service in Britain published in 1993 a guide
for those responsible for purchasing health care for drug users. Seven different
'suitable cases for treatment' were defined:

(1) dependent user (addict)
(2) injector
(3) intoxicated drug user
(4) user in withdrawal
(5) drug user with co-morbidity
(6) individual at risk (tomorrow's patient)
(7) addict in recovery.

Each of these groups has its own health care needs; the same individual may
occupy more than one category at the same time, and the categories occupied
may change as time goes by.

(1) *The dependent user (addict)* will have been taking a drug on a sufficiently
regular basis that a degree of neuro-adaptation exists such that abrupt
interruption of intake of the drug will result in a withdrawal syndrome. The
exact physical and psychological characteristics of the withdrawal syndrome
will be determined by the drug's pharmacological group. Special consideration
should be given to management of the dependent female user who is pregnant,
as there may be associated problems of dependence in the new-born baby
who will experience a neo-natal drug withdrawal syndrome, after interruption
of the placental supply of the drug (see Chapter 10).

(2) *The injector* is at increased risk of various complications – especially if
the injecting behaviour includes the sharing of needle and syringe or the
use of insufficiently cleaned second-hand equipment. As a result of such
needle-sharing, hepatitis B has become widespread among injecting drug users,
so that between 50% and 95% of heroin injectors in different cities in
the UK are infected with the hepatitis B virus. Recent studies have shown

that co-infection with the delta fragment (see Chapter 10) is already extensive in some populations of injecting drug users in the UK, and it is likely that future studies of hepatitis C will also find evidence of existing penetration of the injecting population. In the 1980s, HIV infection was observed among injecting drug users – particularly in Edinburgh and Dundee, but with much lower levels of infection and a slower unfolding of the epidemic in other cities within the UK (see Strang & Stimson, 1990). The Edinburgh epidemic was particularly well documented, and involved the rapid spread of the virus up to a prevalence level of more than 50% among injecting drug users within a period of 18 months. The injecting drug user is also at greater risk of other complications, including those associated with impurities or contaminants within the drug, or the greater risk of inadvertent overdose due to the sudden bolus administration of the drug.

(3) *The intoxicated drug user* often has a remarkable ability for making himself unpopular. Nevertheless, they may have very real health care needs relating either to the immediate management of their intoxication, or to co-morbidities which may well be undetected or untreated. Unplanned overdose is more likely to occur with the novice drug user, or where there are sudden changes in the purity of black market supplies; and it is particularly likely to occur after periods of abstinence (such as after self-discharge from a treatment programme, or on release from prison) when drug users may not appreciate the extent to which they have lost their previous tolerance to the drug.

(4) *The user in withdrawal* will usually be preoccupied with a wish to gain relief from the withdrawal syndrome. The opportunity should be explored as a possible first step to a more fundamental and permanent change in their ongoing drug use. The withdrawal syndrome will only develop in those individuals who have already become dependent, for whom the classical withdrawal syndrome will be determined by their drug of dependent use (e.g. opiate withdrawal syndrome, barbiturate withdrawal syndrome, benzodiazepine withdrawal syndrome – and the alcohol withdrawal syndrome). While the nature of the withdrawal syndrome is determined by the pharmaco-logical group the actual time-course will be determined by the specific drug of recent use (e.g. slower onset and longer duration of withdrawal with methadone, compared with more rapid onset and clearance with heroin). The specific complication of epileptiform fits, in association with alcohol, barbiturate and benzodiazepine withdrawal, makes the unmodified withdrawal syndrome particularly dangerous. Special consideration will need to be given to the management of the withdrawal syndrome for individuals who are suddenly separated from their regular supply – as when admitted to a hospital, detained in police custody, or imprisoned.

(5) *The drug user with co-morbidity* may often be unaware of a co-existing illness. Some complications will be obvious, such as current abscesses or septicaemia. However, others may be sub-clinical (such as sub-acute bacterial endocarditis or acute hepatitis B infection), and the long-term health sequelae

of these infections may not become evident until later in the individual's life. Any contact with a drug user should be used as an opportunity to screen for the presence of any of these co-morbidities, especially when there may be evidence of progressive disease, as with chronic hepatitis B infection and HIV infection. The accurate identification of those with chronic hepatitis B or HIV infection will not only give them an opportunity of modifying their behaviour so as to reduce the infection of others, but will also alert them to the importance of self-monitoring and regular check-ups to detect disease progression at the earliest possible opportunity. Treatments exist to slow down hepatitis B disease progression in the chronic carrier, and it now appears that these may also be available for HIV. It is essential that the psychiatrist is competent at identifying these co-morbidities, and must also be involved either in direct provision of, or arranging the separate provision of, the necessary ongoing physical health care.

(6) *The individual at risk* – we may have an opportunity to prevent him/her becoming tomorrow's patient. Not only should there be primary prevention programmes which may prevent onset of drug use, but we should also look at interventions which may deflect from continued drug use, or from significant progression in a drug using career (for example, the move from occasional to regular use of a drug; or the move from smoking to injecting of the same drug). Interventions at the primary health care level have been found to be effective with drinkers and smokers, and it remains to be seen whether there is scope for a minimal intervention approach with non-dependent users of illicit drugs. Certainly, despite the extensive development of more widely available services for the drug taker (see Chapter 11) there is still usually an interval of several years between the onset of dependent use and the first request for help.

(7) *The addict in recovery* is often overlooked when it comes to considering need for sevices. Specialist rehabilitation houses exist in the UK which are almost exclusively run by non-statutory organisations such as Phoenix House and Turning Point, and these are described later. The psychiatrist may need to be involved in providing backup and support to these non-medical rehabilitation options, and will also need to be particularly involved in providing on-going care to those drug users who also have another psychiatric condition (which may indeed leave them vulnerable to subsequent relapse). The ongoing rehabilitation of the addict in recovery will require consideration of re-training opportunities, housing circumstances, marital and family involvement, etc.

Confusion between perspectives on drug use

The doctor not only forms opinions on the drug user which are based on the available medical evidence, but may also hold views which reveal an underlying medical, social or moral perspective. It is important to be able to identify separately these different positions as, too often, they are

---

**Box 3.1   The Misuse of Drugs Act, 1971 and
Misuse of Drugs Regulations**

Drugs are classed, in the Act, according to the harmfulness attributable to them when misused:

Class A – includes cocaine, LSD, phencyclidine, diamorphine (heroin), morphine, methadone, pethidine, opium, dextromoramide, dipipanone, alfentanil and class B drugs when prepared for injection.
Class B – includes oral amphetamines, barbiturates, cannabis and some opiates.
Class C – most benzodiazepines, buprenorphine and a variety of other drugs deemed liable to misuse.

Drugs are scheduled, in the Regulations, according to sanctions governing their handling:

Schedule 1 – includes cannabis, LSD. Possession and supply prohibited without Home Office authority.
Schedule 2 – most class A and B substances, excluding the barbiturates. Full controlled drug regulations apply to storage, record keeping and prescription.
Schedule 3 – most barbiturates and some other class B and C substances. Regulations apply to prescription writing.
Schedule 4 – the benzodiazepines and pemoline. Minimal control.
Schedule 5 – very low-strength preparations. Little restriction.

A special licence from the Home Office is required to prescribe diamorphine, dipipanone or cocaine for the purpose of treating addiction. These substances may be prescribed without licence for the relief of pain due to organic disease or injury.

Persons in whom drug addiction is suspected must be notified to the Chief Medical Officer if their drugs of misuse include:

cocaine, dextromoramide, diamorphine, dipipanone, hydrocodone, hydromorphone, levorphanol, methadone, morphine, opium, oxycodone, pethidine, phenazocine or piritramide

---

all mistakenly identified as medical perspectives when they emanate from the doctor.

Use of the same drug will hold different meanings for different individuals. It is often convenient to refer to the initial episodes of drug use as experimental; with a subsequent 'recreational' phase of drug use when the individual is deliberately seeking effects which are perceived as positive by the drug user. For some of these individuals, their drug use will become compulsive or dependent. The individual may require medical treatment for a complication of their drug use at any of these three levels of relationship, but concern by the drug users about the drug use itself will not usually result in clinical presentation until the latter stage. In his early work, Stimson (1973) described four types of drug user who may exist in society – loners, stables, junkies, and two-worlders. Although the media stereotype is one of the addict who is heavily involved in a variety of criminal activities (both independent and linked to their drug use) this relationship is not as robust as widely believed. For example, in a study of US opiate addicts, Rounsaville *et al* (1982, 1991) found that the population seemed to be drawn from three main groups of approximately equal size – a group where there was clear evidence of early childhood deprivation or trauma, a group in whom adolescent delinquency pre-dated their significant use of illicit drugs, and finally a group in whom the illicit drug use was the first evidence of significant deviant behaviour. In the UK the diversity is likely to be even greater as the necessary link between opiate use and criminality, for example, is not as strong as has been seen in the US.

Principles of assessment

Physical examination

As with other areas of psychiatric practice, physical examination is an essential part of the assessment and ongoing monitoring of the drug taker. This should include examination for the presence of vein puncture marks – usually on the arms or in the antecubital fossa, but also occasionally in the groin over the femoral vein, or on legs or ankles. The examination should also include a check for the presence of any drug-specific effects or drug withdrawal effects. Thus there are separate lines of enquiry into the particular drug being used on the one hand, and the route and pattern of administration on the other hand. The examining doctor should make full use of the available laboratory support during assessment and diagnosis. A full drug screen of a urine sample taken at first consultation can be an invaluable source of information – especially when consideration is being given to the possibility of a drug-induced psychosis, for example.

The extent of laboratory analysis may depend on the degree of development of local toxicological services, but should include thin layer chromatography, supplemented by either gas chromatography or immuno-assay techniques (often referred to as EMIT – Enzyme Multiplied Immunoassay Technique). A positive result requires interpretation, as the use of different drugs gives a different profile of positive responses in the urine. Thus there may be positive results to cannabis for many days or weeks after a single substantial intake, whereas cocaine may only give a positive result for a specimen collected during the first 24 hours. Heroin use will be detected by the presence of morphine in the urine, but other drugs will also give a morphine positive result, including prescribed drugs such as codeine, as well as some over-the-counter proprietary preparations (for such instances, the presence of a weak morphine positive which accompanies a strong codeine positive would indicate that the morphine result related almost entirely to the ingested codeine). (For a brief review of urine testing for drugs and its clinical application, see *Lancet* Editorial, 1987; for a wider review of approaches to measurement, see Strang *et al*, 1989.)

Box 3.2   Physical assessment in suspected drug misuse

Stigmata of drug use – e.g. needle marks, skin abscesses, pupillary changes, nasal discharge or rash

Signs of intoxication or withdrawal

Comorbidity – e.g. Hepatitis B or C, HIV infection

Laboratory investigations – urine/blood drug assays

Psychiatric disorders and their association with drug use

It is important not to be blinded by the drug use or dependence. Psychiatric disorders may occur in the drug user in a way that is wholly independent of the drug use, in just the same way as physical or psychiatric disorders may occur in the remainder of the population. However, use or dependence may confuse the clinical picture so as to mislead the doctor in the diagnostic process. Just as the casualty officer must be careful not to overlook head injury in the drunk, so the psychiatrist must be clinically vigilant so as to identify an independent psychiatric condition.

Psychiatric disorders certainly do occur as a direct result of the drug use, and these may be considered as either (a) drug-induced disorders or (b) drug-precipitated disorders. Drug-induced disorders are those in which the drug use has a direct causal relationship with the development of the condition, the most famous examples being the drug-induced psychoses with amphetamines and with cocaine (a short-term psychosis which passes with the passage of the drug, and which is not associated with subsequent psychotic episodes). Drug-induced psychiatric disorders can also occur as part of the withdrawal syndrome – for example the depressive reaction during the first few days of amphetamine and cocaine withdrawal, during which the individual may attempt suicide.

Drug-precipitated psychiatric disorders occur when the event of drug use triggers off an otherwise independent psychiatric condition. It is probable that this is more likely to occur when the event of drug use has been particularly profound or disturbing (for example, a bad 'trip' with LSD), as a result of which the anxiety state, or the major depressive or schizophreniform disorder becomes manifest. The significant point here is that the ongoing management of the individual patient, and the likely time-course of the disorder will now be dictated by the characteristics of the independent psychiatric condition itself, and not by any feature of the drug use. Additionally, drug use has been found to be one of the precipitants of relapse among individuals in remission from schizophrenia or manic depressive disorders (see Chapter 9).

Principles of treatment

Doctors on occasion overestimate the importance of their position, and believe that they are the be-all and end-all to the drug user's continued well being. On other occasions, doctors underestimate the importance of their contribution, when they may be the significant additional influence resulting in the drug user going down one pathway rather than another, able to give that key piece of advice which the user incorporates into a revised safer form of the continued behaviour. Thus harm reduction may come in the form of advice on self-help strategies or advice on key changes which the drug user may make (such as the move from injecting to smoking their illicit drug). Similarly, although the drug user should be advised to stop all injecting, it is also important for there to be available advice on effective methods of cleaning needles and syringes so as to protect the determined injector from the risk of infection.

Our concept of treatment must extend beyond the simple prescribing of drugs or the provision of care in an in-patient setting. The environment may be manipulated so as to influence the subsequent course of the drug user who returns home after a period of residential care. It should be possible to identify reinforcers within the environment which encourage the maintenance of healthy changes (such as abstinence from all drugs, or the reliance on oral-only substitutes). The findings of Robins *et al* (1974) demonstrate the extent to which heroin addiction can be reversible. They found that 95% of heroin addicted soldiers in the US army in Vietnam were successful in becoming and remaining drug free on return to the USA (see Chapter 2). There are other effective interventions than treatment out of a bottle.

The goals of treatment

Stable abstinence is probably the most obvious goal. However while it is a worthy goal, the doctor who is only willing to work towards immediate abstinence may miss opportunities for bringing about improvements in the physical, psychological or social conditions of the drug users whom they attend. Going for a goal other than abstinence may be seen as going for second best, but there may be times when going for second best may be best first – especially if this more modest benefit may be achieved in a larger proportion of drug users.

Harm reduction

Since the advent of HIV this broad perspective has become more prominent under the heading of 'harm minimisation' or 'harm reduction'. Implicit in this is the pragmatic approach that accepts that some people will use illicit drugs and some people will inject drugs. It is therefore viewed as best that they incur the least amount of harm from these activities. This involves a hierarchical health message which primarily discourages people from taking drugs; if they take drugs, then it suggests that they avoid injecting; if they inject, then it is suggested that they use sterile injecting equipment and avoid sharing this equipment with other drug users; if they do share, then it is suggested that they clean the equipment.

The most widely publicised aspect of harm reduction has probably been the development of an extensive network of needle and syringe exchange schemes across the UK (Stimson *et al*, 1988, 1990) and this has also extended to pharmacy-based exchange programmes which supply sterile equipment to drug users (Glanz *et al*, 1989).

The adoption of a harm minimisation approach has implications for the specialist and the generalist. Both now have opportunities to help in facilitating significant changes in drug using behaviour. This may on occasion be the achievement of abstinence but on other occasions may legitimately be moves to less harmful forms of continued use. An approach of harm minimisation should not be seen as in competition with the promotion of abstinence, any more than the provision of advice to switch to low tar cigarettes could be criticised as condoning continued smoking. In practice the doctor is well used to circumstances in which more than one message is given simultaneously.

Box 3.3   Harm reduction

Aims
  Reduce or stop drug use
  If using, reduce or stop injecting
  If injecting, reduce or stop sharing of injecting equipment; avoid
    contaminated equipment
  If sharing, clean equipment first

Strategies
  Education on risks of infection and overdose
  Education on safer sex
  Education on how to clean injecting equipment if it is reused
  Provision of needle exchanges and condoms
  Hepatitis B immunisation
  HIV testing
  Substitute oral drugs

The interview as therapy

The therapist traditionally regards the interview (especially the first interview) as an opportunity to gather information. However, to the patient, this first consultation is often a more significant event, and may have a direct therapeutic influence. Thus, the manner in which the doctor conducts the interview may have a profound influence on the options which the drug taker considers, and on the course which he/she subsequently follows – and indeed on the likelihood of engaging in the therapeutic progress at all. The reality of working with the drug user is that each consultation with a new patient could possibly be the only opportunity to impact information to that individual and to influence their choice of the available options. Single brief interventions have certainly been found to be of very real benefit with smokers and drinkers, and it is likely that a similar finding may be made in the future with illicit drug use. Virtually all treatment programmes are beset with problems of drop out from treatment, so that there are substantial losses at every stage of the treatment process – whether the programme is a methadone prescribing programme or a needle exchange scheme.

Miller (1983) has described an explicit style of interviewing which attempts to capitalise on these early opportunities. In his approach of 'motivational interviewing' he describes how the therapist may influence the personal audit being undertaken by the client. One of the covert goals of the therapist is to generate a critical mass of dissonance in the drinker or drug taker, until they become willing to consider alternatives to their continued drug or alcohol use. Although Miller describes this as a complete therapeutic process in itself, this approach could alternatively be included within the armamentarium of the versatile therapist and incorporated into various different treatment approaches (see Chapter 8).

Relapse prevention

This cognitive behavioural approach is specifically designed to enhance individuals' capacity to maintain their chosen changed behaviour. The process of relapse is broken down into various stages, and the former drug user is taught to identify particular high risk situations, and to develop specific coping skills – both for preventing further episodes of drug use, and also for reducing the catastrophic nature of lapses when they do occur. Indeed, it is argued that the overinvestment in absolute abstinence may itself contribute to the catastrophic nature of relapse when it occurs – the 'abstinence violation effect'. Specific treatment approaches include the teaching of skills and awareness, by re-enacting past relapse situations, role playing these occasions, and then *in vivo* visits to the high risk situations themselves – initially accompanied and subsequently alone. Episodes of drug use are viewed, not as evidence of failure, but as opportunities for learning about personal vulnerabilities, for which existing skills must be enhanced, or new skills learnt (for discussion of this and 'cue exposure therapy', see Chapter 8).

Working with the family

Quite apart from the independent need on the part of the partner or family for support or advice, the family has recently been seen as the context in which treatment might be administered. Three main types of family therapy have been applied, including psychodynamic approaches, behavioural approaches, and the 'systems approach'. The interested reader is referred to the family therapy literature for further information.

Residential rehabilitation programmes

The majority of residential provision for drug users occurs within the non-statutory/voluntary sector, with a network of therapeutic communities throughout the UK. Although the original community may have drawn on the work of Maxwell Jones and others, the subsequent development of therapeutic communities in the drugs field have departed considerably from the original model and may now be considered as a separate programme. In the late '60s, several therapeutic communities were established in the UK – usually based on successful projects in the USA, such as Phoenix House, and usually termed 'concept houses'. These therapeutic communities use self-help within a structured hierarchical drug free environment, in which the resident plays a major role in the day to day running of the house. Personal responsibility is emphasised, and privileges and responsibilities increase as the resident progresses, through the achievement of certain goals. There is frequently a confrontational style to the therapeutic sessions, and firm feedback is provided on behaviour, with the setting of clear behavioural limits. The resident is expected to stay from nine to 18 months in the concept house or in the aftercare hostel.

A number of Christian houses have also been established in the UK, in which there is usually a gentler and more explicitly supportive environment, which allows for the gradual recovery of the individual. These may be further sub-divided into those in which the Christian faith is an essential component of recovery, and others in which a religious involvement on the part of the resident is not compulsory. The gentler style of the latter form of Christian rehabilitation house may be particularly well suited to the more vulnerable drug user or the drug user with a dual diagnosis (concurrent other psychiatric disorder).

A small number of community-integrated houses have been established in which there is an explicit attempt to involve the local community in the process of rehabilitation within a residential setting. In these houses, the recovering addict maintains close links with the local community and often contributes to local good works and support, for example providing care to the elderly.

The most recent development has been the establishment of a number of 12 Step residential programmes (see description below). These work to a much shorter timescale than the other residential houses, of about two to three months.

Separate development of self-help support has occurred in the UK, with the formation of family support organisations such as Families Anonymous and ADFAM, which largely exist outside the formal treatment arena.

Narcotics Anonymous, and 12 Step programmes (sometimes known as 'Minnesota Model')

These various approaches are all developments of the original Alcoholics Anonymous (AA) groups (see Chapter 7). The 12 Steps refer to the stages of growth through which the individual must progress in order to achieve and maintain sobriety. A common area of confusion is the statement by those affiliated to AA or Narcotics Anonymous (NA) that there is no cure and that they are still addicted: this may more usefully be seen as part of a coping strategy for ensuring continued vigilance, rather than a statement with scientific origins. Narcotics Anonymous began in California in the '50s, and became a significant movement in some areas in the UK during the 1980s. The initial involvement with NA revolves around regular meetings which are attended on an open basis and which provide a setting for mutual support and self-help in order to maintain a drug free state. Participants give their personal life story, and there is frequently a cathartic quality to the group. Several cities in the UK have a wide network of meetings which take place on a daily basis, so that it is now possible for the addict in recovery to attend at least one meeting every day.

During the 1980s, a number of private or charitable residential programmes based on the 12 Step philosophy were established in the UK, and these have now become a major part of the overall service provision for today's addict seeking to attain and maintain abstinence, with the option of follow-up care in a halfway house.

It is disappointing that little has yet been done in the development of self-help strategies for users of illicit drugs. A recent study in London found extensive evidence of previous attempts at self-detoxification among patients at a drug dependence unit, with a total of 212 previous attempts at self-detoxification being reported by 50 opiate addicts. Their rates of success in the short term were at least comparable with the results of many treatment programmes, and it is likely that there may be an unexploited reservoir of benefit in this area.

The addict doctor

While in absolute numbers, the addict doctor may form a small part of the problem of addiction to alcohol and other drugs such as heroin and cocaine, the characteristics and health care needs of this group warrant special consideration. As a group, doctors are at high risk of developing drug problems and this appears to be particularly among specialities with lower levels of control over access to drugs (such as general practice, anaesthetics and, more recently, diagnostic radiology). The higher incidence is compatible with Winick's model (1980) that the extent of use in a population is determined by three factors: the availability of the drug, the extent of social proscription, and the degree of role strain. Treatment of addicted doctors often employs a highly structured approach (Anker & Crowley, 1982) and has more recently included the supervised administration of naltrexone (Washton *et al*, 1984). The prognosis of addict doctors in recovery is well above normal.

Specific syndromes and treatment options

The opiates

Heroin is the most widely used opiate on the black market in the UK, although there will be major local variations in the availability of prescribed and black market opiates. Thus at times there has been extensive use of Diconal (dipipanone and cyclizine mixture) in a tablet form which is then injected, or Temgesic (buprenorphine) of which the tablets are also injected. Similarly, methadone tablets may be crushed and injected, for which reason the prescribing of oral methadone should probably be restricted to the linctus preparation, which also has the least value on the black market and hence the least probability of diversion. As outlined above, the physical withdrawal syndrome will be similar across all the opiates, although the time course will be influenced by the particular opiate of use. With heroin, the withdrawal syndrome is characterised by an onset of withdrawal symptoms after six to eight hours, reaching a peak at 36 to 48 hours, followed by gradual decline over the next week or two; with symptoms of abdominal cramps, nausea, diarrhoea, goose flesh, sweating, sleeplessness, irritability, rhinorrhoea, excessive lacrimation and uncontrollable yawning.

Diversity came to the heroin scene in the UK during the 1980s. After a brief fashion of heroin by snorting, the use of smoking heroin by 'chasing the dragon' became widespread in some cities in the UK (e.g. London, Glasgow, Liverpool) even though it remained rare in other cities (e.g. Edinburgh). 'Chasing the Dragon' involves the heating of smokable black market heroin on tin foil above a flame until the heroin melts into an oil and then sublimates – at which point the 'dragon's tail' of sublimate can be inhaled through a tube. 'Chasing the Dragon' can no longer be regarded as a passing fashion, and clinical services are now seeing substantial numbers of heroin users for whom this remains their chosen route of use despite the development of high dose and high cost heroin habits. For others, however, the initiation into heroin chasing has been a stepping stone on to their subsequent injecting of the drug. A study in 1991 in London found that there had been a major change in initiation into heroin use, with 95% of all those who had recently started heroin being initiated by 'chasing the dragon', whereas those initiated before 1980 were most likely to inject on their first occasion (Strang *et al*, 1992).

Various prescribing options have recently been described by the Department of Health in *Drug Misuse and Drug Dependence: Guidelines on Clinical Management* (1991). It is suggested that there could be considerable improvement to the quality of the debate around the appropriateness and the practicalities of prescribing substitute drugs to the heroin addict: in particular it is suggested that prescribing drugs such as oral methadone should be considered in one of four contexts:

(1) the rapid detoxification over the course of a week or so (as might be considered for the patient dependent on alcohol, barbiturates or opiates following general hospital admission or detention in police custody or prison)
(2) gradual outpatient withdrawal over several weeks or months (as is often employed in out-patient/community drug treatment services)
(3) maintenance-to-abstinence approaches in which an initial stable dose is given with the expectation of progression to a withdrawal within a period of a few months
(4) maintenance, in which the goal is stabilisation of opiate intake on prescribed oral methadone so as to effect separation from other sources of opiate and encourage stabilisation of lifestyle.

Recommended dosages for methadone are likely to vary over time as the purity of black market heroin varies. In the US, two dose ranges are considered: low dose methadone at a daily dose of 30–40 mg of oral methadone, and high dose methadone at approximately 80–100 mg daily. It is uncertain whether the US reports of methadone blockade at the higher dose range have relevance in the UK where black market supplies of heroin are so much purer (approximately 40% versus 5% in the UK and US respectively at the time of writing). The recent guidelines on clinical management from the Department of Health (1991) advise consultation with a local specialist in drug dependence to obtain information on the current applicable conversion rate: for example, at present, a dependent dose of half a gram of black market injectable heroin daily is regarded as equivalent to approximately 40 mg of oral methadone daily.

For treating withdrawal, there has been interest in non-opiate alternatives, for example the anti-hypertensive drug clonidine, or possibly later generations of such drugs which may be less prone to side-effects. As an alpha-adrenergic agonist, clonidine appears effective in suppression of some of the autonomic features of the opiate withdrawal syndrome, although it is complicated by postural hypotension, which may be pronounced. As a result, many specialists regard this as a drug which should only be used on an in-patient basis for the management of opiate withdrawal. Dosage schedules typically start at between 0.2–0.4 mg daily (e.g. 0.1 mg tds) increasing incrementally up to a maximum of 1.2 mg daily, with each increment being subject to satisfactory monitoring of blood pressure.

In recent years attention has turned to elements of care required in the post-detoxification phase (or at least separate from the task of detoxification). These may include specific relapse prevention strategies as outlined in the book by Marlatt & Gordon (1985) and/or specific behavioural approaches

Table 3.1 Methadone equivalents of other opiates (Department of Health, 1991)

Drug	Dose	Methadone equivalent
Street heroin	Cannot accurately be estimated because street drugs vary in purity. Titrate dose against withdrawal symptoms	
Pharmaceutical heroin	100 mg tablet or ampoule	20 mg
	30 mg ampoule	50 mg
Methadone	10 mg ampoule	10 mg
	Mixture (1 mg/1 ml) 10 ml	10 mg
	Linctus (2 mg/5 ml) 10 ml	4 mg
Morphine	10 mg ampoule	10 mg
Dipipanone (Diconal)	10 mg tablet	4 mg
Dihydrocodeine (DF118)	30 mg tablet	3 mg
Dextromoramide (Palfium)	5 mg tablet	5–10 mg
	10 mg tablet	10–20 mg
Pethidine	50 mg tablet	5 mg
	50 mg ampoule	5 mg
Buprenorphine hydro-chloride (Temgesic)	200 μg tablet	5 mg
	300 μg ampoule	8 mg
Pentazocine (Fortral)	50 mg capsule	4 mg
	25 mg tablet	2 mg
Codeine linctus 100 ml	300 mg codeine phosphate	10 mg
Codeine phosphate	15 mg tablet	1 mg
	30 mg tablet	2 mg
	60 mg tablet	3 mg
Gee's linctus 100 ml	16 mg anhydrous morphine	10 mg
J. Collis Brown 100 ml	10 mg extract of opium	10 mg

to interfere with craving. (For further detail, see Chapter 8.) In the US there has been much investigation of the potential benefit from general, social and occupational rehabilitation of the recovering addict, but there has been little systematic study of this area in the UK. Successful methadone maintenance programmes in the US and Australia include a substantial commitment to these broader aspects of treatment and rehabilitation, and are associated with better outcome.

Specific opiate antagonists now exist, and are available in oral forms. Naltrexone is a highly efficient opiate antagonist which can be taken by mouth and has a duration of action of 48 to 72 hours. Thus the addict who 'decides to relapse' must wait until the effect of the naltrexone has passed before they can obtain an opiate effect. As naltrexone wears off, there is a gradual loss of the competitive blockade. There has now been extensive research into the potential applications for naltrexone (mainly in the US): so far the pharmacological promise of the drug has not been accompanied by a wide range of clinical applications, but work is ongoing (for review see Kleber, 1985). Work is currently underway on the development of a sustained release form of naltrexone so that a depot preparation or implant can be administered with a duration of action of many weeks – although there may need to be a reconsideration of the ethical issues around antagonists with the development of this longer acting form. As yet it still remains unclear what place will be occupied by such antagonist drugs in the future management of the addict in recovery.

Stimulants

Amphetamines remain the most widely abused stimulant in the UK, although cocaine use has been increasing greatly in recent years. Both of these drugs may be taken either by snorting or by intravenous injection. During the late 1980s, a new form of cocaine appeared, known as 'crack' or 'rock' which was a stable form of free-base cocaine, which could be smoked in a purpose made or home made crack pipe. This new form of cocaine could be inhaled across the lungs and would hence give a rapid onset to the psychoactive effect, such as to be comparable to intravenous injection. In 1991, there were reports of drug users smoking methyl amphetamine, sometimes known as 'ice', but this remains rare in the UK to date.

Effects

Amphetamine and cocaine can both result in the development of a drug induced psychosis, in which paranoia and persecutory delusions may occur in clear consciousness, alongside ideas of reference and auditory or visual hallucinations. Symptomatic treatment and management is sufficient, and the condition will recover spontaneously over the course of a few days (or a week or two at the most), and should not recur unless there are further episodes of high dose stimulant use. Urine analysis on admission is essential to assist in differentiation from an acute schizophreniform episode (see Chapter 9).

Withdrawal treatment

Treatment of the withdrawal syndrome has, until recently, been entirely symptomatic. However, recent work from the USA in the management of cocaine withdrawal has been exploring the potential therapeutic value of various drugs, including desipramine. It is postulated that desipramine exerts a moderating effect on the acute cocaine withdrawal syndrome via a mechanism different from its anti-depressant effect. Other drugs which have been used include bromocriptine and lithium, although it is doubtful that these drugs should yet be considered in regular clinical practice.

Non-pharmacological strategies and a longer term perspective should also be used in planning the after care of the cocaine or amphetamine addict in recovery, along the lines similar to those described above for the opiate addict.

Intravenous hypnotics and tranquillisers

Intravenous barbiturate abuse is now fortunately rare, but became widespread for a number of years during the '70s, and was associated with high morbidity and mortality. Not only were the barbiturates poorly soluble for intravenous use, and likely to produce cold abscesses associated with leakage around the injection site, but there was also a particular risk of respiratory depression or arrest, as the rate at which tolerance developed to this effect was less rapid than the development of tolerance to the sought-after psychoactive effect. Consequently the dependent barbiturate injector would steadily increase dose up to a point where the therapeutic margin of safety became very narrow.

During the late 1980s, intravenous abuse of benzodiazepines became evident with extensive intravenous injecting of the contents of temazepam capsules. At the time of writing, it remains unclear whether the reformulation of the liquid filled capsule into a hard gel fix capsule has been a sufficient change to reduce the overall extent of harm resulting from intravenous abuse. So far, the injecting of benzodiazepines is almost exclusively a UK phenomenon and has mainly involved the temazepam capsules. However, other benzodiazepines are also being injected. The benzodiazepines and barbiturates produce an effect similar to alcohol, and are sometimes used as a substitute for, or as an enhancer of, the effect of alcohol.

Dependence on prescribed benzodiazepines is now widespread in the UK, with an estimated two million adults taking benzodiazepines each day in the UK. Consideration of this problem is given in Chapter 4.

LSD, ecstasy, and other hallucinogens

The most famous hallucinogen of all is LSD. Despite early work with the drug by psychiatrists using it as an enhancer or short-cut for individual or group psychotherapy, the drug became discredited after its extensive use in the '60s and association with the new hedonistic drug taking culture. Like Aldous Huxley before him, Timothy Leary and the Merry Pranksters and the League of Spiritual Discovery taught a whole generation of western adolescents how to 'turn on, tune in and drop out'. The extent of this phenomenon extended way beyond the individuals who actually took the drug, so that the whole music industry, fashion and art were influenced by this social phenomenon, which has now been assimilated within society.

Other hallucinogens exist. In the UK, there are naturally occurring hallucinogenic mushrooms, with an extensive seasonal crop of these 'magic mushrooms' (notably *Psilocybe semilanceata*, known as the liberty cap).

More recently there has also been increasing use of a synthetic amphetamine analogue (MDMA, commonly known as ecstasy or E) which has combined stimulant and hallucinogenic properties.

Hallucinogens are taken specifically for the effects they have on perception and mood. The drug taker may seek treatment after a 'bad trip' in which the perceptual distortions, visual hallucinations or intense emotions have taken a frightening or disturbing turn – in contrast to the usual 'good trip'. The LSD user will usually retain a degree of contact with reality, although at times the phenomena seems so real that there is a serious risk of suicide. Drug users frequently develop a degree of competence at coping with fellow drug users who experience a bad trip, who can be helped considerably by reassurance and a link with reality until the natural passage of the effects. If pharmacological treatment is required, then it may be best for this to be restricted to a minor tranquilliser, as there have been reports that phenothiazines may aggravate the condition after the use of some of the more unusual hallucinogens.

Flashbacks are described by former LSD users, in which there is a recurrence of all or part of the original LSD experience. The pharmacological basis of the phenomenon is not understood, as these may occur months, or even years, after the original use of the drug. However it is notable that the flashback is usually a recurrence of a bad 'trip', or is associated with distress, and in many ways it seems similar to a panic attack. The intensity of the flashback is usually significantly less than the original drug effect, but flashbacks may be associated with anxiety or depression.

Growing use of ecstasy in the 1990s has been followed by reports not only of transient psychotic states but also serious physical illness: recurrent episodes of jaundice; acute severe chest pain; epilepsy; and spontaneous intracerebral haemorrhage (Henry, 1992).

Cannabis, Marijuana

Cannabis is far and away the most widely used illicit drug in the UK, accounting for more than three-quarters of arrests for possession of drugs by the police. The drug is usually smoked with a mixture of tobacco and dried leaves (marijuana) or with the resin (hash). There are various psychoactive components within cannabis, but the most active constituent is delta 9 tetrahydrocannabinol (delta 9 THC, often abbreviated to THC). As with all drugs, the effects of cannabis depend greatly on the circumstances of use, and particularly on the individual's expectations and previous experience.

For most users, and for most episodes of use, there will be no serious untoward physical or psychiatric complications. However, short term adverse reactions do occur, including anxiety states and panic attacks, brought on by the drug – particularly in novice users, and may occur in the absence of any prior psychopathology. Short-term psychotic reactions may occur, although it remains unclear whether these reactions may only occur within vulnerable individuals or in any drug user. Anxiety, depersonalisation and confusion are prominent features of the acute cannabis psychosis, and, as with other drug-induced psychoses, the condition is usually managed adequately by symptomatic relief and reassurance.

Chronic psychotic episodes have been described in association with cannabis use, but the evidence for this causal link between prior use of the drug and subsequent psychosis remains inconclusive and unsubstantiated. Use of cannabis can certainly act as a trigger to the recurrence of schizophrenia or manic depressive states, but the existence of a specific motivational syndrome is less clear. The extent to which cannabis interferes with motor performance is often overlooked. Studies of simulated driving conditions, or simulated air pilot flying demonstrate the considerable extent to which cannabis interferes with estimations of time and distance, as well as impairment of attention and short term memory – with these effects still being discernible 24 to 48 hours after use of the drug. Cannabis is fat-soluble, and is only slowly eliminated, so that urine tests after high dose cannabis use can remain positive for several weeks.

Volatile substances

Inhalation for pleasure of substances which alter consciousness and cause euphoria or disinhibition was practised, and still is occasionally, with the early anaesthetics such as ether and nitrous oxide. Nowadays a wide range of over-the-counter substances are purchased by young people for 'recreation'. Some users develop dependence (Esmail *et al*, 1992); deaths have occurred due to large doses in a single session causing unconsciousness and inhalation of vomit, and in isolated cases of chronic use due to toxic damage to liver or kidneys. Brain damage has resulted from repeatedly inhaling gasoline containing lead.

Mode of use

Adhesives (or paint strippers) are poured into empty plastic bags such as crisp packets and the vapour inhaled often with exhaling into the bag and rebreathing carbon dioxide. Fluids such as typewriter correcting fluid or dry-cleaning solvents (which contain trichlorethane) are poured on to a sleeve or a cloth and the vapour inhaled.

Gases from cigarette lighters, camping gas containers (butane, propane), or aerosol products (butane, halons) are inhaled via a plastic bag or directly from the containers. Aerosols sprayed directly into the mouth or pharynx have caused cold burns, laryngospasm or cardiac arrest from vagal stimulation.

Recognition

The regular user begins to behave in a more disorganised way, is erratic at school or truant, may often be out of the house and secretive when he is at home. When the child is intoxicated, disinhibition, perhaps giggling, may be noticed by an alert parent. These changes may not seem dissimilar from other adolescent behaviour. More conclusive will be a smell of solvent on the breath or clothes, and adhesives may leave marks on clothes or sores around the nose or mouth from compound sticking to the edge of the plastic bag.

Physical effects and detection

Larger doses or prolonged use may lead to ataxia, tinnitus, visual and auditory hallucinations, or confusion.

Urinary and blood analysis can detect certain of these compounds (Meredith *et al*, 1989). Ideally, the specimen should be placed in a glass container, which is well filled, with a cap tightened on metal foil.

Conclusion

A sound grasp of syphilis and the protean manifestations of infection was an essential requirement for the clinical and research psychiatrist of yesterday. Today it is becoming apparent that an appreciation of drug and alcohol misuse and dependence are similarly essential requirements for the competent clinician and researcher in the mental health arena. The full-time addiction specialist may be particularly interested in the characteristics of addict doctors in recovery; the general psychiatrist with special responsibility for drug services may be involved in developing shared care practices with local general practitioners; and the general psychiatrist may be confronted by the overlap between drug use and other possible causes of the acute psychotic episode. For each of these psychiatrists, a sound grasp of the potential role of substance abuse is now essential.

Recommended reading

Ghodse, H. & Maxwell, D. (eds) (1990) *Substance Abuse and Dependence: an Introduction for the Caring Professions*. London: Macmillan.
Royal College of Psychiatrists (1987) *Drug Scenes*. London: Gaskell.

References

Advisory Council on the Misuse of Drugs (1984) *Report on Prevention*. London: HMSO.
Anker, A. L. & Crowley, T. J. (1982) Use of contingency contracting in specialty clinics for cocaine abuse. In *Problems of Drug Dependence, 1981* (NIDA Research Monograph No. 41) (ed. L. S. Harris), pp. 452–459. Rockville, MD: National Institute on Drug Abuse.

Department of Health (1991) *Drug Misuse and Dependence. Guidelines on Clinical Management.* London: HMSO.

Esmail, A., Anderson, H. R., Taylor, J., Pottier, A. & Ramsay, J. D. (1992) Controlling deaths from volatile substance abuse in under 18s: the effects of legislation. *British Medical Journal,* **305**, 692.

Glanz, A., Byren, C. & Jackson, P. (1989) Role of community pharmacists in prevention of AIDS among injecting drug misusers: findings of a survey in England and Wales. *British Medical Journal,* **299**, 1076–1079.

Henry, J. A. (1992) Ecstasy and the dance of death. *British Medical Journal,* **305**, 5–6.

Kleber, H. D. (1985) Naltrexone. *Journal of Substance Abuse Treatment,* **2**, 117–122.

Lancet Editorial (1987) Screening for drugs of abuse. *Lancet,* **1**, 365–366.

Marlatt, G. A. & Gordon, J. (eds) (1985) *Relapse Prevention: Maintenance Strategies in the Treatment of Addictive Behaviours.* New York: Guilford Press.

Meredith, T. J., Ruprah, M., Liddle, A., *et al* (1989) Diagnosis and treatment of acute poisoning with volatile substances. *Human Toxicology,* **8**, 277–286.

Miller, W. (1983) Motivational interviewing with problem drinkers. *Behavioral Psychotherapy,* **11**, 147–172.

Robins, L., Davis, D. H. & Goodwin, D. W. (1974) Drug use by U.S. Army enlisted men in Vietnam: a follow-up on their return home. *American Journal of Epidemiology,* **99**, 235–249.

Rounsaville, B. J., Carrol, K., Budde, D., *et al* (1991) Psychiatric diagnosis of treatment-seeking cocaine abusers. *Archives of General Psychiatry,* **48**, 43–51.

——, *et al* (1982) Heterogeneity of psychiatry diagnosis in treatment opiate addicts. *Archives of General Psychiatry,* **39**, 161–166.

Stimson, G. V. (1973) *Heroin and Behaviour.* Shannon, Ireland: Irish University Press.

——, Alldritt, L., Dolan, K., *et al* (1988) Syringe exchange schemes for drug users in England and Scotland. *British Medical Journal,* **296**, 1717–1719.

——, Donoghoe, M., Lart, R., *et al* (1990) Distributing sterile needles and syringes to people who inject drugs: the syringe-exchange experiment. In *AIDS and Drug Misuse: the Challenge for Policy and Practice in the 1990s* (eds J. Strang & G. Stimson). London: Routledge.

Strang, J. & Stimson, G. V. (eds) (1990) *AIDS and Drug Misuse: the Challenge for Policy and Practice in the 1990s.* London: Routledge.

——, Bradley, B. & Stockwell, T. (1989) Assessment of drug and alcohol abuse. In *The Instruments of Psychiatric Research* (ed. C. Thompson). Chichester (UK): John Wiley.

——, Griffiths, P., Powis, B., *et al* (1992) First use of heroin: changes in route of administration over time. *British Medical Journal,* **304**, 1222–1223.

Washton, A. M. Gold, M. F. & Pottash, A. C. (1984) Successful use of naltrexone in addicted physicians and business executives. *Advances in Alcohol and Substance Abuse,* **4**, 89–96.

Winick, C. (1980) A theory of drug dependence based on role, access to, and attitudes towards drugs. In *Theories on Drug Abuse* (eds. D. J. Lettieri, M. Sayers & H. W. Pearson). Washington: National Institute on Drug Abuse.

4 Dependence on prescribed and socially tolerated substances
John Marks

This chapter groups three types of substance, tranquillisers, tobacco and caffeine, which are not generally associated with acutely harmful effects but which can lead to dependence. Dependence *per se* has little medical significance until the drug is discontinued. Toxicity from chronic ingestion encouraged by the dependence is, of course, important (Marks, 1985; Jaffe, 1990*a*).

Minor tranquillisers

'Minor tranquillisers' (now usually termed 'tranquillisers') embrace a series of compounds used for symptomatic relief of anxiety. They merge with the sedative hypnotics on the one hand (many minor tranquillisers can be used as hypnotics, while sedatives are effective anxiolytics), and with neuroleptics on the other (some neuroleptics are used in low dosage as anxiolytics).

The range of dependence and abuse liability among sedatives is shown in Table 4.1. Some of these are no longer used, several because they were associated with severe dependence and abuse, and banned or restricted in many countries.

Epidemiology of tranquilliser dependence

The peak of benzodiazepine use was passed in the late 1970s, with the annual number of UK prescriptions having fallen by a third to 20 million by 1990. The drop in prescribing was almost entirely due to reduction in anxiolytic use, rather than hypnotic use.

Use is greater in women and in the elderly. The US mental health national survey interviews found that those prescribed benzodiazepines have an elevated incidence of criteria for depressive disorders as well as anxiety disorders. In Europe long-term use is greatest in Belgium and France, least in Sweden, with the UK in between. A study in 1985 found that one in 50 of a typical UK general practice population had received a prescription for a benzodiazepine continuously for a year or more (Rodrigo *et al*, 1988). Many long-term users do not take their drugs regularly, according to self-report studies and to findings of plasma drug levels. Prevalence rates of regular long-term use may therefore sometimes be overestimates.

Table 4.1   Estimates of dependence/misuse risk of the 'sedatives class' of drugs

	Dependence/misuse liability	Medical/social problems	Extent of current use
Barbiturates	+ + +	+ + +	+
Bromides	+ / −	+	+ / −
Chloral hydrate	+ +	+	+ / −
Paraldehyde	+ / −	−	+ / −
Meprobamate & derivatives	+ +	+	+ / −
Methaqualone	+ + +	+ +	nil
Benzodiazepines	+	+	+ + +
Phenothiazines	−	+	+ +
Buspirone	−	+ / −	+
Cyclopyrrolone (Zopiclone)	+ / −	+ / −	+

+ + +, high level; + +, moderate level; +, low level; + / −, negligible if any.

What proportion of long-term users should be deemed dependent is not known. The highest estimate comes from certain self-help groups who report that most long-term users expect discontinuance symptoms. When less selected samples are asked about such symptoms the rates are lower. For example, in a survey of patients presenting prescriptions for diazepam, of those patients who said they had tried to stop, 86% reported a return of old symptoms but only 18% the development of new, different symptoms (Haskell *et al*, 1986). Around a half of long-term users nowadays say that they would like to come off benzodiazepines but this proportion is almost the same for all patients receiving long-term therapy of any type.

When compared to patients prescribed a drug for hypertension, the average patient on a benzodiazepine does not tend to renew the prescription early or to duplicate prescriptions from another physician. However, these practices do occur in a small number of users, especially those who are polydrug abusers.

Among polydrug abusers, use of benzodiazepines has become common. Local fashions and availability influence the prevalence. Injecting the contents of temazepam capsules, with risk of vascular occlusion, was not eliminated by changing the formulation from liquid contents to gel.

Clinical features

The varying characteristics of 'sedative' dependence

The World Health Organization (WHO) had the barbiturates in mind when defining dependence in 1964:

"a state arising from repeated administration of . . . an agent . . . generally in amounts exceeding therapeutic dose levels. Its characteristics include:

(1) a strong desire to continue taking the drug . . .
(2) a tendency to increase the dose, partly owing to the development of tolerance
(3) a psychic dependence . . .
(4) a physical dependence on the effects of the drug requiring its presence for maintenance of homeostasis and resulting in a definite, characteristic, and self limiting abstinence syndrome when the drug is withdrawn" (World Health Organization, 1964).

However, when applied to dependence to the benzodiazepines when used in therapeutic doses, many of these features do not occur. There is usually not a strong desire to continue taking the drug, even after prolonged ingestion; tolerance to the anxiolytic effect is not great, so there is relatively little escalation of the dose; the occurrence of florid withdrawal manifestations is rare. Indeed the dependence to the benzodiazepines which occurs during therapeutic use shows very little resemblance to that found, for example, with barbiturates or methaqualone. Thus the term 'dependence' covers in practice a very wide range of phenomena even within a single WHO class.

So far as the benzodiazepines are concerned, there was increasing evidence during the 1980s that a clear distinction should be drawn between the classical physical dependence which occurs very rarely with this group of substances and an entirely different phenomenon which can occur during therapeutic dose use. There is currently a dispute as to whether this latter reaction should really be classed as dependence. For practical purposes the group of minor tranquillisers which currently requires the greatest consideration is the benzodiazepines and this group can therefore be considered in detail as the current most important example.

The features of, and issues surrounding, benzodiazepine dependence have been extensively reviewed – see Owen & Tyrer (1983), Petursson & Lader (1984), Marks (1985), Woods *et al* (1987) and Lader (1989). A balanced current view is provided by the APA (American Psychiatric Association) Task Force Report (1990).

Clinical features of benzodiazepine 'dependence' at therapeutic dosage

Although there is presumptive evidence that psychological dependence is a feature of the dependence to therapeutic doses of benzodiazepines, craving and drug seeking behaviour are not florid manifestations. For practical purposes the vast majority of those who are regarded as being dependent on benzodiazepines as a result of therapeutic administration can be best regarded as examples of physical dependence.

Physical dependence produces no symptoms or signs while the benzodiazepine is being administered and it is only when the substance is withdrawn that symptoms occur. These have usually been termed 'the abstinence syndrome', 'abstinence manifestations' or 'the withdrawal reaction' but the recent APA Task Force Report (1990) prefers the terms 'discontinuance syndrome' and 'discontinuance symptoms' to take account of the fact that all such phenomena do not necessarily represent physical dependence.

Since the half-lives of many of the widely used benzodiazepines are substantially longer than many sedatives, blood levels low enough to precipitate discontinuance symptoms often occur somewhat later. Thus they often first appear between the second and fifth day after withdrawal, reach a maximum intensity by about the seventh to tenth day and rarely persist in established form beyond four weeks.

In their most minor form discontinuance symptoms consist only of minor anxiety, insomnia, dizziness and anorexia which may probably be regarded as rebound manifestations.

The typical symptoms of discontinuance are shown in Table 4.2 in which an estimate of their frequency of occurrence as assessed by the APA Task Force is also recorded. There is some dispute about whether all these are true manifestations of physical dependence. For example some are mainly associated with one benzodiazepine (e.g. psychotic reactions with triazolam; Oswald, 1989) and may represent a specific toxic reaction, although this is strongly debated.

The differential diagnosis of withdrawal reactions after therapeutic dosage

It is vital to appreciate that the only objective and specific sign of a withdrawal reaction to any sedative compound is a convulsion which occurs at a time sequence which is compatible with the elimination of the substance. The remaining manifestations are all subjective or non-specific and suffer from the problems associated with subjective phenomena, particularly those of confirmation and quantification.

Convulsions are virtually unknown after the withdrawal of therapeutic doses of most benzodiazepines. When they occur in the absence of a co-existing alcohol dependence they are commonly the result of immediate total withdrawal usually coupled with the substitution of neuroleptics or tricyclic antidepressants both of which classes of drugs lower the seizure threshold. The only exception to this general low incidence of convulsions is the sudden withdrawal of high doses of short-acting compounds with a high potency.

Because there are so few examples of objective signs of benzodiazepine discontinuance the differential diagnosis must usually be made on the subjective symptoms. At therapeutic dose levels there are considerable difficulties in determining if these symptoms really represent an abstinence syndrome, for the following reasons:

Table 4.2 Manifestations of sedative abstinence syndromes

Psychological manifestations of anxiety including
    irritability (+ +)
    difficulty in concentration
    restlessness (+ +)
    insomnia (+ +)
    agitation (+ +)
    nightmares (+)
Physiological correlates of anxiety including
    tremor
    shakiness
    profuse sweating (+)
    palpitations
    lethargy (+)
Hyperexcitability and hyperacuity including
    muscle tension (twitching and aches and pains) (+ +)
    hyperacuity to light, smell, sounds (+)
    metallic taste
    rarely convulsions (+ / −)
Other physical reactions including
    nausea (+)
    loss of appetite
    weight loss
    'flu-like' illness (+)
Other psychological reactions including
    dysphoria
    impaired memory/confusion (+ / −)
    depersonalisation and derealisation (+ / −)
    psychotic reactions (+ / −)
    hallucinations (+ / −)

(+ / −) to (+ +) Estimate of frequency of occurrence as assessed by the APA Task Force (1990): (+ +) = very frequent; (+) = common; (+ / −) = uncommon. Those for which no estimate of frequency is provided are not mentioned in the APA Report.

Non-specific symptomatology   It has been shown (Merz & Ballmer, 1983) that about one in ten of the normal population and a higher proportion of those with anxiety present with the symptoms that are reputedly pathognomonic of withdrawal in physical dependence (Table 4.2). Several authors have suggested that sensory hyperacuity is an important distinguishing feature for dependence. However hyperacuity can be a feature of a typical normal anxiety reaction which develops in young adults prior to an examination.

Rebound   Rebound reactions are very common with many drugs, the majority of which are not implicated in any way with dependence (Lupolover *et al*, 1982).

Several of the manifestations reputed to be related to abstinence in physical dependence (e.g. insomnia, anxiety) can be shown to occur after even a single administration of a short-acting high potency benzodiazepine. For example rebound insomnia has been said to occur after even a single dose of an ultra short-acting benzodiazepine administered as an hypnotic (Woods *et al*, 1987). Hence these reactions i.e. insomnia, anxiety and the symptoms associated with them, cannot be regarded as pathognomonic of physical dependence. Some authorities have even suggested that the majority of withdrawal reactions may be rebound effects (Owen & Tyrer, 1983). This may however be merely a question of semantics.

Recurrence of anxiety   Morbid anxiety is typically a recurrent disorder. Experience has demonstrated that too short a period of treatment can lead to a risk of recurrence, the symptoms of which are virtually indistinguishable from those of the abstinence syndrome.

This is not to say that physical dependence is not a concern when the benzodiazepines are administered. Moreover, it is a concern that a proportion of patients become dependent as a result of the physician reinstituting therapy in the belief (which may have been correct initially) that they were treating a recurrent and inadequately treated anxiety state.

It is important to appreciate that the diagnosis of physical dependence to therapeutic doses of benzodiazepines is far from easy. A substantial proportion of such patients do show symptoms that can be ascribed to either rebound or recurrence of the anxiety.

If an attempt is made to make the diagnosis then the main characteristics upon which physical dependence can be regarded as being the most likely diagnosis are:

(1) a time sequence in which the symptoms start approximately two to three days after the drug is withdrawn (assuming a medium or long-acting benzodiazepine is being administered), reach a maximum after about seven or eight days and then reduce in intensity. In contradistinction to this, the typical recurrence of an anxiety state comes on more slowly, gradually reaches a higher level after about two to three weeks and persists.
(2) a triad of clinical manifestation, namely a 'flu-like' dysphoria; significant levels of hyperacuity; an unpleasant metallic taste. However even this triad cannot be regarded as pathognomonic.

The pragmatic approach is to regard any patient who has received sedative drugs for over six weeks as potentially physically dependent and to withdraw the sedative gradually.

The post-withdrawal syndrome

It has been suggested that there is a dysphoric state which may persist for months or years in those withdrawn from benzodiazepines. It has also been

---

Box 4.1   Differential diagnosis of physical dependence/recurrent anxiety

	Physical dependence	Recurrent anxiety
Time sequence (approximate)		
Onset	2–3 days	7 days
Maximum intensity	7–8 days reduces 14 days	14+ days continues
Symptoms	New symptoms, often with 'flu like' dysphoria, hyperacuity, metallic taste	Typically, return of old symptoms

---

referred to as 'the persistent benzodiazepine dependence syndrome'. There is no biochemical or pharmacological mechanism yet described which could explain such a phenomenon and the symptoms are probably best interpreted as those of a recurring anxiety state. In some patients it emerges that there is a relapsing depressive disorder.

Erroneous beliefs, expectations and attributions appear to play a part. Anxiety attributed to dose reduction is experienced by many patients too early to be consistent with the drug's known elimination half-life, and sometimes does not persist as long as the pharmacokinetics would predict (Higgitt & Fonagy, 1992). Patients pay attention more intensely than others to normal bodily sensations. They focus on the irreversibility of their condition and the need for the drug 'to cope'.

Aetiology of tranquilliser dependence

Changes in receptor sensitivity related to the gamma-aminobutyric acid (GABA) portion of the receptor complex have been reported as a consequence of chronic administration of benzodiazepines. This is one potential explanation for short-term benzodiazepine dependence. Alterations in receptor numbers and sensitivity are also possibly implicated. Although the basic neuropharmacology clearly requires much further exploration, clinical study has revealed that various factors affect the propensity and severity of discontinuance symptoms.

Factors influencing incidence, severity or timing of discontinuance symptoms

Although the clinical features described above are seen, to a greater or lesser extent, in a substantial proportion of withdrawal reactions, various factors can influence the frequency, severity or time course of the reactions:

High doses   The higher the dose, the more likely it is that the patient will experience withdrawal symptoms. There is however no known threshold for dosage below which abstinence symptoms do not occur. It was several years before it was recognised that withdrawal symptoms could occur at normal therapeutic doses, but this has now been established quite clearly.

Duration of use   The duration of use is probably the single most important factor which determines the proportion of patients who will experience abstinence symptoms. However there is a shorter time frame for the development of withdrawal symptoms when higher doses are administered.

Since rebound phenomena have been reported after single dose administration of short-acting sedatives it is impossible to give a reliable indication of the minimum time to the onset of withdrawal symptoms. In practical terms, symptoms of anything other than a minor level are extremely rare under one month of therapeutic use and clinically meaningful symptoms are low during the first three to four months of regular therapeutic dose administration. The incidence after longer administration is considered later.

Drug characteristics   Abstinence symptoms are encountered with both short half-life and long half-life drugs and with those that are used mainly as anxiolytics, hypnotics and muscle relaxants. However the time of onset after withdrawal is less and the symptoms are often more florid after the sudden withdrawal of short half-life benzodiazepines.

How far drug potency (as opposed to elimination half-life) is a factor in the genesis of withdrawal phenomena is a matter of dispute. There is no unequivocal evidence, but a general clinical impression of more numerous and more severe symptoms after a shorter period of administration with some of the high potency short half-life benzodiazepines like alprazolam, lorazepam and triazolam (Hallfors & Saxe, 1993).

Patient type   The fact that duration of continuous administration influences the risk of abstinence symptoms means that certain types of patient e.g. chronic dysphoric state, chronic insomnia are at greater risk. The risk is also greater in those with a prior or current history of drug abuse and those who have been termed 'dependence prone' individuals (Marks, 1985). Woods *et al* (1987) have described this group as having a 'passive dependent personality'. The evidence suggests that such patients are more prone to develop symptoms on cessation of equivalent dose levels. They have also suggested that those with an obsessional personality are less likely to show symptoms on withdrawal. Cognitive processes likely to presage persistent symptoms attributed to withdrawal have been described as low self-efficacy, and tendency to amplify bodily sensations, assuming catastrophic causes for them (Higgitt & Fonagy, 1992).

Variation of incidence of withdrawal reactions with
length of therapeutic dose administration

The main determination of the incidence stems from an examination of case reports since there are no satisfactory prospective studies. When the errors inherent in such a technique are compounded by the difficulties of definition of what constitutes a withdrawal reaction it is scarcely surprising that there are very variable views about the incidence.

The best current estimate of incidence of withdrawal reactions with length of continuous use for an 'average' benzodiazepine (i.e. not one for which there is presumptive evidence of high risk) is given in Table 4.3. It should perhaps be restated that this is the incidence of withdrawal reactions and this does not equate to the incidence of physical dependence, which would be less than this.

Even if there are varying views of the incidence during the first year of continuous use there is substantial agreement that at least 50% of patients treated with therapeutic doses for more than one year show no withdrawal effects. The reasons for this are far from clear.

Table 4.3   Variation in the incidence of discontinuance syndrome with length of continuous use of a long acting benzodiazepine at therapeutic dosage

Up to 3 months	virtually nil
3–12 months	10–20%
over 12 months	20–45%

The proportion of these reactions which represent a true physical dependence is a matter of dispute.

Management

Reducing the risk of withdrawal reactions after long-term use

Gradual withdrawal should be used in all patients who have received benzodiazepines for more than about six weeks continuously. The rate of reduction that avoids the risk of withdrawal reactions varies from one patient to another and depends on the length of previous continuous administration and the dose. Despite the fact that at least 50% of those treated continuously for some years can be withdrawn rapidly without problems, it is good medical practice to always withdraw steadily.

As a working guide:

(1) up to about four to six weeks of therapeutic doses, reduction by three halving steps over a total of seven to ten days and then discontinuation is normally appropriate unless the patient is a heavy user of alcohol

(2) from six weeks to about six months of therapeutic doses, stepwise reduction over 10–20 days is desirable

(3) beyond six months continuous use or if there is doubt about the patient's previous use of alcohol or sedatives it is wise to reduce the dose stepwise over about four to six weeks.

Box 4.2 Influences on severity of symptoms of discontinuance from benzodiazepines

High dose
Longer period of use
Shorter drug half-life
Personality: 'dependence prone' (chronic dysphoria; passive dependent)
Cognitive style: low self-efficacy, tendency to catastrophise

---

Withdrawal where there is evidence of dependence

The most important single factor in achieving successful and long-term withdrawal in such patients is the sustained support of the practitioner. The process of withdrawal is unpleasant and uncomfortable when the patient is dependent. This should be recognised by the practitioner and appropriate advice, sympathy and consolation accorded the patient. At the same time, firm though kind management is essential.

If the patient is currently taking a rapidly eliminated benzodiazepine this should be substituted by an equivalent and adequate dose of one of the slowly eliminated benzodiazepines (usually diazepam) (Table 4.4). The dose is then reduced very gradually. The rate of reduction that avoids withdrawal sequelae varies from one such patient to another. As a general rule in cases of established dependence at least four to eight weeks is necessary to reduce the problems to a level which is acceptable to the patient. In the majority of patients it is possible to reduce to half the therapeutic dose fairly rapidly but later reduction

Table 4.4 Withdrawal from benzodiazepines facilitated by transfer to the longer acting drug, diazepam. The following are equivalent to 5 mg diazepam

Chlordiazepoxide	15.0 mg
Oxazepam	15.0 mg
Lorazepam	0.5 mg
Lormetazepam	0.25 mg
Nitrazepam	5.0 mg
Temazepam	10.0 mg
Triazolam	0.25 mg
(no longer prescribable in the UK)	

should be slower. It is suggested that the maximum reduction step should be a quarter of the current dose at intervals of four to six days. If the patient experiences a level of discomfort that is unacceptable then the dose should be held just above the level that provokes the reaction and then further gradual reduction reinstituted more slowly. However a steady firm approach is essential to achieve good results.

The administration of propranolol will reduce the physical but not the emotional problems associated with the abstinence syndrome. The author believes that tricyclic antidepressants and phenothiazine neuroleptics should be given with great caution over the withdrawal period because their administration increases the risk of convulsions by reducing the convulsion threshold.

**Box 4.3 Withdrawal in patients with evidence
of dependence**

Firm but kind management by the physician is essential. Provide advice about the likely problems but do not overstress them

Substitute current therapy with a slowly eliminated benzodiazepine (usually diazepam)

Administration of propranolol will reduce the physical manifestations

Reduce the dose in maximum steps of about one-quarter of the current dosage

Each reduction step interval should be at least 4–6 days

The whole course should last for 4–8 weeks

Avoid administration of tricyclic antidepressants and phenothiazine neuroleptics during withdrawal

---

Various self-help patient groups exist to assist withdrawal (e.g. 'TRANX'). Their value is variable depending in major part on the personality, experience and ability of the group leaders.

The later management of anxiety in those
withdrawn from benzodiazepines

When patients withdrawn after dependence on benzodiazepines require support for recurring morbid anxiety, it is rational and prudent to try non-pharmacological methods first. The cognitive–behavioural approach which has been recommended (Higgitt & Fonagy, 1992) includes teaching relaxation, distraction, graded exposure and re-framing catastrophic thoughts. Relabelling symptoms as anxiety rather than drug-withdrawal is important, followed by reappraisal of anxiety, for example, "feeling anxious is not dangerous, it's just damned unpleasant".

If psychological treatment fails, then pharmacological methods other than the benzodiazepines should be tried e.g. buspirone or a sedative neuroleptic. Theoretically buspirone, which still appears to have no dependence potential would appear to be ideal, but unfortunately some patients experience dysphoria when taking it and, in general, it is perceived as not being so effective as an anxiolytic by patients who have previously been prescribed a benzodiazepine. Hence there is often patient resistance to its use.

Unfortunately substitution is not always successful and a long acting benzodiazepine has now been used in a substantial number of such patients. In theory a rapid return to a dependent state would be expected. In practice, a surprisingly high proportion of such patients can return to controlled variable dose intermittent benzodiazepine use to cover periods of pronounced distress.

Clearly the technique should only be undertaken when absolutely necessary. The patient requires extensive counselling about the use of the drug and a full understanding and acceptance by the patient of the risk involved is essential. The management requires careful control by a psychiatrist who has considerable experience in the management of patients with severe disabling recurrent anxiety.

Is the use of benzodiazepines justified?

The group of the anxiety disorders is not only among the most common seen in medical practice but is also among the most difficult to manage given the constraints imposed by shortage of time and money. Many of the most appropriate and probably most effective forms of treatment (such as cognitive therapy, behavioural therapy, relaxation techniques) are only feasible given access to extensive facilities on a long-term basis. Even when they are used the results are not universally good. This is not surprising when it is appreciated that morbid anxiety often represents a failed coping mechanism to environmental problems, at home, at work or in life in general. Since these can rarely be removed entirely it follows that permanent cure is rare even in expert hands.

Since morbid anxiety is very disturbing for the patient, doctors must perforce use all available effective methods of treatment to achieve rapid symptomatic relief. Hence, although it can only help to alleviate symptoms rather than effect a permanent cure of the underlying disorder, those who have a biological approach to psychiatry believe that pharmacotherapy should form part of the therapeutic armamentarium, but used with the other forms of medical management. Although tricyclic and serotonin uptake inhibitor antidepressants have a role, it is still accepted that for a substantial proportion of patients with morbid anxiety judiciously used benzodiazepines still offer effective and safe symptomatic relief.

Guidelines for benzodiazepine use

Physicians must accept that if there is a problem of dependence with a therapeutic agent then efforts should be made to reduce the risk. Guidelines for appropriate benzodiazepine use should be designed to reduce the risk. They represent in fact the normal techniques of good medical practice.

(1) Select very carefully the patients for whom a benzodiazepine will be prescribed. If anxiety is not a prominent feature of the clinical manifestations then there are grave doubts about the wisdom of using a benzodiazepine. If there are features of depression then consider the use of an antidepressant or, if both anxiety and depression appear to be present it may be useful to give both a benzodiazepine and one of the more sedative antidepressants initially, withdrawing the benzodiazepine after about ten days when the antidepressant activity is present. Some psychiatrists prefer to try tricyclic antidepressants first in those with panic disorders or phobic anxiety, while buspirone should certainly be considered for any patients who are considered to be possibly 'dependence prone'.

(2) Always consider whether the level of 'distress' is such that the use of any pharmacotherapeutic agent is required. Remember that a cure can best be effected if, with the practitioner's help, the patient can either avoid the cause of the anxiety or at least come to terms with it. Pharmacotherapeutic agents are not necessary for the normal stresses of life and should not be used as a replacement for medical discussion and counselling.

(3) One particular area which requires attention is the management of insomnia. Short-term or intermittent pharmacotherapy with a benzodiazepine has a place when linked to education on 'sleep hygiene' (Nicholson & Marks, 1983). A particular area for care is in the management of bereavement, a circumstance in which inappropriate long-term prescription of an hypnotic benzodiazepine appears to be all too frequent.

(4) Additional care during the use of any pharmacological agent will be necessary with patients who show a dependence on other substances (e.g. alcohol) or who show a dependent personality. Remember it is better to seek and define this problem before initiating therapy than after.

(5) It is important to keep the daily dose as low as possible compatible with achieving the desired therapeutic effect.

(6) Therapy should always be stopped as soon as this is justified on clinical grounds. Benzodiazepine therapy is symptomatic and adjunctive rather than curative and there are no merits in further continuous therapy once the distress has been relieved.

(7) An intermittent variable dosage schedule in which both the administration and the dosage is graded according to the level of distress has great merit and the concept is normally understood well by the patient if time is taken to explain it.

(8) Since it is impossible to be certain whether a discontinuance syndrome may occur, whatever this may represent, it is important to reduce the dose gradually after any period of administration. This should apply to any chronically administered therapeutic agent. The longer the administration the longer the period of dose reduction.

Box 4.4   Guidelines for benzodiazepine use

Select carefully for anxiety which is causing distress

If depression is a feature try tricyclic antidepressant first

Use only as part of overall management strategy

Use lowest effective dose for shortest period to achieve therapeutic response

Always reduce dose gradually on discontinuation

Length of administration and the question of chronic use of benzodiazepines

In the early 1980s various UK medical bodies made dogmatic statements defining the maximum length of benzodiazepine administration as one month. Few other countries reacted in this fashion and some patients may have lost rather than gained as a result of the advice.

Ultimately, the patient has the right to decide the general form of therapy which they receive. All physicians have the duty to act as advisers and not deities. Indeed some authorities now suggest that it is unethical to withhold treatment which the patient requests. However in order that the patient can reach the right decision for his own circumstances it is vital that the doctor provides adequate information about both the pros and cons of the proposed therapy. It is even more important to adopt this policy in a subjective phenomenon like anxiety, in which only the patient can define their level of distress and the physician has no reliable objective measurements. This information should be expressed in comprehensible terms.

Providing that the patient has enough comprehension, it is important to explain the nature, the possible causes and the anticipated course of the disorder. It is vital to explain that current anxiolytics do not produce a cure but reduce the distress to a level at which the patient is able to determine and attempt to overcome the fundamental cause.

The doctor should explain that as the level of anxiety is reduced from that which causes distress to that which can be tolerated the patient will be given other assistance to solve the fundamental problem. This will probably include some form of individual psychotherapy or relaxation therapy and attempts at environmental modification management. To be effective, the management should be a combined operation involving both doctor and patient.

From what has been said it is clear that there cannot be a fixed period of benzodiazepine use but that the time to achieve the required therapeutic effect will vary from one patient to another. However good medical practice requires review of the patient's state on a regular basis, particularly at the early stage.

After two weeks.   If a pronounced improvement has not been seen by this stage the diagnosis should be reviewed. Lack of considerable improvement after two weeks suggests that anxiety is not the prime feature and that the diagnosis is more likely to be depression. The administration of a sedative antidepressant should be considered. There is no merit in continuing the administration of a benzodiazepine beyond the two week period if there is no improvement.

After four weeks.   By this stage any distress should have been controlled for some two to three weeks and, if doctor and patient have used the time wisely, a substantial proportion of the patients should have solved or come to terms with their problems.

Box 4.5   Time constraints on benzodiazepine use

Onset: Prescription only as part of overall management strategy of anxiety

2 weeks: If negligible improvement withdraw benzodiazepine and consider alternatives e.g. tricyclic antidepressant

4-6 weeks: Review carefully and withdraw gradually noting response to withdrawal

Thereafter: Only advise benzodiazepines for unacceptably high level of distress from anxiety which cannot be controlled by other means.

(1) Ensure patient understands the risks/benefit balance and accepts it
(2) Use intermittent variable dosage
(3) Withdraw therapy very gradually

Since the maintenance of continuous benzodiazepine administration beyond this time carries some risk of dependence it should be avoided if possible. It is important to withdraw the benzodiazepine gradually over a period of some seven to ten days and review the situation. There are three possible outcomes:

(1) The anxiety was either of short duration or the problem has been solved and the patient is cured. Administration of a benzodiazepine is no longer required.
(2) There is an intermittent identifiable cause for an acute anxiety state. If this leads to a level of distress and the cause cannot be avoided, the provision of a small number of benzodiazepine tablets which can be carried may be adequate to avoid distress. Alternatively short intermittent courses may be necessary.

(3) An unacceptable level of anxiety may still be present. The doctor should discuss with such patients the therapeutic needs and the risks involved in continuing therapy. Some patients can only live in society if given some form of support. In the opinion of many physicians the benzodiazepines represent a more effective and certainly safer support than readily available alternatives (e.g. alcohol, cigarettes). Such patients if counselled well may decide that the risk of dependence is of less concern to them than an intolerable level of anxiety. It is suggested that it is useful at this stage if the patient provides informed signed consent for the decision to continue therapy to avoid later dispute.

Even in these patients it is possible to reduce the risk of dependence. Anxiety rarely, even in the most severe case, runs at a steady level of high distress. Environmental circumstances vary and the level of distress changes. Therefore the dosage schedule should be based upon the principle of variable intermittent dosage with the patient encouraged to tailor their own use of the benzodiazepine to their needs. The important point is that dosage reduction should always be gradual.

One particular group that must be considered in this respect is that embracing people who are already chronic abusers of narcotics, alcohol or a mixture of drugs. While this group of patients are at greater risk of developing dependence, such dependence if it occurs (and it is not universal) may not be the overriding concern. The important points to assess are whether the administration of a minor tranquilliser enables the person to live more comfortably in society, to reduce their dependence on the substances which have a higher level of toxicity or, arguably, whether it protects society and the patient from the more extreme forms of their anti-social behaviour. This approach must be controversial but harm reduction by this approach is worth considering. The important point is that other methods of management of the dependence should have been considered fully before this is contemplated. Equally in this group, as in any other, it is essential to try to reduce the dose of the benzodiazepine if it is at all possible.

Benzodiazepine misuse potential

There is no totally accepted definition of the terminology related to inappropriate use of therapeutic substances and the term 'misuse' is therefore used here to signify 'persistent or sporadic use which is inconsistent with or unrelated to acceptable medical practice i.e. use within the socio-recreational drug scene'. I exclude from consideration inappropriate or misguided therapeutic use.

Misuse of the benzodiazepines may be either primary, or secondary to misuse of other substances. On a world-wide basis it is clear that primary benzodiazepine misuse is rare, although it does occur, perhaps more commonly in the Far East than in other parts of the world. It appears that the effect which is sought is a disinhibition. Even in these primary benzodiazepine misusers, it is far more common to find a simultaneous ingestion of alcohol and a high potency short-acting benzodiazepine than a long-acting benzodiazepine used alone.

There have been some reputed social consequences of this primary misuse namely aggression and burglary, but it is often difficult to be certain how much the misuse is being used as an excuse for the anti-social behaviour. However even if there are some unfortunate social consequences of the primary misuse, medical or public health sequelae are not encountered. Specifically, there is no evidence that primary benzodiazepine misuse leads on to misuse of other substances.

Secondary benzodiazepine misuse is a feature of the mixed drug misuse which is encountered in many countries at the present time. The exact combination which is misused varies from one community to another. It depends both on availability of the preferred drugs and also national fads and fashions and these vary from year to year, even in the same community. In many countries narcotics are the primary drugs of misuse in such a mixture but most of the other primary drugs of misuse have been implicated at some stage.

There would appear to be three main reasons for the inclusion of a benzodiazepine in the mixture which is being misused:

(1) As a substitute drug when the narcotic drug of primary misuse is not available. Benzodiazepines are not true substitutes for the narcotics in the pharmacological sense and have a low preference rating among narcotic abusers. On the other hand they do make a reduced narcotic dose more tolerable when there are difficulties over supply. There are parts of the UK where intravenous misuse, particularly of short-acting, high potency benzodiazepines has become more frequent in the 1990s (see p. 48).

(2) To reduce the side effects which may occur during narcotic misuse and particularly to overcome the anxiety which can be provoked by a 'bad' trip.

(3) Combined with alcohol to produce an euphoriant effect as a component of the socio-recreational misuse of narcotics. The extent of this effect is a matter of considerable controversy.

There is dispute currently about the merits of the 'harm reduction' concept by the deliberate attempt to substitute part or all narcotic misuse by benzodiazepines in those dependent on narcotics. In favour of such a procedure is the fact that a less toxic substance is being administered, even though dependence to the benzodiazepine is extremely likely to result. Against this approach is that true substitution may not be achieved, the patient becomes dependent on both drugs and may even utilise the prescribed benzodiazepine for further gratification. Certainly such attempts at substitution are not the first choice in the early stages of narcotic misuse but may have merit when it is apparent that complete withdrawal is very unlikely to be achieved and reduction of toxicity is an important feature. The increased incidence of HIV infections among narcotic drug users has certainly caused more experts in the field to re-examine the possibility.

Tobacco

There is now no doubt that tobacco is a substance of physical and psychological dependence although there is still doubt about the mechanism (Raw, 1982; Jaffe, 1990*b*). This applies to tobacco when smoked, chewed or sniffed (as snuff).

The nature of tobacco dependence

The current evidence suggests that smoking is mainly taken up originally by teenagers, not initially because of the physiological effects, because these are unpleasant at first. The onset is usually the result of social or psychological factors which include curiosity, assertion of independence, rebelliousness or perhaps more than any other factor by actual or supposed peer pressure.

Once established, smoking is maintained by a number of factors both social (peer expectation, widespread availability) and economic (relative cheapness). To this must be added a very high level of dependence, which, if one judges from the difficulties experienced over withdrawal and the poor results that have been achieved during encouraged withdrawal, is at least as severe as most drugs which are under international control as a result of UN/WHO action.

The mechanism of tobacco dependence is a complicated and multi-factorial one, as is the dependence to other substances. Pharmacological dependence to one or more of the chemical agents released from cigarettes is only one factor in this. To date it appears that the most powerful pharmacological agent in tobacco dependence is nicotine. Certainly there is clear evidence that nicotine can be the subject of dependence and that those who smoke heavily seem to do so in such a way that the blood nicotine level is kept constant (Raw, 1982).

There is a moderate genetic influence on the initiation and maintenance of cigarette smoking, on the level of dependence, and on the ability (or inability) of a smoker to quit smoking. The basis of these genetic influences has not been determined. Possible mechanisms include genetically determined differences in the pharmacological response to nicotine, differences in personality, and the presence or absence of dysthymia, particularly depression. The high concordance found in genetic studies between smoking and alcoholism indicates a genetic component shared between these two addictions. Thus a proportion of the genetic predisposition to tobacco addiction may be specific to nicotine, but some is linked to alcoholism or to other drug addictions (Benowitz, 1992).

The main withdrawal symptoms and signs include craving (i.e. psychological dependence), irritability, impatience, frustration or anger, anxiety, difficulty concentrating, restlessness, increased appetite, weight gain, depression, insomnia, constipation, increased slow waves in the EEG and performance decrement. Some of these are the direct effect of the loss of the pharmacological actions of nicotine, some the results of central nervous system modifications. Social and environmental circumstances change the intensity of these withdrawal effects, indicating that there are other factors involved in the dependence. Nevertheless there is now wide acceptance within medicine that the opt-out term 'habit' to describe chronic tobacco misuse is not appropriate and that it should be regarded as true 'dependence'.

The toxicity of chronic tobacco misuse

In the light of this dependence it is important to try to assess the level of damage to the individual and society as a result of this abuse. This subject has been reviewed *in extenso* over the past two decades since the health risks of smoking were first really appreciated. The most recent UK review is that published by the Health Education Authority (1991) and those who seek further information are referred to this recent publication.

It should perhaps be sufficient here just to point out the conclusions of the Royal College of Physicians (1983), that smoking accounts for 15–20% of all British deaths and that a reasonable estimate of the annual death total which should be ascribed to smoking will not be less than 100 000.

Management

As with any dependence, psychological and/or physical, there is no painless or easy way to withdraw. The will to succeed is a major factor in all of them and this is true of tobacco dependence. There have been four approaches to the management of tobacco dependence in the UK.

The first of these has been peer pressure restriction on smoking, backed sometimes by legislation (perhaps for different motives, such as fire safety) on smoking in public places and in the workplace. This attempt to encourage smoking abstinence has been backed by massive public sector advertising on the dangers of smoking and legislative restrictions on cigarette advertising. There seems to be little doubt that it has had some effect in reducing the number of existing smokers, but very little on discouraging new teenage smokers.

The second approach has been that of the development of less harmful cigarettes. The rationale for this is that the success rate for permanent cessation is small (only 35% of UK smokers succeed in stopping smoking before the age of 60 years (Jarvis & Jackson, 1988)). Hence the aim is to produce a cigarette that provides the same nicotine load while delivering less tar and carbon monoxide. This approach has not so far had any major success.

The third approach, largely unsuccessful, involved various forms of behaviour therapy including electric aversion, rapid smoking and cue aversion.

The fourth and most effective current approach has been by the provision of 'clean' nicotine in the form of chewing gum, skin patch or nasal spray. This is coupled with either group therapy in special smokers clinics or more informal advice within general practice. A combination approach of this type more than doubles the success rate from the low level of success achieved with just general support to a decline of 1 % per year in self-reported smoking prevalence. Pooling the results of outcome after one year from all the 28 randomised trials available in 1993 showed that on average nicotine replacement therapy could enable 15 % of smokers who seek help in stopping smoking to give up the habit (Tang *et al*, 1994). (See also Russell, 1989; Fould, 1993.)

Caffeine

The nature of caffeinism

Although caffeine is the most widely used psychoactive drug in the world there have been relatively few studies in either animals or humans of its toxicity or its potential dependence. The best current reviews of the subject are those of Griffiths & Woodson (1988) and Hughes (1992).

Caffeine is indeed a substance to which physical and psychological dependence can occur. The main withdrawal symptoms are craving, headache, fatigue, anxiety and impaired psychomotor performance and these manifestations can vary between mild and incapacitating.

The withdrawal syndrome starts after about 12-24 hours, peaks at one to two days and normally lasts up to about a week. This time sequence accords well with the short average plasma half-life of caffeine which is about 3-6 hours. Experimental studies have indicated an incidence among heavy caffeine users of between 25 % and 100 % and with high exposure (greater than 600 mg/day) withdrawal effects have been reported after as little as six to 15 days of use. The pharmacological specificity has been established. Whether there is a threshold of intake below which dependence does not occur is still unclear – there is anecdotal evidence of withdrawal symptoms after prolonged intake of even very modest amounts.

Although the manifestations of caffeine dependence are different, as one would expect from the pharmacology, it is interesting to note the similarities of time sequence, incidence and aetiology between caffeine and benzodiazepine dependence. The relationship is made even more cogent when it is appreciated that coffee overuse has been suggested as one factor in the continued intake of benzodiazepines (Marks, 1985).

Is caffeine a clinically significant drug of misuse?

If we accept that drugs of misuse have two major characteristics (Griffiths *et al*, 1985), namely they have reinforcing properties and produce harm to the individual and/or society, then it is abundantly clear that since caffeine can serve as a reinforcer and that physical dependence potentiates this reinforcing effect the first of the characteristics is met. It is therefore important to determine whether caffeine is toxic.

The evidence indicates that caffeinism can produce medical problems. It has been encountered as a serious problem in the rehabilitation of chronic schizophrenics and those with moderately severe learning difficulties. Caffeinism has been demonstrated to be a precipitant of panic attacks (Nutt & Lawson, 1992) and may also be a factor encouraging the continuation of benzodiazepine use (Marks, 1985).

Acute toxicity with death, although it has been reported, is rare. Untoward reactions are however common at plasma concentrations above about 30 μg/ml. This is equivalent to the ingestion of about 10 cups of strong coffee or equivalent intakes of other caffeine containing beverages. The symptoms include insomnia, restlessness, excitement, tachycardia and muscle tension, which may progress to mild delirium, emesis and convulsions in some people.

Hence we must regard caffeine as a drug of misuse. While the ready availability of the drug in the social environment encourages habitual caffeine use it also reduces the incidence of the abstinence syndrome. Thus we should probably class caffeine as a socially acceptable drug of mild misuse, with little evidence of chronic health impairment, but with increasing recent evidence of a precipitant role in other psychiatric disorders.

References

American Psychiatric Association (1990) *Benzodiazepine Dependence, Toxicity and Abuse: a Task Force Report of the American Psychiatric Association.* Washington, DC: APA.

Benowitz, N. L. (1992) The genetics of drug dependence: tobacco addiction. *New England Journal of Medicine*, **327**, 881-883.

Foulds, J. (1993) Does nicotine replacement therapy work? *Addiction*, **88**, 1473-1478.

Griffiths, R. R., Lamb, R. G., Ator, N. A., *et al* (1985) Relative abuse liability of triazolam: experimental assessment in animals and humans. *Neuroscience and Biobehavioural Research*, **9**, 133-151.

—— & Woodson, P. P. (1988) Caffeine physical dependence: a review of human and laboratory animal studies. *Psychopharmacology (Berlin)*, **94**, 437-451.

Hallfors, D. H. & Saxe, L. (1993) The dependence potential of short half-life benzodiazepines: a meta analysis. *American Journal of Public Health*, **83**, 1300-1304.

Haskell, D., Cole, J. O., Schniebolk, S., *et al* (1986) A survey of diazepam patients. *Psychopharmacology Bulletin*, **22**, 434.

Health Education Authority (1991) *The Smoking Epidemic - Counting the Cost.* London: Health Education Authority.

Higgitt, A. & Fonagy, P. (1992) Withdrawal from benzodiazepines and the persistent benzodiazepine dependence syndrome. In *Recent Advances in Clinical Psychiatry*, Vol. 7 (ed. K. Granville-Grossman), pp. 45-59. Edinburgh: Churchill Livingstone.

Hughes, J. R. (1992) The clinical importance of caffeine withdrawal. *New England Journal of Medicine*, **327**, 1160-1161.

Jaffe, J. H. (1990*a*) Drug addiction and drug abuse. In *The Pharmacological Basis of Therapeutics*, 8th edn (eds A. G. Gilman, L. S. Goodman, T. W. Rall, *et al*), pp. 522-573. New York: Macmillan.

——— (1990*b*) Tobacco, smoking and nicotine dependence. In *Nicotine Psychopharmacology: Molecular, Cellular and Behavioural Aspects* (eds S. Wannacott, M. A. H. Russell & I. P. Stolerman), pp. 1-37. Oxford: Oxford University Press.

Jarvis, M. J. & Jackson, P. H. (1988) Cigar and pipe smoking in Britain: implications for smoking prevalence and cessation. *British Journal of Addiction*, **83**, 323-330.

Lader, M. (1989) Benzodiazepine dependence. *International Review of Psychiatry*, **1**, 149-156.

Lupolover, R., Dazzi, H. & Ward, J. (1982) Rebound phenomena: results of a 10 years' (1970-1980) literature review. *International Pharmacopsychiatry*, **17**, 194-237.

Marks, J. (1985) *The Benzodiazepines: Use, Overuse, Misuse, Abuse*. 2nd edn. Lancaster: MTP Press.

Merz, W. A. & Ballmer, U. (1983) Symptoms of the barbiturate/benzodiazepine withdrawal syndrome in healthy volunteers: standardised assessment by a newly developed self-rating scale. *Journal of Psychoactive Drugs*, **15**, 71-84.

Nicholson, A. N. & Marks, J. (1983) *Insomnia: a Guide for Medical Practitioners*. Lancaster: MTP Press.

Nutt, D. & Lawson, C. (1992) Panic attacks: a neurochemical overview of models and mechanisms. *British Journal of Psychiatry*, **160**, 165-178.

Oswald, I. (1989) Triazolam syndrome 10 years on. *Lancet*, **2**, 451-452.

Owen, R. T. & Tyrer, P. (1983) Benzodiazepine dependence: a review of the evidence. *Drugs*, **25**, 385-398.

Petursson, H. & Lader, M. (1984) *Dependence on Tranquillisers*. Oxford: Oxford University Press.

Raw, M. (1982) The nature and treatment of cigarette dependence. In *The Dependence Phenomenon* (eds M. M. Glatt & J. Marks), pp. 179-198. Lancaster: MTP Press.

Rodrigo, E. K. (1988) Health of long-term benzodiazepine users. *British Medical Journal*, **296**, 603-606.

Royal College of Physicians (1983) *Health or Smoking*. London: Pitman.

Russell, M. A. H. (1989) The Addiction Research Unit of the Institute of Psychiatry University of London - II The Work of the Unit's Smoking Section. *British Journal of Addiction*, **84**, 853-863.

Tang, J. L., Law, M. & Wald, N. (1994) How effective is nicotine replacement therapy in helping people to stop smoking? *British Medical Journal*, **308**, 21-26.

World Health Organization (1964) WHO Expert Committee on Addiction - producing Drugs, 13th Report. World Health Organization Technical Report Series No 273. Geneva: WHO.

Woods, J. H., Katz, J. L. & Winger, G. (1987) Abuse liability of benzodiazepines. *Pharmacological Reviews*, **39**, 251-419.

5 Epidemiology and primary prevention of alcohol misuse
Bruce Ritson

Drinking in the general population ● Alcohol-related harm ●
Levels of consumption and risk ● Primary prevention ● Social measures
to reduce risk of harm

Drinking in the general population

In Britain and many other parts of the world alcohol is, to quote a Royal College of Psychiatrists (1986) report, "our favourite drug". It is drunk by more than 90% of the adult population in the UK. Alcohol has been prepared for thousands of years and references to it can be found in the earliest writings. From early on in history the production and sale of alcohol have been closely regulated and taxed. One consequence of this has been that data about alcohol trade, production and consumption has been available at least in rudimentary form for several centuries.

National per capita consumption data is commonly derived by the equation: consumption = production + imports − exports. It is assumed that the result of this equation represents the alcohol consumed in the population. This figure does not take into account illicit and unrecorded home production which in some countries may be considerable. If per capita consumption is based on consumption divided by total population then it will be influenced strongly by the age structure of that population. When the age distribution is reasonably constant this may be of no great consequence, however it becomes very important when assessing changes in the consumption of populations in which rapid demographic change is occurring. Comparisons are more reliable using estimates of per capita consumption based on the total population over the age of 15.

Spring & Buss (1977) studied changes in alcohol consumption in the UK over the last 300 years. Figure 5.1 shows the dramatic decline in consumption over that time and also the evident changes in beverage choices. This is a salutary reminder that there is nothing fixed or unchanging about a nation's drinking habit. It also shows that the period from 1930 to 1950 was one of exceptionally low levels of drinking which has been followed by a rapid growth in consumption until the late 1970s when there was a levelling off and even a slight decline, followed by a continuing but rather less steep rise in consumption (see Fig. 5.2).

During the last 50 years a similar trend in per capita consumption is evident in most European countries. Many shared a peak in alcohol consumption in the 1970s. In approximately a third of European countries a downward trend

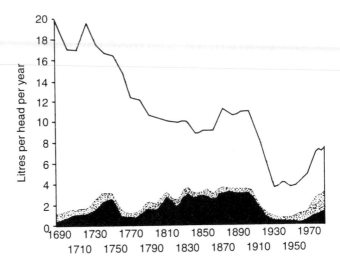

Fig. 5.1 Changes in alcohol consumption in Britain over the centuries. □, Beer;
⊡ , Spirits; ■ , Wine. (From Spring & Buss, 1977)

Fig. 5.2 Per capita alcohol consumption in the UK (1900–1990; Thurman, 1991)

has continued. In another third it has levelled off and in the remainder
(including the UK) there is evidence of a slight rise. Changes in per capita
consumption in selected countries are shown in Table 5.1. The UK is not
conspicuously high on this list. There is no clear correlation between the
relative prosperity of each country and per capita consumption. However within
country trends often demonstrate a close relationship between prosperity
(particularly disposable income in relation to the price of alcohol) and per capita
consumption.

Table 5.1 Per capita alcohol consumption, litres per year per person over 15 years of age

	UK	Ireland	France	Spain	Sweden	Denmark	USA	Australia	USSR
1961	5.5	4.9	23.9	9.6	5.3	6.0	7.4	9.1	5.7
1965	6.0	6.5	23.4	15.6	5.8	6.6	8.1	10.0	7.1
1970	6.7	8.5	21.6	16.8	7.3	8.8	9.3	11.4	9.4
1975	8.6	11.2	21.2	19.3	9.0	11.8	10.1	12.9	8.4
1980	9.5	10.4	19.1	16.8	7.1	11.5	10.6	12.8	8.4
1985	8.8	9.6	16.8	15.3	6.3	12.1	10.3	11.8	7.7
1988	9.1	8.6	16.6	15.5	6.7	11.8	9.6	10.9	4.8
1991	9.0	10.1	15.3	13.7	7.3	11.9	8.8	10.8	6.4 (1990)

General population surveys

The figures described above provide no indication about the distribution of alcohol use within the population. There are two principal sources of this data available in more developed countries. One relies on household survey data and the other on specially commissioned drinking surveys. In the UK the General Household Survey and Family Expenditure Survey are conducted annually. These provide some measure of alcohol use. More importantly in the past 25 years there have been a number of carefully conducted surveys of drinking habits within the UK. These have been concerned specifically with drinking habits and alcohol-related consequences; most are based on a detailed report on the past week's drinking. They represent the most valuable sources of data for studying groups at risk and the prevalence of various alcohol-related problems in the population. Surveys of this kind have a number of shortcomings. It is commonly observed that the reported consumption of the population is well below, often by 50%, the known consumption levels identified by trade figures. There is evidence that the heaviest drinkers are the most unreliable in recording their consumption (not necessarily because they are most dishonest but because the task is more difficult). It is often also more difficult to reach the heaviest drinkers in national surveys either because they are not at home or have no settled accommodation. Nonetheless population surveys are the most useful means of understanding the drinking habits of the population and monitoring changes arising out of preventive and other policies.

A general population survey in England and Wales was conducted in 1989 (Goddard, 1991). This showed that the average weekly amount of alcohol consumed per head was 8.8 standard units. One unit contains approximately 8 grams of ethanol. This corresponds with the quantity of alcohol contained in a half-pint of beer, lager or cider (3-4% alcohol by volume), a measure of spirits (40% by volume) or an average sized glass of wine (10-12% by volume) or a small glass of sherry. These measures are very rough and based on average strengths for each beverage in pub measures. At home drinks are often dispensed in much more generous quantities. Some extra strong beers or lagers are two or three times stronger (6-8.5%) than their weaker namesakes.

This report showed little overall change in consumption levels over the preceding ten years. There had been a slight decline in consumption among the youngest age groups and an increase among older men and women. Men report drinking three times as much as women. The differences between men and women are less apparent in the younger age groups (particularly those aged 16-17). Adults drink less with advancing years. Approximately one in three men and one in six women report drinking on more than four days in the previous week. Men had more drinking occasions per week (4.4) compared with women (3.2) and drank more quickly on average consuming one unit of alcohol in 21 minutes (women 30 minutes). Goddard (1991) characterised "light" drinkers as men consuming 1-21 units in the past week;

Table 5.2 Consequences of drinking experienced in the last year, by sex and type of drinker based on last week's consumption; 1989 (Goddard, 1991)

Recent drinkers aged 16 and over (%)

	Men				Women		
	Light	Moderate	Fairly heavy	Very heavy	Light	Moderate	Heavy
Drank too much	39	72	75	87	33	73	65
Difficulty getting up	16	33	50	45	14	35	35
Memory loss	10	30	47	57	7	30	29
Felt effects at work	12	28	36	42	9	26	23
Felt should cut down	7	28	39	51	5	31	25
Advised by others	6	20	32	52	2	14	15
Drunk weekly	5	18	23	38	4	16	21
Been in argument	6	11	19	29	4	18	27
Felt aggressive	6	11	20	28	3	15	10
Broke promise to self	5	12	15	27	2	13	10
Been criticised	2	10	13	18	1	8	8
Shaking hands	2	10	10	25	2	4	15
Felt ashamed	2	5	8	10	1	8	8
Out of control	1	7	8	10	1	7	4
Afraid was alcoholic	1	3	6	10	1	4	4
Advised by doctor	2	5	8	18	1	2	2
Been violent	1	2	10	9	1	4	6
Drank secretly	2	3	4	7	2	5	6
Been unable to stop	2	6	3	9	1	4	4
Drank first thing	1	4	3	8	0	2	4
Base = 100%	773	159	80	81	856	90	32

(For definitions of drinking categories see text.)

women 1-14 units; "moderate" drinkers 22-35 units men and 15-25 units (women); "fairly heavy" as 36-50 units (men) and 26-35 units (women). "Very heavy drinkers" reported drinking above these levels.

This survey was based only on England and Wales; earlier surveys conducted in Scotland and Northern Ireland reveal only slight differences. Northern Ireland has more abstainers than other parts of the UK and in Scotland drinking tends to be concentrated in fewer days per week. There is some regional variation in drinking patterns among men (less so for women) with the highest weekly consumption being found in the north of England.

Alcohol and occupation

Survey reports show that men employed in unskilled manual occupations are more likely to be heavy drinkers. For women the heaviest drinkers are in non-manual occupations and professional and managerial jobs (Goddard, 1991).

Cirrhosis mortality data provide another window on the prevalence of excessive drinking and occupation (see Chapter 6 and Fig. 6.4), with publicans and others in the drink trade being at high risk.

The prevalence of alcohol dependence

No UK population studies have been published using structured interviews which will yield diagnoses of alcohol dependence based on the currently accepted international criteria specified in DSM–III–R or ICD–10 (see Chapter 1). The UK surveys have included questions linked with dependence (hands shaking, inability to stop, drinking first thing in the morning) as well as questions related to harmful consequences, chiefly social. Survey data of the kind shown in Table 5.2 reveal that among those who have drunk some alcohol in the past year, 4% report having had shaking hands related to drinking and 2% being unable to stop drinking in that period. Surveys in the USA, to take the 1988 National Data for example, find that ICD–10 criteria are met for the preceding 12 months by 6.8% of those interviews. DSM–III–R criteria of dependence in the same study were met by 10% (physical withdrawal symptoms, such as shakes, are not necessary conditions in either diagnostic system) (Grant, 1993).

Alcohol-related harm

Alcohol-related harm may be physical, social or psychological. It may occur as a consequence of intoxication or prolonged excessive use. There is overlap and the heaviest drinkers will commonly report problems in every category. There are a number of indices which can be taken to reflect alcohol-related harm to the community. Some are more readily and reliably measured than others.

Alcohol-related mortality

Excessive drinkers have an increased risk of premature death. The contribution which alcohol makes to various conditions is shown in Table 5.3.

Death from hepatic cirrhosis is the most commonly used measure of health damage due to alcohol. The contribution which alcohol makes to cirrhosis is also influenced by other factors such as the level of nutrition in the community and the prevalence of hepatitis from other causes. In the UK alcohol is thought to be a significant factor in 80% of cirrhosis deaths.

Table 5.3   Estimate of proportion of deaths (age 15+) attributable to alcohol in England and Wales, 1984

	Percentage of deaths	
	Men	Women
Malignant neoplasms (ICD 140-239)	4	3
Cerebrovascular disease (ICD 430-438)	12	3
Respiratory disease (ICD 460-519)	11	2
Digestive disease (ICD 520-579, excluding 571)	12	3
Chronic liver disease (ICD 571)	80	80
Injuries and poisonings (ICD 800-899)	40	40
Other	6	1
All deaths	12	3

(From Anderson, 1991.)

Excessive drinking increases the risk of cancer of the oropharynx threefold, the oesophagus twofold and of the larynx fourfold. The risk of oesophageal cancer increases multiplicatively when smoking and alcoholic excess are combined. Like cirrhosis the prevalence of these cancers is closely related to per capita consumption. Similar but less clear cut associations have been observed between level of consumption and breast cancer (Garro & Lieber, 1990).

Morbidity

Injudicious drinking makes a significant contribution to medical morbidity of many kinds (Royal College of Physicians, 1987) (Chapter 10). Many studies have shown that around 20% of men and 5-10% of women admitted to general medical wards have characteristics indicative of problem drinking. Similar levels have been observed in psychiatric practice. In the USA Moore *et al* (1989) interviewed admissions to a wide range of medical facilities and screened for 'alcoholism'. The overall prevalence was 25% in psychiatry; 30% in medicine; surgery 23%; neurology 19% and obstetrics/gynaecology 12.5%. These diagnoses were frequently missed by clinicians providing treatment. The protean health problems associated with alcohol and the distress which it causes families combine to make it a significant factor in the workload of family practitioners. The exact size of this contribution needs to be more carefully studied.

Accidents form a significant part of alcohol-related morbidity - they have been documented at home, in the workplace, during sporting activities but particularly in relation to road traffic accidents. It is estimated that 20% of road traffic accident fatalities occur where at least one of those involved had a blood alcohol concentration of over 80 mg per cent and that one in ten non-fatal casualties occur in drink–drive accidents (Faculty of Public Health Medicine, 1991). Increased risk applies not only to the drinking driver but also to the drinking pedestrian.

The most conclusive study of the relationship between drinking, driving and accidents undertaken was in Grand Rapids, USA. Blood alcohol concentration (BAC) was measured in every individual involved in an accident and a similar measure taken from a control group of drivers at the same location. At 150 mg % BAC the accident risk was raised ten times and by 200 mg % increased 20 times. There is also evidence that excessive drinkers as revealed by a raised serum GGT are more likely to be involved in road traffic accidents (Dunbar *et al*, 1985). The relationship between per capita consumption and the level of road traffic accidents is often confounded by factors such as level of police activity, enforcement, car ownership and road conditions. The introduction in the UK of breath testing in 1967 had an immediate effect on the level of accidents but the influence of the new law quickly diminished as drivers came to realise that the likelihood of detection was low.

Social harm

The level of social disruption caused by alcohol is well known but hard to measure. It is also very much influenced by what is regarded as culturally acceptable behaviour. What is seen as acceptable drunken comportment at one time or context may meet with strong social disapproval in another. Alcohol misuse that may cause havoc in a complex industrial plant may pass unnoticed in a less demanding or hazardous environment. Recording of social indices of harm is variable and often more influenced by available resources than true levels of harm. Reporting on the presence of alcohol as a contributing factor to social problems is often inconsistent.

Nonetheless it has been estimated that alcohol misuse makes a massive contribution to crime in the UK. Studies of prisoners suggest that between half and two-thirds of men and 15 % of women have serious drinking problems. Drunkenness offences increased in the UK throughout the '60s and '70s and paralleled the rising consumption level in the population. The introduction of new cautioning procedures and diversionary schemes in England in 1984 was associated with an immediate decline in reported arrests. This is a revealing example of the way in which an index of alcohol-related harm can misleadingly convey that a problem is declining when it has simply been dealt with in another way and is no longer recorded. Similar factors are probably at work in the changing prevalence of admission to psychiatric hospital with a variety of alcohol-related problems. Here the figures rose steadily (more so in Scotland than England) for 20 years until 1980 when there was a downward trend, not, it is thought, because the level of alcohol problems had suddenly declined but because services were responding in a different way and no longer placing so much reliance on admission as the principal treatment response. Similarly the variation in admission rates to psychiatric hospitals round the UK most probably represents differences in patterns of care and the availability of resources (Crawford *et al*, 1984).

The social harm attributable to alcohol is particularly evident in the damaging effect which it has on family life and the mental health of spouse and children. These effects are hard to measure; drunkenness is frequently cited in divorce and found in many cases of child abuse and neglect.

Alcohol and employment

Alcohol misuse is a common cause of absenteeism and industrial accidents. Impaired efficiency due to hangover and intoxication is hard to measure but probably very common. A recent survey recorded 7% of men as saying that they have been to work with a hangover in the preceding 3 months. Box 5.1 gives a breakdown of factors contributing to the economic cost of alcohol-related problems in England and Wales, lost working time making a very significant contribution.

Box 5.1   The economic costs of alcohol misuse

Cost to industry
  Sickness absence
  Reduced productivity
  Unemployment
  Premature death

Social cost to National Health Service
  Psychiatric in-patient costs
  Non-psychiatric in-patient costs
  GP visits

Cost of society's responses to alcohol problems
  National bodies and research

Road traffic accidents

Social costs of criminal activity including
  Police involvement in traffic offences, and other offences

Alcohol-related accidents (home, work, fires)

Costs to social services and other agencies arising from alcohol-related family disputes, child neglect, etc.

Emotional pain and suffering from alcohol-related problems

Levels of consumption and risk

It is clear that the heaviest drinkers in a population run the greatest risk of alcohol-related damage. The exact nature of this association for each harmful consequence is less clear cut. For cancer, the relationship is linear; for liver cirrhosis there is a threshold (Anderson *et al*, 1993).

The levels of consumption that are safe are up to approximately 21 units of alcohol per week for a man and 14 units per week for a woman. Above these levels harm of various kinds becomes increasingly likely. For pregnant women limits are much lower at two or three units per week because of the risks of foetal damage. These guidelines which have been widely supported and frequently published in health promotion materials are of course crude generalisations but they have the benefit of simplicity. They are based on a number of studies which point to an increased risk even at relatively low levels of drinking.

Longitudinal studies in the UK and many countries find mortality among middle-aged men begins to be associated with drinking when admitted consumption passes about 30 units per week (Shaper *et al*, 1988; Marmot & Brunner, 1991; Anderson *et al*, 1993). Chick *et al* (1986) studied a population in a general hospital and compared this with a local community control sample. This showed admitted alcohol consumption of over 21 units per week was associated with an increasing risk of admission for certain categories of illness such as liver disorders, upper-gastrointestinal disease, coronary heart disease and respiratory illness. The classic studies of alcohol consumption and liver cirrhosis in France showed that the relative risk of cirrhosis was six times greater at 5–8 units of alcohol per day and 14 times greater at 8–10 units per day, but a slightly increased risk had been visible at as little as 3–4 units per day. The risk of interpersonal and social problems also begins to increase even with moderate consumption (Table 5.2).

The relationship between per capita consumption and death from coronary heart diseases is a U-shaped curve and because heart disease is the commonest cause of death in middle age, the relationship between consumption and overall mortality is also U-shaped for that age-group. Many studies of middle life have found reduced mortality among light and moderate drinkers (1–30 units per week). This relationship is not seriously doubted but there has been controversy about its explanation. Some studies have found that abstainers contain a disproportionate number of individuals who have abandoned drinking because of ill health or have reduced their consumption at the first indications of cardiac disease (Shaper *et al*, 1988). More recent studies have taken this possibility into account and shown that the relationship still holds true with lifetime abstainers having a higher mortality (Marmot & Brunner, 1991; and Chapter 10). It is possible that the higher mortality in abstainers may relate in part to abstainers being from a different sub-culture, who are prone to greater stress for example but this has not been shown to date. Men who drink lightly or regularly (1–2 units a day) have favourable risk factor status in terms of social

---

Box 5.2   Alcohol and mortality: the U-shaped curve

The evidence
   Longitudinal studies in the middle aged show higher mortality in
   abstainers than light drinkers
   Some abstainers are already ill but relationship holds up if only lifetime abstainers included

The cause?
   ?Protective effect of ethanol for cardiovascular disease
   ??'Stress' factor in abstainers
   Light, regular drinkers have most favourable risk factor status in
   terms of social class, smoking, body weight, blood pressure, exercise

Health message?
   Risks of harm if population advised to increase drinking

---

class, smoking, body weight, blood pressure and exercise, perhaps also blood lipid concentration (Shaper *et al*, 1988). Or, ethanol may have a protective biochemical action for cardiovascular disorder. Reduction in the prevalence of problems due to heavy drinking which might follow reduction in per capita consumption needs to be set against loss of possible benefits in reduction of coronary heart disease among light and moderate drinkers and any psychological/social solace that alcohol may bring (Kemm, 1993). The benefits of guidelines to sensible drinking are that they provide material for health promotion at a community level and for secondary prevention in clinical populations.

Primary prevention

The mean alcohol consumption of a population and the prevalence of heavy drinking are closely correlated ($r = 0.97$) (Rose & Day, 1990). A mean reduction of per capita alcohol consumption of 10% would reduce the number of heavy drinkers by a similar percentage. Although heavy drinkers have many more alcohol-related problems than other drinkers their contribution to the total of alcohol-related harm in the community is less compared to that attributable to the much greater number of moderate and light drinkers. Focusing preventive measures only on those in the high risk group would have less impact on overall harm than would a population based approach termed the 'preventive paradox' (Kreitman, 1986). A 'high risk' strategy benefits those excessive drinkers who can be identified although the efficacy of treatment is far from certain. A population approach aimed at all drinkers with the goal of reducing per capita consumption is likely to be much more effective but involves all drinkers taking responsibility for moderating their consumption. These two strategies can be combined.

Box 5.3   Determinants of population alcohol consumption

Factors influencing demand
   Traditions
   Consumer purchasing power
   Advertising
   Health promotion and education
   Alcohol costs in relation to disposable income

Factors influencing supply
   The size of harvest and agricultural controls
   The volume of beverage produced and/or imported and controls
   on these
   The number and opening hours of retail outlets and
   controls on these (licensed premises and licensing hours)
   Controls on purchasers (the age limit)

The major determinants of the quantity of alcohol consumed by a population are shown in Box 5.3.

An ounce of prevention is worth a pound of cure but often seems a less attractive proposal to politicians, professionals and the public. Primary prevention is aimed at reducing the prevalence of hazardous drinking – this may entail separating drinking from hazardous activities such as driving or reducing the overall level of per capita consumption. We have already seen that a rise in per capita consumption is usually followed by an increase in all the readily measurable indices of harm such as cirrhosis morbidity, drunkenness offences and admission to hospital for alcohol-related conditions. The principal strategies available to reduce the level of alcohol related harm in the community are demand reduction and supply reduction.

Demand reduction

Measures which limit demand by influencing culture and religious traditions are rarely feasible but it is important to note that attitudes toward alcohol in a culture do change gradually over time. It is thought that 'wet' generations in which alcohol is prominent are often followed by 'dry' generations which react to this extreme by introducing social controls.

The importance of consumer purchasing power depends on economic factors which are outside the influence of health professionals but times of prosperity usually are associated with increasing alcohol use. To a certain degree this depends on the alternatives available both in terms of beverage choice and other social activities (discussed later). The importance of advertising and health education is discussed below.

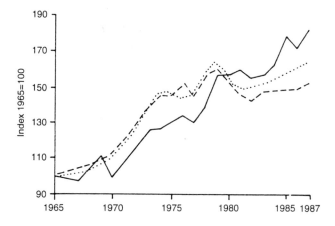

Fig. 5.3   Relative index of alcohol consumption (-----), affordability (· · · ·) and deaths from chronic liver disease (——) (UK, 1965–1987)

Fiscal policy

Measures which influence the price of alcohol in relation to disposable income have more immediate impact than any others on per capita consumption. Many studies have shown that when relative cost rises consumption declines. In the UK during the period 1979 to 1982 there was an unusually steep rise in the cost of alcohol relative to disposable income. This was associated with an 11% decline in per capita consumption and a fall of 49% in cirrhosis mortality (England and Wales), 7% decline in drink-driving conviction and 19% reduction in first admission to English psychiatric hospitals for alcohol dependence (Kendell, 1984). Because much of the retail price of alcoholic beverage in the UK is attributable to tax (60% for spirits, 40% for beer and wine) the Government can have a major influence in this respect. In many countries Governments have been reluctant to use tax as a health promoting measure as far as alcohol is concerned although this approach is generally accepted for tobacco.

The Royal College of Psychiatrists (1986) in common with many other medical organisations recommended that 'government taxation policies should be intentionally employed to ensure that per capita consumption does not increase beyond present levels and is by stages brought to an agreed lower level'.

In the UK the retail price index is deduced from a shopping basket of essential commodities. The price of alcohol is incorporated in the index. Not only does this reinforce the belief that alcohol is an 'essential' part of household spending but it ensures that any rise in the price of alcohol has an inflationary influence because the retail price index is used as a standard for wage negotiations. It has therefore been recommended that alcohol should be removed from this index (Faculty of Public Health Medicine, 1991).

The European Union has resolved to eliminate tariff barriers between member states. If this were to occur then tax on alcohol in countries such as Denmark, Ireland and UK would decline with likely damage to public health. Conversely prices would rise steeply in the Mediterranean wine producing areas. It had been estimated that such a change would have increased alcohol consumption in the UK by 46%. The original proposal for harmonisation will probably not be implemented abruptly but a gradual change will occur. This is a useful illustration of the potential impact of international agreements on public health. Many similar illustrations exist in world trade particularly in Africa where the importation or promotion of commercially produced alcohol has had a damaging effect on established consumption patterns (Beckmann, 1988).

Advertising

Evidence concerning the impact of advertising on alcohol consumption is contradictory. Critics point to the very high consumption in some countries where no advertising exists. It seems likely that the effects are marginal. Advertisers stress that they are only concerned with influencing brand choice. In the UK the Independent Broadcasting Authority has agreed a code of Advertising Standards governing alcohol. This proscribes advertisements which are misleading or directed toward young people, the linking of alcohol with sexual fulfilment, work, or driving. Aitken *et al* (1988) have shown that young teenagers are very familiar with alcohol advertisements well before they are permitted to drink, and particularly enjoy their humour and songs.

Alcohol promotion has a major role in sports sponsorship which again increases public awareness of the brand but also links alcohol with sporting and cultural activities. Although there is no evidence in either direction that these promotions have any impact on consumption they do form part of a general background of acceptability that may influence public perceptions about the desirability of alcohol. No restrictions on alcohol and sports sponsorship currently exist in UK.

Education

Education about the hazards of alcohol and promoting sensible drinking habits are the traditional standby of many prevention programmes. They vary considerably in both target and aim. Some are concerned with providing information about sensible limits, the dangers of drinking, the social and health problems associated with drinking and more recently the promotion of healthy life styles and choices. Targets include:

(1) *The general public* or segments of it – most commonly school children but also for instance young people, the elderly, ethnic minorities

(2) *Specific high risk groups* such as pregnant women, drivers, those in high risk occupations

(3) *Professional workers,* such as nurses, social workers, doctors, police usually aimed to enhance their understanding so that they can advise clients and recognise alcohol-related problems at an early stage (see chapter 11)

(4) *Opinion leaders* – particularly those who may have to plan policies and assign priorities so that they have a broad understanding of alcohol and its attendant problems.

Mass media campaigns have been shown to reach the target audience, and in some cases increase knowledge but the effect on attitude and behaviours has been minimal. Similarly bleak conclusions can be drawn from most school education programmes. After a major review of education programmes in the USA Maskowitz (1989) was forced to conclude that "there is currently little evidence to support the efficiency of primary prevention programmes". This experience has not been shared in Holland where a public education campaign has produced demonstrable benefits. Health educators stress the importance of ensuring that material is tailored to the customs of the target group, and much health promotion is now centred on facilitating decision making about healthier life styles and acquiring social skills rather than being preoccupied with particular forms of substance misuse. Without education aimed at increasing public knowledge it will prove difficult to ensure an informed debate about alcohol policies. This goal seems more attainable and is a further illustration of the need to combine a number of approaches in developing a coherent alcohol policy at national level.

Alternatives

The promotion of alternatives to alcohol includes the provision of alternative (non-alcoholic) beverages as well as alternative recreational activities.

Low alcohol and non-alcohol wines, lagers and beers have become increasingly available in recent years. Products labelled as 'alcohol free' are required to contain less than 0.05% alcohol by volume. Low alcohol drinks can contain up to 1.2% alcohol. Above this level excise duty is payable. Manufacturers have been criticised for the high costs of these low alcohol beverages and it would be a healthy policy to maintain their prices at a low level. The promotion of non-alcoholic drinks such as coffee and tea plus the availability of meals is one way of relieving some of the concentration on alcohol evident in some licensed premises in the UK.

Second to watching television, 'going out for a drink' is reported by the British as the most popular leisure activity. In some areas few alternative activities are available. Some communities have tried to promote alternative centres of recreation such as alcohol free pubs and clubs or by ensuring the provision of a diverse range of sporting and leisure resources. The impact of such approaches has never been effectively evaluated. Health promotion concerned with helping individuals choose healthier life styles needs to ensure that there is an environment which supports and facilitates such choices.

Supply reduction

Most countries try to restrict the place of purchase of alcohol by means of licensing and further influence availability by restricting hours of opening. These regulations have often been introduced in the interests of public order. During the period of the First World War there was a concentration on workers around munition factories near Carlisle. In an attempt to improve work efficiency and reduce accidents the local licensed premises were taken under Government control and availability greatly restricted. This had the desired effect.

It may be argued that restrictive hours create a pressure toward rapid consumption releasing intoxicated individuals on to the streets at closing time. The hours immediately following this are certainly a time when most drink-related accidents occur and violence around licensed premises increases. Recent increases in hours of opening at a national level in the UK did not produce significant changes in reported consumption (Duffy & Plant, 1986; Goddard, 1991). This may be because availability of alcohol had already reached saturation point as the trend toward fewer restrictions on hours of opening had increased steadily during the preceding 40 years. Off-sales availability had been enhanced by permission to sell alcohol in supermarkets, a move which is believed to have contributed to a noticeable increase in alcohol consumption among women. Some countries such as Norway and Sweden have a state alcohol monopoly allowing much greater control of sale and marketing of alcohol while in some countries particularly the wine growing areas sales are virtually unrestricted. Davies & Walsh (1983) observed that countries which were restrictive toward the availability of alcohol tended to have lower per capita consumption than those which were more liberal in their policies. Arguments about the association between controls and consumption need to recognise that in a democracy prohibitionistic laws require a background of public opinion which supports such measures. It also seems likely that restricted availability coupled with high cost promotes home production and bootlegging. This link was clearly documented during the period of prohibition in the USA in the 1920s and more recently in the consequences of reduced availability of alcohol in the former USSR where severe restriction gave rise to an immediate and alarming growth in illicit production. Nevertheless, prohibition in the USA was a time when accidents, liver cirrhosis and other measures of alcohol-related harm declined steeply.

Age restrictions on purchase and consumption are common. Their impact on consumption is variable. Younger drinkers may simply shift their place of drinking to parks or private premises. In general a lower permitted age promotes drinking more at an earlier age with worrying consequences for accidents and hazardous behaviour. In the USA, where the minimum age for driving is low, States which raised their drinking age experienced an accompanying reduction in drinking-driving offences and accidents.

Social measures to reduce risk of harm

Prevention can be effective when focused on a particular risk behaviour. Education and antenatal counselling to reduce the risk of fetal alcohol syndrome has been an example. Women in many countries are now reducing their alcohol consumption during pregnancy. Some of these specific control strategies are outlined below. They may be particularly suitable for local action programmes (see Tether & Robinson, 1986).

Drinking and driving

The hazards of drinking and driving are well known. The level of road traffic fatalities is declining in the UK and many other countries and the percentage of drivers and riders killed in road traffic accidents who are over the legal blood alcohol limit has declined from approximately 30 to 20% over the past decade. Education campaigns about the hazards of drinking and driving are of uncertain benefit. The impact of harsher penalties is diminished when the likelihood of detection is low and it is evident that many continue to take the risk. Increasing the likelihood of detection by random breath testing with highly visible road checks has been shown to be the most effective preventive policy.

Alcohol and disruptive behaviour

The prevalence of hooliganism at sporting events has been reduced by banning the sale of alcohol near grounds and excluding drink and drunken spectators. There have also been local laws forbidding the consumption of alcohol in public in certain areas of towns in the UK. The impact of such regulations on certain troublesome behaviour is not yet known. Policing policy has a demonstrable influence on drunken behaviour. The procedure of police officers visiting pubs shortly before closing time was shown in a controlled study to have a significant impact on the level of street crime in an English seaside town (Jeffs & Saunders, 1983).

In the workplace

In some occupations alcohol has been effectively excluded by breathalysing and searching employees. Such measures have usually been confined to particularly hazardous work environments such as oil-rigs. Random breathtesting (and urine testing for drugs) of train drivers and personnel in the armed forces, now occurs in several countries. In addition to controls of this kind an increasing number of employers are introducing alcohol education as part of employee assistance programmes (see Chapter 7) and ensuring that the workplace is alcohol free.

Coordination of prevention policy

It is important to acknowledge that preventive approaches do not exist in isolation. They can work in concert as part of a coherent health policy or they can be at odds. In the UK more than 14 government departments have some concern with different aspects of alcohol policy, including trade and industry, treasury, law enforcement, agriculture, health, and social welfare. To be effective a coherent response to alcohol problems should be well coordinated and recognise the benefits as well as the problems associated with alcohol. The Ottawa Charter has emphasised the need for healthy, public policies which take into account the health and welfare implications of *all* measures concerning alcohol and other commonly misused substances.

References

Aitken, P. P., Leather, D. S. & Scott, A.C. (1988) Ten to sixteen year-olds perceptions of advertisements for alcohol drinks. *Alcohol and Alcoholism*, **23**, 491–500.

Anderson, P. (1991) *Management of Drinking Problems*, WHO Regional Publications. Euro Series 32, Copenhagen: WHO.

——, Cremona, A., Paton, A., *et al* (1993) The risk of alcohol. *Addiction*, **88**, 1493–1508.

Beckman, V. (1988) Alcohol, another trap for Africa. *Bokförlaget Libres*. Örebro.

Chick, J., Duffy, J. C., Lloyd, G. G., *et al* (1986) Medical admissions in men: the risk among drinkers. *Lancet*, **2**, 1380–1383.

Crawford, A., Plant, M., Kreitman, N., *et al* (1984) Regional variation in British alcohol morbidity rates. *British Medical Journal*, **289**, 1343–1345.

Davies, P. & Walsh, D. (1983) *Alcohol Problems and Alcohol Control Policy in Europe*. London: Croom Helm.

Duffy, J. & Plant, M. (1986) Scotland's liquor licensing changes an assessment. *British Medical Journal*, **292**, 33–36.

Dunbar, J. A., Ogston, S. A., Ritchie, A., *et al* (1985) Are problem drinkers dangerous drinkers? *British Medical Journal*, **290**, 827–830.

Faculty of Public Health Medicine (1991) *Alcohol and the Public Health*. London: Macmillan.

Garro, A. J. & Lieber, C. S. (1990) Alcohol and cancer. *Annual Review of Pharmacology and Toxicology*, **30**, 219–249.

Goddard, E. (1991) *Drinking in England and Wales in the Late 1980s*. London: HMSO.

Grant, B. F. (1993) ICD-10 harmful use of alcohol and the alcohol dependence syndrome: prevalence and implications. *Addiction*, **88**, 413–420.

Jeffs, B. N. & Saunders, N. M. (1983) Minimising alcohol related offences by enforcement of existing licensing legislation. *British Journal of Addictions*, **78**, 67–77.

Kemm, J. (1993) Alcohol and heart disease – the implications of the U-shaped curve. *British Medical Journal*, **307**, 1373–1374.

Kendell, R. E. (1984) The beneficial consequences of the United Kingdom's declining per capita consumption of alcohol in 1979-1982. *Alcohol and Alcoholism*, **19**, 271-276.

Kreitman, N. (1986) Alcohol consumption and the preventive paradox. *British Journal of Addiction*, **81**, 353-363.

Marmot, M. & Brunner, E. (1991) Alcohol and cardio-vascular disease: the status of the U-shaped curve. *British Medical Journal*, **303**, 565-568.

Moore, R. D., Bone, L. R., Geller, G. *et al* (1989) Prevalence, detection and treatment of alcoholism in hospitalised patients. *Journal of American Medical Association*, **261**, 463-507.

Moskowitz, J. M. (1989) The primary prevention of alcohol problems; a critical review of the research literature. *Journal of Studies on Alcohol*, **50**, 54-88.

Rose, G. & Day, S. (1990) The population mean predicts the number of deviant individuals. *British Medical Journal*, **301**, 1291-1298.

Royal College of Psychiatrists (1986) *Alcohol - Our Favourite Drug*. London: Tavistock.

Royal College of Physicians (1987) *The Medical Consequences of Alcohol Abuse: A Great and Growing Evil*. London: Tavistock.

Shaper, A. G., Walker, M. & Wanamethee, G. (1988) Alcohol and mortality in British men: explaining the U shaped curve. *Lancet*, **2**, 1267-1273.

Spring, J. A. & Buss, D. H. (1977) Three centuries of alcohol in the British diet. *Nature*, **270**, 567-572.

Tether, P. & Robinson, D. (1986) *Preventing Alcohol Problems: a Guide to Local Action*. London: Tavistock.

Thurman, P. (1992) Personal communication. In *Risk Takers* (eds M. Plant & M. Plant), p. 17. London: Routledge.

6 Aetiology of alcohol misuse

Christopher Cook

Vulnerability to alcoholism - biological markers and genetic effects •
Psychological factors • *Personality* • *Psychiatric disorder* •
Environmental factors • *Summary*

Alcoholism has been attributed by various groups and societies at different points in history to various root causes. For example, the temperance movement suggested either that alcohol itself is the cause of alcoholism or that society is responsible for allowing alcohol to be available. At other times that same movement treated the drunkard as a victim, suffering from a disease (Levine, 1978), thus implying that the cause lies within the individual. The 'moral' model, also associated with the temperance movement, has ascribed aetiology to personal responsibility or sin, and this approach still colours popular attitudes today. Similarly medical and scientific views have undergone their vicissitudes. Genetic factors, long popular in one form or another, were almost totally eclipsed in the 1930s and '40s, only to reappear with renewed vigour in the '50s, culminating in their present popularity.

Modern reviewers rightly tend to see alcoholism as having a multifactorial aetiology, with no easy answers. However, alcoholism is also heterogeneous, and for each patient alcoholism is the result of a different interaction of different aetiological factors.

Definitions and pathogenesis

Alcohol misuse and 'alcoholism' may be defined in various ways (see Chapter 1). Heavy drinkers do not inevitably progress to severe problem drinking and dependence, and 'moderate' drinkers do sometimes experience problems. However, given a population distribution of vulnerability to the development of problems and dependence, increased levels of consumption do appear to increase the probability that an individual will develop drinking problems, including dependence. Level of consumption of alcohol, complications secondary to consumption, and physical dependence thus represent three interacting conceptual levels at which aetiological factors appear to operate (Murray *et al*, 1983; see Fig. 6.1).

Strictly, the terms 'heavy drinking', 'alcohol misuse' or 'alcohol dependence' should be used in preference to the term 'alcoholism'. However, as already indicated, these concepts are not independent of each other. In the following discussion, for the sake of brevity, the term 'alcoholism' will therefore be used to refer to alcohol misuse (or 'problem' drinking) and/or alcohol dependence, except where special distinction is to be made between these concepts.

Aetiological influences upon liability to alcoholism

Characteristics of the individual ('constitutional' factors), the properties of alcohol itself, and the environment all contribute to the aetiology of alcoholism.

No study of aetiological factors in alcoholism would be complete without a consideration of the properties of alcohol as a drug. Its depressant effects, leading to disinhibition, anxiolysis and impaired psychomotor performance are all pertinent to an understanding of why people drink and why they develop problems when they do. Its ability to induce dependence is clearly also important. Alcohol exerts a rapid onset of action, often associated with pleasurable effects, but in excess causes organ damage which is not experienced as 'unpleasant' until drinking has been established for some time (usually a period of years). This immediate reinforcement, with delayed adverse consequences, is significant in an understanding of psychological models of the aetiology of alcoholism.

The properties of alcohol itself, however, do not explain why some individuals drink heavily, develop complications, or become dependent, while others encounter none of these difficulties. For such explanations we must turn to individual characteristics and environmental variables.

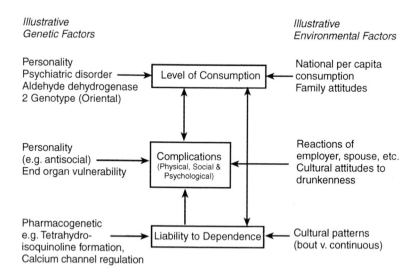

Fig. 6.1 Model of genetic and environmental effects in the aetiology of alcoholism.

Vulnerability to alcoholism – biological markers and genetic effects

Given similar environmental circumstances, including the ready availability of alcohol, not all individuals in a population will drink heavily. Among

---

Box 6.1   Individual factors influencing vulnerability to alcoholism

Biological markers of vulnerability to alcoholism:
(See Table 6.1)

Genetic effects:

(1) Level of consumption of alcohol:
   Subjective effects less in alcoholics
   Restoration of physiological or biochemical deficiency
   Protective 'flushing' effect of alcohol – 'Oriental' ALDH2
(2) Vulnerability to complications of alcohol consumption:
   Social & Psychological
   End-organ damage
     Cirrhosis
     Pancreatitis
     Cardiomyopathy
     Psychosis
(3) Vulnerability to physical dependence upon alcohol:
   Increase in calcium channels?
   TIQ production

Psychological factors:

(1) Psychodynamic theories:
   Oral (or anal) fixation
   Repressed homosexuality
   'Slow suicide' – Introjected anger
   Transactional analysis – Gains from alcoholic behaviour
(2) Cognitive, behavioural & social psychological theories:
   Classical conditioning
   Operant conditioning
   Combined model of classical and operant conditioning
   Stimulus generalisation
   Extinction
   Modelling
   Self-handicapping
   Social learning
   Expectancy

Personality:
(See Table 6.5)

Psychiatric disorder:
(1) Affective disorders
(2) Anxiety disorders
(3) Others? (See text)

---

those drinking similar amounts, some will develop dependence or other alcohol related problems, while others will not. This can only be convincingly explained by a consideration of physical and psychological differences between individuals. Individual factors that have been implicated in the aetiology of alcoholism are listed in Box 6.1.

Biological markers

Biological markers fall into three main groups. State markers reflect the consequences rather than the causes of prolonged heavy drinking (although, in theory at least, a 'state' marker might appear only in those individuals with a premorbid susceptibility to alcoholism). They are useful in screening for alcoholism, but offer little or no information about its aetiology and will not be considered further here. Genetic markers may offer clues as to which genetic loci are responsible for conferring a predisposition to alcoholism, and they will be considered in the next section, on genetic effects. Trait markers demonstrate enduring individual differences which may be indicators of a premorbid liability to alcoholism. They are often, although not necessarily, thought to reflect underlying genetic differences and the extent to which they are involved in aetiological processes, rather than simply being epiphenomena, is not always clear. The rest of this section will be devoted to a closer study of trait markers of alcoholism (see Table 6.1).

A popular method of studying trait markers (also employed in psychological studies) has been to study the adolescent or young adult, non-alcoholic, offspring of alcoholics (Family History Positive or 'FHP' subjects). On the basis that these subjects are a known high risk group, differences from controls with a negative family history of alcoholism (FHN), are assumed to indicate

Table 6.1 Biological markers of vulnerability to alcoholism

EEG – Alpha activity	Reduced
ERP – P300 potential	Reduced amplitude and increased latency
Static ataxia	Increased
Subjective intoxication*	Reduced
Autonomic Nervous System	Hyperreactive
Prolactin*	Lower levels than controls
Cortisol*	Reduced peak levels relative to controls
TSH	Enhanced response to TRH
	(Blunted response in abstinent alcoholics)
MAO	Reduced activity?
Acetaldehyde	Increased relative to controls?
Transketolase	High K_m

*Following alcohol consumption

Table 6.2 Twin studies of alcoholism

Author	Twin Pairs (n)	Sex	Criticisms	Criteria	Concordance MZ (%)	DZ (%)	MZ/DZ
Kaij (1960)	174	M	Antisocial subject bias	Official records All records Chronic alcoholism	25.4 53.5 71.4	15.8 28.3 32.3	1.6 1.9 2.2
Hrubec & Omenn (1981)	7962	M	No interviews Low ascertainment (?DZ>MZ)	V-A Records: Alcoholism Alcoholic psychosis Cirrhosis	26.3 21.1 14.6	11.9 6.9 5.4	2.2 3.5 2.7
Kendler (1985)	81	M	As for Hrubec & Omenn (1981) (Represents a subset of their sample)	V-A Records (Probands identified with both alcoholism & schizophrenia): Results here are for ICD-8 Alcoholism only	64.7	8.5	7.6
Gurling *et al* (1981), Gurling (1989)	79	M+F	? Validity of twin method in alcoholism	ICD-9 Alcoholism RDC Alcoholism	23.0 30.0	36.0 36.0	0.6 0.8
Koskenvuo *et al* (1984)	244	M	No interviews ? Migration DZ>MZ Low ascertainment	Hospital admission Death certification ICD-8 Alcoholism	23.1	10.8	2.1

Continued

Table 6.2 *Continued*

Author	Twin Pairs (n)	Sex	Criticisms	Criteria		Concordance MZ (%)	DZ (%)	MZ/ DZ
Pickens *et al* (1991)	169	M + F	? Validity of twin method in alcoholism	DSM-III Alcohol:				
				Male	Abuse	74.0	57.8	1.3
					Dependence	59.0	36.2	1.6
				Female	Abuse	26.7	27.3	1.0
					Dependence	25.0	5.0	5.0
Caldwell & Gottesman (1991)	154	M + F	? Validity of twin method in alcoholism	DSM-III Alcohol:				
				Male	Abuse	68	46	1.5
					Dependence	40	13	3.1
				Female	Abuse	47	42	1.1
					Dependence	29	25	1.2

V-A: Veterans Administration; ICD: *International Classification of Diseases*; ICD-8: 8th Revision (World Health Organization, 1977); ICD-9: 9th Revision (World Health Organization, 1965); DSM-III: *Diagnostic & Statistical Manual of Mental Disorders*, 3rd Edn (American Psychiatric Association, 1980); RDC: Research Diagnostic Criteria (Spitzer *et al*, 1978).

pre-morbid traits which predispose to the development of alcoholism. This is a useful strategy, but few researchers have followed up subjects through adulthood to determine whether or not individuals with a particular trait actually do go on to develop alcoholism. The design does not distinguish between genetic and environmental effects.

Several investigators have shown that FHP subjects and alcoholics demonstrate relatively low levels of slow wave (alpha) activity on electro-encephalograms (EEGs) and in some of these studies slow wave activity increased relatively more than in controls following an ethanol challenge. Perhaps ethanol consumption in these individuals corrects for a low level of alpha activity, thus producing more feelings of relaxation. However, these changes are not specific to alcoholism.

Electrophysiological studies have also suggested a reduced amplitude and/or increased latency of the P300 event related potential (ERP) in alcoholics with a family history of alcoholism and in their non-alcoholic first degree relatives. However, results from different studies have not always been consistent and, in at least some of these studies, latency may have increased as a consequence of previous alcohol consumption (see introductory review by Polich *et al*, 1988).

It has now been shown by several groups that body sway or 'static ataxia' is increased in the first degree relatives of alcoholics. However, other researchers have demonstrated that the increase in body sway following ingestion of alcohol is significantly smaller in FHP than in FHN subjects.

Several studies have shown inter-individual differences in the subjective effects produced by a dose of ethanol, with FHP groups demonstrating less subjective intoxication.

Autonomic responsiveness to stress, as measured by various cardiovascular parameters, has been shown to be increased in FHP subjects.

Hormonal markers that have been studied include the response to ethanol of prolactin and cortisol. Following ethanol ingestion, levels of prolactin are lower in FHP subjects than in controls (Schuckit *et al*, 1983). The rise in cortisol and ACTH following an oral dose of ethanol is significantly less among FHP than FHN men (Schuckit, 1984). A blunted response of Thyroid Stimulating Hormone (TSH) to Thyrotropin Releasing Hormone (TRH) has been demonstrated in abstinent alcoholics, but the response is enhanced in non-alcoholic FHP subjects.

A large number of studies have addressed the issue of monoamine oxidase (MAO) activity in alcoholism. This is of particular interest in view of its relevance to the aetiology of affective disorders, which are themselves associated with alcoholism. MAO activity has been found to be reduced in the brains of alcoholic suicides, and platelets of abstinent alcoholics and first degree relatives of alcoholics. Others have found that platelet MAO was reduced in Type II alcoholism but not in Type I (Table 6.4), and still other studies have generated negative results. Clearly this marker warrants further research.

Genetic effects

A now considerable body of research has addressed the question as to whether a predisposition to alcoholism may be inherited. Family studies have consistently shown that alcoholism occurs more frequently among the relatives of alcoholics than among the relatives of non-alcoholics (Cotton, 1979), but this alone does not distinguish between genetic and environmental influences in aetiology. Twin and adoption studies offer the opportunity for separating genetic and environmental effects. It is therefore worth considering the evidence provided by these and other genetic studies, before going on to consider the mechanisms by which genetic effects may influence vulnerability to alcoholism.

Twin studies of alcoholism employing clinically ascertained samples are summarised in Table 6.2. Of these six (independent) studies, five show greater monozygotic (MZ) than dizygotic (DZ) concordance suggesting a significant genetic effect. However, several of these studies are subject to various methodological criticisms. There is also some question as to whether the classical twin method, used in these studies, is appropriate for studying alcoholism. The twin method assumes that any excess in concordance for MZ over DZ twins can be attributed to heredity and not to unequal family environments in MZ and DZ families. However, MZ twins are more likely to live together in adult life than DZ twins and this proximity could increase their concordance for alcoholism. Unequal family environments may also reduce concordance by a within pair 'competition' effect, whereby heavy drinking effects reduce consumption in the co-twin. A competition effect has been shown to exist for DZ twins in studies of normal drinking. The current evidence for a genetic effect in alcoholism is thus weak as far as data from twin studies are concerned.

Adoption studies have been widely employed in psychiatric research as a means of disentangling genetic and environmental influences, since adoptees receive their genes from one set of parents and their family upbringing from another. Four different groups of researchers have used the adoption strategy to study alcoholism (see Table 6.3). Roe's study is the only one to have shown absolutely no evidence of a genetic effect, and there is some doubt as to the diagnosis of alcoholism in the fathers of her subjects. The methodology of the other studies has also been criticised on various grounds, but they continue to provide strong evidence in favour of a genetic influence upon the aetiology of alcoholism.

The Iowa studies (Cadoret & Gath, 1978; Cadoret *et al*, 1985, 1987) are of interest by virtue of having shown a genetic effect in females as well as males, and an environmental effect in males (but not females). However, the Copenhagen study (Goodwin *et al*, 1973, 1974, 1977) is probably the best to date on methodological grounds. It showed a fourfold increase in the incidence of alcoholism among male adoptees adopted away from their alcoholic parent(s) soon after birth. An effect of alcoholism in the adoptive family was not demonstrated (except in terms of the increased incidence of depression

Table 6.3   Adoption studies of alcoholism

Authors	Influence of adoptive family demonstrated	Increased incidence of alcoholism among adoptees with alcoholic biological parents
Roe (1944)		Male & Female – No
Cadoret & Gath (1978)		Male & Female – Yes
Cadoret *et al* (1985)	Males – Yes	Males – Yes
Cadoret *et al* (1987)	Females – No	Females – Yes
Goodwin *et al* (1973, 1974)	Males – No	Males – Yes
Goodwin *et al* (1977)	Females – No	Females – No
Bohman (1978)		Males – Yes
		Females – No

among female adoptees). Goodwin's criteria for 'alcoholism' may have been too lenient and overinclusive, but nevertheless they produce a curious anomaly. If the cut off point for abnormality is widened to include an even broader group of 'problem drinkers', then there is no significant difference between index and control adoptees. This finding contradicts the evidence of numerous twin studies, and of Cloninger's analysis of Bohman's adoption study (Cloninger *et al*, 1981), that not only alcoholism but also milder alcohol abuse is under some degree of genetic influence. It also runs counter to the evidence that heavy drinking and alcoholism are closely related.

Bohman (1978) also demonstrated a genetic effect in males but not females. Since alcohol abuse was uncommon among women at the time this study was carried out, it may have been that the sample was too small to show any significant effect. Adoptees who lived with their biological mother for more than 6 months had 1.5 times more risk of later alcohol abuse than others, but this did not account for the differences between the biological children of alcoholics and controls. Cloninger *et al* (1981) re-examined and enlarged Bohman's data on male adoptees. They identified two types of alcoholism (see Table 6.4). Taken together, the findings of Bohman and Cloninger are quite remarkable, but it remains to be seen whether their classification of alcoholism will stand the test of time. It has certainly not received universal support, and many subjects appear not to fit clearly into either category.

Half-siblings of offspring of alcoholics also offer opportunities for separating possible genetic and environmental effects on drinking behaviour. Schuckit *et al* (1972) found that it seemed to matter little whether the half-sibs were raised by an alcoholic parental figure or not, since the same proportion of both groups became alcoholic. The only consistent predictor of alcoholism in half-siblings was the presence of an alcoholic biological parent.

Table 6.4 Two types of alcoholism (Cloninger *et al*, 1981)

	Type I 'Milieu Limited'	Type II 'Male Limited'
Drinking pattern	Loss of control	Inability to abstain
Sex	Male and female	Male
Heritability	Parents mild/non-abusers	Highly heritable
Criminality	No association	Associated
Post-natal environment	Determines severity and frequency	May influence severity
Severity	Usually mild	Moderate/Severe
Age of onset	> 25 years	< 25 years

Another method of studying alcoholism has been to search for association with genetic markers. A recent study employing DNA markers (Blum *et al*, 1990) revealed a strong association between alcoholism and the A1 allele of the dopamine D_2 receptor gene. Some research groups have been able to replicate this finding, but others could not. If valid, it implies that either the D_2 receptor gene or very closely linked genes must be candidate loci for conferring a susceptibility to alcoholism. It is worthy of note that a dopamine receptor blocking agent, tiapride, has beneficial effects in the treatment of alcoholism (Shaw *et al*, 1987). Cloninger's theories of personality and alcoholism suggest that dopaminergic pathways are involved in reinforcement of alcohol seeking behaviour (Cloninger, 1987), and Modell *et al* (1990) have proposed theories of craving and loss of control attributable to dopaminergic dysfunction.

Given that there is evidence in favour of a genetic effect, but that the particular genetic loci concerned are not yet definitely identified, how may a genetic predisposition to alcoholism be mediated? Genetic effects may influence levels of alcohol consumption, incidence of alcohol-related problems, and onset of physical dependence.

Possible mediators of a genetic effect

(1) Level of consumption of alcohol

A large number of twin studies of 'normal' drinking have revealed a modest but significant heritability of drinking behaviour. However, the relevance of these studies to the genetics of alcoholism is uncertain because the relation of normal drinking to variation of alcoholism may be complex. There are four main suggestions as to how genetic effects may influence levels of alcohol consumption.

First, pharmacogenetic factors may determine a less intense reaction to alcohol (see above) such that vulnerable individuals drink more before feeling intoxicated, and thus tend to consume more alcohol than their peers.

Second, it is hypothetically possible that alcohol may correct a deficiency of a biochemical or physiological nature found in certain, vulnerable, subjects.

The effect of alcohol in restoring EEG alpha activity (see above) may fit such a model. If alcohol has a biphasic effect on this hypothetical system, whereby it causes first stimulation and then subsequent underactivity, the propensity to become addicted is also explained. Kent *et al* (1985) have produced some preliminary evidence that serotonin metabolism may fit this model, and drugs which modulate serotonergic neuro-transmission have shown some potential in the treatment of alcoholism (Tollefson, 1989; Naranjo *et al*, 1990).

Third, at least in some populations, genetic effects operate by tending to reduce the level of intake among certain individuals, thus protecting them against the risk of becoming alcoholic. Metabolism of alcohol is dependent upon a number of enzymes: the two most important being alcohol dehydrogenase (ADH) and aldehyde dehydrogenase (ALDH) (see Fig. 6.2). Around 50% of Chinese and Japanese subjects possess a deficiency of the active mitochondrial form of aldehyde dehydrogenase (ALDH2). Ingestion of alcohol by these individuals results in high levels of acetaldehyde which induce a 'flushing response' that includes tachycardia, a sensation of heat in the stomach, palpitations, muscle weakness, and facial flushing.

Fourth, alcohol consumption may also be elevated as a consequence of an underlying psychiatric disorder, personality disorder or personality trait which is genetically determined. This possibility will be discussed further below.

(2) Susceptibility to complications of alcohol consumption

To some extent any factor increasing consumption of alcohol by an individual will be likely to increase liability to complications, simply on the grounds of increased risk of accidents or other social consequences of intoxication. Antisocial personality disorder may be expected to increase not only the amount of alcohol consumed (see below), but also the behavioural complications arising from a given level of consumption. Furthermore, some of the psychological complications of heavy drinking are disorders which have an established genetic basis independent of alcoholism. Thus, for example, we may expect that an independently inherited susceptibility to affective disorder will render a heavy drinker more susceptible to depression as a 'complication'

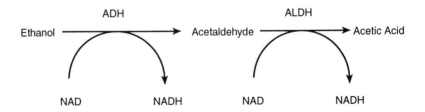

Fig. 6.2 Metabolism of ethanol in man.

of his drinking. However, the individual variation in liability to accidents or other social complications remains an area in which little genetic research has been conducted.

Genetic factors probably also influence susceptibility to alcohol-induced end organ damage. Research to date has focused mainly on the liver and the brain, although it is quite likely that similar effects influence vulnerability to damage of the pancreas, heart and other organs. Hrubec & Omenn (1981) demonstrated greater MZ than DZ concordance rates for alcoholic cirrhosis in their twin study, suggesting a genetic effect in the predisposition to alcoholic liver damage. Much attention has been devoted to the use of HLA antigens as genetic markers for liability to alcohol-induced liver damage, but this field is plagued by conflicting results and numerous different HLA loci have been implicated. There is some evidence that the ALDH2 locus not only affects alcohol consumption in oriental populations but possibly also the incidence of alcohol-induced liver disease (Enomoto *et al*, 1991).

Hrubec & Omenn (1981) demonstrated greater MZ than DZ concordance for alcoholic psychosis in their twin study. However, the significance of this is uncertain because they incorporated heterogeneous diagnoses (61% delirium tremens, 21% unspecified, 12% hallucinosis or paranoia and 6% Korsakoff's psychosis) under the heading of 'alcoholic psychosis'. A high K_m variant of transketolase has received some attention as a possible mediator of genetic susceptibility to alcoholic psychosis of the Wernicke–Korsakoff type (Blass & Gibson, 1977). This enzyme variant is seen in patients with the Wernicke–Korsakoff syndrome, but also in familial chronic alcoholism and in the unaffected sons of such alcoholics as well as (less commonly) in the normal population.

(3) Liability to physical dependence upon alcohol

Tolerance and dependence, although closely related, are not inseparable phenomena. Decremental adaptation is that form of tolerance resulting from a simple reduction in end organ (or target cell) responsiveness. Withdrawal of the drug is not associated with any untoward effects. In oppositional adaptation, tolerance appears through development of a physiological state opposing the effects of the drug. Withdrawal of the drug thus leaves an unopposed hyperexcitable state which is manifested clinically as a withdrawal syndrome.

Little is known about the mechanisms underlying decremental adaptation. A plausible theory would be that the neuronal membrane becomes more resistant to penetration of ethanol, such that it is less able to exert its effects upon membrane proteins.

Oppositional adaptation occurs to both the anaesthetic and anxiolytic effects of ethanol. The latter is probably mediated by reduced sensitivity of $GABA_A$ receptors to GABA, thus leading to CNS disinhibition. The former, which is associated with increased risk of epileptiform seizures, is thought to be mediated by a compensatory increase in the number of voltage operated calcium channels in the neuronal membrane (Littleton, 1991).

A completely different line of research, which is in direct contrast to studies of the low incidence of alcoholism among ALDH2-deficient Oriental subjects, demonstrates that ALDH activity (in red blood cells, and liver) is reduced in alcoholics. Perhaps because of this, following the ingestion of ethanol, serum acetaldehyde may be elevated in alcoholics or their relatives, relative to controls. The low activity of ALDH2 in alcoholics does not appear to be due to abnormal isoenzyme patterns and other investigators have been unable to replicate these results. However, elevated levels of acetaldehyde could explain a predisposition to alcohol dependence, conferred by the production of condensation products of acetaldehyde with certain biogenic amines. In animal studies intraventricular administration of small amounts of these substances (tetrahydroisoquinolines and beta-carbolines) has been shown to induce a prolonged and marked increase in voluntary alcohol consumption. Not all investigators have been able to replicate these results, and there have been few studies in humans. However, such a mechanism may underlie the induction of craving and dependence (see review by Myers, 1989).

Psychological factors

Psychological theories of the aetiology of alcoholism, both dynamic and behavioural, tend to originate from either or both of two common underlying assumptions. Firstly, alcohol consumption is seen as being highly pleasurable and effective in relieving subjective distress or discomfort (i.e. it is 'rewarding' or 'reinforcing'). Secondly, for one of a number of reasons, the alcoholic may be seen as deficient in avoiding the negative consequences of heavy drinking. Dynamic and behavioural perspectives also both tend to view alcoholism, other forms of drug dependence, and a range of other behaviours (exercise dependence, eating disorders, certain sexual perversions, 'pathological' shopping, etc) as varying forms of 'psychological' dependence. In almost every other respect, cognitive–behavioural and psychodynamic approaches differ.

Psychodynamic theories

Psychodynamic explanations of the aetiology of alcoholism have not been popular in recent years, perhaps because of their disappointing failure to realise any great value when implemented in treatment. Freud made little reference to alcoholism in his published work, but did suggest that the consumption of alcohol provided relief from the conflict generated by an oral fixation, or repressed homosexuality. Later theorists have developed upon these two main ideas.

Psychoanalysts have also developed theories of a 'self-destructive' motive for alcoholism (Barry, 1988). According to this theory, the disinhibitory effects of alcohol weaken normal avoidance of the adverse consequences of drinking. Alcoholics are seen to be particularly vulnerable to this effect because they already have deficient mechanisms for avoidance of these consequences, by virtue of an unconscious motivation to self-destruction. This is said to be generated by anger and destructive feelings directed towards the internalised parent in their superego. This line of reasoning, developed by Knight (1937, 1938) and Menninger (1938), led to the view of alcoholism as a form of 'slow suicide'. A similar line of reasoning suggests that alcohol intoxication represents a rebellion against obsessional traits which are the product of an underlying anal fixation.

Psychoanalytic theories of alcoholism suffer from the usual criticisms of such work. They are based upon inference, they are difficult to prove or disprove, and were developed in a context (late 19th century Europe) from which extrapolation may not be valid.

One modern school of psychotherapy which has generated theories with rather more value to the treatment of alcoholism is Transactional Analysis. This model of alcoholism highlights the gains from alcoholic behaviour. For example, the disinhibition associated with intoxication allows expression of aggression, and the self-damage consequent upon drinking attracts care and attention from others. Benefits may also be more altruistic, such as distraction of attention from a partner's emotional deficiencies. While such dynamics undoubtedly do occur, their aetiological significance is far from clear. For a vivid popular account of "Games alcoholics play", see Steiner (1974).

Cognitive, behavioural and social psychological theories

In contrast to the demise of psychodynamic explanations of alcoholism, cognitive, behavioural and social psychological theories have all become increasingly popular in recent years. Nine representative models or processes are described below in order to illustrate the breadth of research and the ready applicability of these theories to the aetiology of alcoholism. It is not to be imagined that these processes are viewed as mutually exclusive alternatives, or that this list is in any sense complete.

(1) According to the traditional Pavlovian theory of *classical conditioning*, neutral (unconditioned) stimuli may become associated with drinking over a period of time such that they become conditioned stimuli triggering a desire to drink ('craving') or actual drinking as a conditioned response. Similarly, a clinical or subclinical withdrawal syndrome may become a conditioned response to certain non-specific physiological states or to environmental cues (Ludwig & Wikler, 1974). Conditioned stimuli relevant to alcoholism may include social occasions, meals, finishing work, passing a pub, and so forth.

(2) Based upon general theories of *operant conditioning*, alcohol consumption may be seen to produce positive subjective effects, and to relieve the negative effects of internal aversive drives, such that it is a reinforced behaviour

(Conger, 1956). The positive effects produced by drinking include social factors as well as pharmacological effects. The negative effects relieved by drinking may include stress or tension (see discussion of the tension reduction theory below), but in later stages of development may also encompass physical (and psychological) symptoms of withdrawal (Wikler, 1961).

(3) A *combined model* of classical and operant conditioning includes the development of withdrawal symptoms as a conditioned response to certain stimuli, such as those described above under the heading of classical conditioning. Drinking then occurs as an operant conditioned response to relieve these symptoms.

(4) Once drinking occurs as a conditioned response to one situation or stimulus, it may be subject to the process of *stimulus generalisation*, whereby it is eventually elicited in a wide variety of differing circumstances. Thus, for example, drinking used initially to deal with problems at work may become a habitual means of dealing with all problems.

(5) Because alcohol and drug use are strongly reinforcing, they may lead to *extinction* of alternative responses to given stimuli. This leads not only directly to increased drinking but also to increased stress and anxiety as the individual's range of strategies for problem solving becomes more and more limited. Further drinking may then be generated along the 'tension reduction' pathway.

(6) *Modelling* or 'vicarious learning' occurs in relation to the drinking behaviour of both peers and family. Patterns of drinking behaviour are copied without reinforcement, although some patterns are apparently more likely to be copied than others.

(7) The *self-handicapping* model is of interest as an example of failure to avoid the harmful consequences of alcohol consumption (cf. the psychodynamic 'self-destructive' model). The theory is that alcohol misuse may follow positive, 'success', experiences because of poor self-confidence and fear of future failure. Subsequent failures are then attributed to alcohol misuse rather than to lack of ability and in that way the individual maintains a positive but fragile self-image, based on past achievement (Jones & Berglas, 1978).

(8) Orford (1985; p. 170) defines *social learning* thus: 'the outcome of a behavioural choice . . . is the result of the balance of expectations of positive outcomes over negative outcomes (rewards over punishments) for engaging in rather than desisting from appetitive behaviour'. These outcomes include intrinsic effects (of alcohol upon the mind and body) and extrinsic effects (social consequences, etc). Orford builds a powerful argument for the operation of a social learning model not only in the case of alcohol consumption, but also for a range of other behaviours including gambling, eating and sexuality.

(9) *Expectancy* of particular effects of alcohol or of particular outcomes of drinking can be important determinants of drinking behaviour. This approach to drinking has led to a cognitive model of craving which is distinct from the model of classical conditioning. In this model, certain 'high risk situations', in which the individual has few resources to cope, may lead to craving.

Craving is thus defined as a 'subjective state that is mediated by the incentive properties of positive outcome expectancies' (Marlatt, quoted by Wilson, 1987).

The implementation of these models in treatment (for example in relapse prevention models) is showing great promise, but their role in aetiology, as distinct from maintenance, of alcoholism and their interaction with other factors (genetic and environmental) is yet to be fully evaluated (for further discussion see Chapter 8).

Personality

Personality has long been a popular contender in the bid to explain the aetiology of alcoholism. Many alcohol counsellors today still speak of the 'addictive personality' as though it were an incontrovertible feature of the treatment landscape. This is perhaps understandable in view of the striking, and dysfunctional, personality traits that are seen so commonly among alcoholics in treatment. However, extensive research over the last 50 years, seeking to distinguish the consequences of prolonged heavy drinking from its causes, has failed to identify any specific personality type which goes on to develop alcoholism. Evidence does exist for a non-specific increase in risk of alcoholism among individuals with certain traits (see Table 6.5), but only antisocial traits emerge from the research with any substantial support.

Windle (1990) reviewed 27 studies of personality of FHP (compared with FHN) subjects. He found salient methodological deficiencies in these studies, and largely negative results, but three variables did demonstrate significant differences. These were external locus of control (locus of control is a concept describing the extent to which an individual believes that his personal actions may influence his environment. An individual with external locus of control is likely to attribute events in his environment to fate or to influences beyond his control); increased alexithymia (alexithymia is characterised by an inability to express emotions, in which there is an apparent mismatch between somatic, psychological and behavioural components of an emotional state,

Table 6.5 Personality traits conferring vulnerability to alcoholism

Antisocial personality disorder
Hyperactivity or undersocialised aggression in childhood
Neuroticism?
External locus of control?
Alexithymia?
Borderline personality disorder?
High 'harm avoidance' and 'reward dependence', low 'novelty seeking' (Type I alcoholism)?
Low 'harm avoidance' and 'reward dependence', high 'novelty seeking' (Type II alcoholism)?

particularly in response to stress); and behavioural undercontrol (including antisocial behaviour and impulsivity).

Vaillant (1983, pp. 45–106) has reviewed six prospective studies which attempted to elicit premorbid predictors of alcoholism in young people who were followed-up into adult life. Of these projects, those conducted by McCord & McCord (1960), and Robins (1966), are the most widely quoted. The McCords found that alcoholism in later life was more likely to develop in those individuals who displayed unrestrained aggression, hyperactivity, denial of their fears, and feelings of inferiority. Robins compared adults who as children had attended a child psychiatrist with a control group who had not. The clinic attenders were more likely to develop alcoholism later in life, and this outcome was specifically associated with antisocial childhood traits (theft and running away), inattention and daydreaming. Vaillant notes that there were methodological shortcomings with all of these prospective studies. In particular, the McCords and Robins both introduced a sample bias in favour of antisocial behaviour. The McCords also failed to take account of the confounding effect of alcoholism in the parents of their subjects.

Vaillant's own prospective study (the 'Core City sample', 1983) found that premorbid personality did not predict alcoholism, except for a minority of future alcoholics with behaviour problems in adolescence. Family history of alcoholism, and ethnicity (see pp. 113–114) were the only other important predictors of future alcoholism.

Prospective studies have thus tended to disprove the importance of personality as an aetiological factor in alcoholism, with the possible exception of antisocial traits and hyperactivity or attention deficit in childhood (which have also both been implicated in the aetiology of antisocial personality). Winokur *et al* (1971) have suggested that the link between alcoholism and antisocial personality is a genetic one. However Reich *et al* (1981) and Cadoret *et al* (1987) have produced evidence that alcoholism and antisocial personality are inherited independently, albeit with interaction between the two conditions. Other, largely retrospective, research has also implicated hyperactivity as a premorbid, childhood or adolescent personality trait of alcoholics. Recent studies suggest that it is actually 'undersocialised aggression' in childhood rather than hyperactivity *per se* that is associated with both parental/adult alcoholism and antisocial personality (Windle, 1990).

Two other personality traits that have attracted particular interest in the study of the aetiology of alcoholism are emotional 'dependency' and anxiety. The former personality type (including traits of passivity, self-doubt, inhibited aggression, etc) has now been excluded in a series of prospective studies (Jones, 1968; Kammeier *et al*, 1973; Vaillant, 1980). The latter, in contrast, continues to attract support and has particular relevance to treatment.

According to the 'tension' or 'anxiety' reduction theory, the alcoholic uses alcohol as an anxiolytic, to reduce levels of anxiety which would otherwise, to a greater or lesser extent, be disabling. In his excellent review, Wilson (1988) discusses the range of evidence against this theory, including conflicting research which demonstrates that alcohol increases, reduces or does not affect human anxiety. In summary, he shows that this theory is extremely limited in its ability to account for the development of alcoholism, except when it is combined with other mechanisms, such as those proposed by learning theory (see above). However, genetic research has also cast helpful light upon this subject. Mullan *et al* (1986), in their twin study, showed that higher neuroticism scores on the Eysenck Personality Quotient (and a range of neurotic disorders) were more common in the alcoholic probands and co-twins than in the normal co-twins, suggesting that they are more often a consequence than a cause of alcoholism. Clifford (1982), also using the twin method, found evidence that the link between anxiety (and depression) and 'escape' drinking in males was genetic in origin (i.e. her subjects were genetically predisposed to both anxiety and a tendency to use alcohol to relieve their symptoms). Anxiety traits do not, therefore, appear to be an important *causal* factor in alcoholism.

Alcoholism has also been found to be associated with Borderline Personality Disorder. Loranger & Tulis (1985) found a two to three fold increase in alcoholism among the relatives of borderline probands, as compared with the relatives of schizophrenic and bipolar disorder probands. However, there were no significant differences once alcohol abuse among probands was controlled for. In view of the methodological shortcomings of this study, the significance of these results is uncertain.

Cloninger (1987) has described a tri-dimensional model of personality, with an underlying genetic structure, which attempts to explain both the aetiology of alcoholism and also its heterogeneity. 'Novelty seeking' is a tendency to respond to novel stimuli with exploratory behaviour and exhilaration. 'Harm avoidance' represents a tendency to inhibit behaviour in response to aversive stimuli. 'Reward dependence' shows a tendency to resist extinction of previously rewarded behaviour. Cloninger suggests that these personality dimensions correlate with the activity of dopamine, serotonin, and noradrenaline neuromodulators each acting in a particular brain system. Each dimension is inherited independently of the others.

High novelty seeking may be associated with alcohol seeking behaviour. High harm avoidance is associated with low alcohol seeking behaviour but rapid development of behavioural tolerance and psychological dependence. High reward dependence will make it difficult to stop using alcohol when it has previously been rewarding. Type I alcoholism (see Table 6.4) is thought to be associated with high harm avoidance, high reward dependence and low novelty seeking. Type II alcoholism shows high novelty seeking but low harm avoidance and reward dependence. Space prevents a full consideration of this elaborate hypothesis, which has implications far beyond the field of alcoholism genetics. It remains to be seen whether future studies employing this typology will support its relevance as a genetic basis for alcoholism.

Psychiatric disorder

Various studies have shown that alcoholism coexists with other psychiatric disorders. In two-thirds or more of cases, at least one additional psychiatric diagnosis may be made. (This is discussed in detail in Chapter 9). These most commonly include affective disorders, neuroses and antisocial personality disorder. It is frequently difficult to establish whether a comorbid psychiatric disorder is secondary to prolonged heavy drinking, or else in some way contributory to the development of it. Frequently, chronology of development, or else severity, are assumed to indicate which disorder is primary and which is secondary (Schuckit, 1986). In the case of some common disorders, comorbidity may also occur simply by chance, or as a result of other factors, such as assortative mating. However, where alcoholism is secondary to another psychiatric disorder, this may hold important implications for treatment and prognosis.

Environmental factors

At the most basic level, the availability of alcohol constitutes a fundamental and necessary environmental factor for the development of alcoholism.

Box 6.2   Environmental factors

Epidemiological factors
  Cost, income, legislation, etc (see Chapter 5)

Cultural factors
  Induced tensions and needs for adjustment
  Attitudes towards drinking
  Availability of alternatives to drinking as means of adjustment

Occupation
  Ready availability of alcohol at work
  Frequent absence from home
  Lack of supervision
  Long and irregular working hours
  Very high or very low income
  Social pressure to drink at work
  Social isolation
  Very high stresses or hazards in the workplace

Family environment
  Psychological effects – modelling, social learning, etc
  Deprivation, cruelty and abuse?
  Disruption of family rituals

Stress and life events

Factors which increase or reduce the availability of alcohol may thus be expected to influence the incidence of alcoholism. This relationship has in fact proved almost invariably true across a wide range of countries at almost every time in history. Thus cost, taxation, income, legislation and a range of other socio-political factors constitute important aetiological agents in determining per capita consumption and the incidence of alcohol related problems within any given population (see Chapter 5 for a more detailed discussion of these issues). These are, arguably, the most important environmental factors influencing the aetiology of alcoholism, and are also those which are (at a social and political level) the most accessible to preventative interventions. However, given that alcohol is available, to a greater or lesser extent, to all members of a particular population, other environmental factors may influence the acceptability of alcohol use, either for the wider population or else within narrower sub-groups of that population. It is these factors (see Box 6.2) that will constitute the focus of the remainder of this discussion of environmental factors in the aetiology of alcoholism.

Cultural factors

In a classic paper, Robert Bales (1946) described three general ways in which culture and social organisation can influence rates of alcoholism.

First, the degree to which the culture operates to bring about acute needs for adjustment, or inner tensions, in its members. Bales listed culturally induced anxiety, guilt, conflict, suppressed aggression, and sexual tensions as examples of this category. Such a theory, implicating subsistence anxiety, had earlier been proposed by Horton (1943) based upon an extensive review of 'the functions of alcohol in primitive societies'.

Second, the attitudes to drinking which the culture produces in its members. These determine whether drinking is seen as a positive response of an individual to his inner tensions or whether the thought of drinking in such circumstances arouses guilt and anxiety. Bales described four different attitudes under this heading. Complete abstinence, as seen for example in Islamic culture, or in America during the prohibition, denies the acceptability of alcohol use under any circumstance. Paradoxically, Bales and others (e.g. O'Connor, 1975) suggest that such a taboo is often ineffective or even counterproductive. To be effective social controls, such attitudes need to be learnt, reinforced and internalised from the earliest age. A ritual attitude towards drinking is usually religious in nature and derives from use of alcohol in a sacred, ceremonial, context. Such attitudes, ingrained from an early age, lead to strong counteranxiety against the misuse of alcohol. This is proposed as an explanation for the low rates of alcohol-related problems in Jewish culture. Convivial drinking or 'social' drinking ascribes a symbolic meaning of solidarity or social unity to the use of alcohol, but when seen in extreme form tends to break down toward purely utilitarian drinking. Irish culture provides a classic example, where all principal social occasions are marked by drinking and where, traditionally, refusal to accept a drink (or to buy a round) would be construed as a grave insult. Utilitarian drinking is motivated by personal interest and is thus often, but not exclusively, a solitary affair. This would include 'medicinal' use of alcohol and drinking to 'escape' from unpleasant personal circumstances. Absence of counteranxiety associated with drinking, suggests that such attitudes are likely to lead to high rates of alcoholism.

Third, the degree to which the culture provides suitable substitutes for dealing with the inner tensions and needs for adjustment which it creates. Other drugs may be more acceptable than alcohol, as may other behaviours such as rituals or trance states. Lack of suitable alternatives increases the likelihood of alcohol use and thus eventually the development of alcohol-related problems.

Numerous alternative classifications and explanations for differences in rates of alcoholism between cultures have been proposed since Bales' 1946 paper. For example, Pittman (1967) describes Abstinent, Ambivalent, Permissive and Over-Permissive cultures. As with Bales' earlier classification, the balance of attitudes promoting drinking with those producing counteranxiety is seen as important. Ambivalent cultures contain opposing beliefs – that drinking is part of the accepted social order on the one hand, and yet that abstention is promoted on the other (for example Irish society). Permissive and over-permissive groups both attach positive connotations to drinking, but in the former case with strong sanctions against excessive use or abuse (examples are Jewish or Italian societies), and in the latter case with tolerance of deviant drinking behaviour (for example the French). Under this schema permissive societies were seen as being at the lowest risk of alcoholism, although a rather socially influenced definition was being used. The high incidence of cirrhosis, other alcohol-related physical disorders, and severe physical dependence in, for example, Italy is now well known.

Stacey & Davies (1970) have reviewed drinking behaviour in childhood and adolescence. Based on their analysis of the literature, O'Connor (1975) has listed nine habits and attitudes considered to be associated with the lowest incidence of alcoholism:

(1) Exposure of children to alcohol (diluted, small quantities) early in life, in the context of a strong family or religious group
(2) Commonly used beverages contain relatively large non-alcoholic component
(3) Alcoholic beverages considered mainly as a food and usually consumed with meals
(4) Parents present a constant example of moderate drinking
(5) Drinking is morally neutral; it is considered to be neither a virtue nor a sin
(6) Drinking is not viewed as proof of adulthood or virility
(7) Abstinence is socially acceptable
(8) Excessive drinking or intoxication is considered socially unacceptable
(9) Wide social acceptance of drinking norms or 'ground rules'.

There is continuing debate as to the correct explanation for cultural differences in rates of alcoholism, the correct classification of particular cultures, and the importance of such concepts as 'ambivalence' (Room, 1976). However, it is clear that cultural factors do exert considerable influence upon alcohol consumption at a population level and that they are an important component of aetiology to be considered in the assessment of the individual patient.

Occupation

One of the most important social or environmental factors affecting the alcohol consumption of particular groups of individuals within the wider population is occupation. Figure 6.3 shows the standardised mortality ratios for cirrhosis for a range of occupations which may be considered to be 'at risk' groups for alcoholism. (Cirrhosis mortality is known to be strongly correlated with,

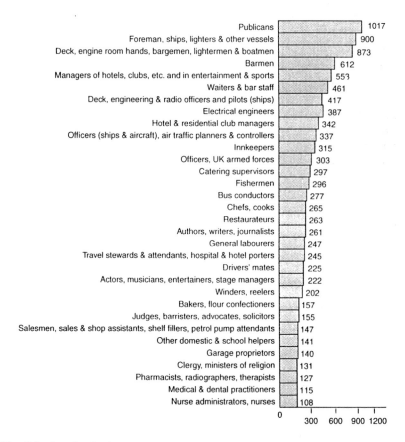

Fig. 6.3 Standardised mortality ratios for liver cirrhosis by occupation – UK Males 1979–1980 and 1982–1983.

and thus provides a good indicator of, levels of alcohol consumption. See Chapter 5). There is much speculation as to wh at the common denominators may be that link such apparently diverse occupations. Ready availability of alcohol at work, frequent absence from home, and lack of supervision are among those most commonly mentioned. Long and irregular working hours, very high or very low income, social pressure to drink at work, social isolation, and very high stresses or hazards in the workplace are also thought to be important.

Plant (1979) conducted an important study of men starting work in a brewery, in an effort to distinguish the effects of working in such an industry from those of employment selection. He was able to show that brewery workers were already drinking more than workers in other industries at the point of their employment, but that their drinking increased further over the subsequent two year period. It thus appears that occupation exerts a causative effect in the generation of heavy drinking, but that there is also a selection effect at the point of employment.

Family environment

Until twin and adoption studies provided evidence suggesting that there was a genetic predisposition to alcoholism, family environment provided a major line of argument to explain the strong familiality of alcoholism. To a large extent these theories relied upon psychological hypotheses, such as those discussed above under 'constitutional' factors. However, the non-specific disruption of childhood by the deprivation and cruelty experienced secondary to being the child of an alcoholic parent have also been thought to play a part. Few research designs have been able to separate these environmental effects of alcoholic parentage from the concomitant genetic effects. For example, there is evidence of an association between childhood sexual and physical abuse and later alcoholism, but such abuse is also associated with a family history of alcoholism (Brown & Anderson, 1991). Is the childhood abuse, the genetic inheritance, the 'alcoholic' environment (or a combination of these) the truly causative variable?

Longitudinal studies of children at risk, behaviour genetic studies, and family systems research have each suggested possible family environmental mechanisms of intergenerational transmission of alcoholism.

Longitudinal studies of children of alcoholics

Two of the best prospective studies of alcoholism (McCord & McCord, 1960; Robins, 1966) showed that future alcoholism was predicted by unstable childhood. However, the subject sample in both of these studies was biased towards underprivileged and delinquent youths. Vaillant (1980), in a longitudinal study of a more privileged group of subjects (college students) found that childhood environment did not predict future alcoholism. In a subsequent study of underprivileged but non-delinquent subjects childhood environmental weaknesses were associated with both future alcoholism and alcoholic parentage (Vaillant, 1983). However, among 51 men with an alcoholic parent, but having few childhood environmental weaknesses, 27% became alcohol dependent, and among 56 men with no alcoholic parent but many childhood environmental weaknesses, only 5% became alcohol dependent. This work thus suggests that although having an alcoholic parent increases the likelihood of experiencing childhood problems, childhood problems are not themselves causally implicated in the future development of alcohol dependence.

Behaviour genetic studies

Behaviour genetic research allows deductions to be made not only concerning genetic effects in alcoholism, or drinking behaviour, but also concerning environmental effects. In twin studies, newer models of analysis allow decomposition of environmental variance into common environmental (CE; between pair effect) and specific environmental (SE; within pair effect) components. The CE component represents the non-genetic source of between family variance (i.e. the family effect).

   Twin studies of personality have revealed that CE has remarkably little effect upon a wide range of personality traits, the environmental effect being contributed almost entirely by the SE component. Similar results have been obtained for some aspects of alcohol use. For example, in a twin study of drinking patterns in normal twins, Clifford *et al* (1984) found little effect of CE upon 'escape' drinking, 'social' drinking, and 'psychological effects' in males. 'Total weekly consumption', 'severe drinking problems' and 'mild drinking problems', showed a more significant effect of CE, but in every case the SE effect was greater than the CE effect (Table 6.6). Results for females were complicated by evidence of a within pair competition effect. Pickens *et al* (1991) showed in their twin study that alcohol misuse in men was determined largely by CE and genetic effects, while alcohol dependence was determined largely by genetic effects (Table 6.6). The results for women showed absence of a genetic effect in alcohol misuse, and absence of a CE effect in alcohol dependence.

   The adoption method offers superior separation of genetic and environmental effects upon alcoholism. Of the three studies which have demonstrated a genetic effect (see above), that of Goodwin *et al* (1974) is the only one to fail to find an environmental effect of the adoptive family upon alcoholism in adoptees. Cadoret *et al* (1985) found that for men (but not women) drinking problems in the adoptive family home significantly increased the risk of alcoholism in the adoptee (by a factor of approximately 3 times). Cloninger *et al* (1981) did not find that alcoholism in the adoptive family increased the risk of alcoholism in adoptees, but they did discover other 'postnatal variables' that increased frequency and severity of Type I ('milieu limited') alcoholism. For Type II alcoholism they showed that post-natal

Table 6.6 Contribution of genetic, specific environmental and common environmental effects to total variance in twin studies of normal drinking (Clifford *et al*, 1984) and alcoholism (Pickens *et al*, 1991) in males

	Characteristic	Genetic effect	Specific environment	Common environment
Clifford *et al* (1984)	Total weekly consumption	0.40	0.32	0.28
	'Escape' drinking	0.40	0.52	0.08
	'Social' drinking	0.49	0.51	0.00
	'Psychological effects'	0.16	0.66	0.18
	Severe drinking problems	0.00	0.61	0.39
	Mild drinking problems	0.25	0.42	0.33
Pickens *et al* (1991)	Alcohol abuse (DSM-III)	0.38	0.14	0.48
	Alcohol dependence (DSM-III)	0.60	0.23	0.17

environment did not influence frequency, although it may influence severity, of alcoholism in adoptees.

Family systems research

Rituals, according to family systems theory, are symbolically rich, consciously employed and perpetuated ways of conducting 'everyday' family affairs (including traditions, celebrations and routines), which are seen as 'special' and which play an important role in organising family behaviour. Family rituals serve two important functions. They conserve family identity, preserving ideals, standards and roles across time, and they transmit family values, affects and perceptions from one generation to the next (see Steinglass *et al*, 1987, pp. 293–323).

Wolin *et al* (1979) have studied the role of family rituals in the inter-generational transmission of alcoholism. 'Subsumptive' families, in which rituals are disrupted or altered secondary to the alcoholism of a parent, are more likely to 'pass on' alcoholism to the next generation than are 'distinctive' families, in which rituals are preserved despite the alcoholic drinking of a parent. Bennett & Wolin (1986) further showed that transmission of alcoholism between generations was less likely where children had low to moderate contact with the alcoholic family of origin, and where they displayed a high degree of 'deliberateness' in selecting and establishing their own rituals following marriage. This important work was conducted on relatively small samples and is as yet unreplicated. However, it offers a valuable theoretical framework as to ways in which environment may serve to transmit alcoholism from one generation to the next, and it suggests promising possibilities for preventative interventions using a family therapy model.

Stress and life events

Implicit in Bales' (1946) model of cultural influences upon the incidence of alcoholism (see above) is the idea that people drink in response to tension or stress, presumably as a means of 'coping' or of reducing subjective distress (see discussion of the tension reduction theory, above). External stresses and life events which lead to anxiety or other aversive emotional states may thus become the stimulus to which alcohol consumption is a reinforced, learned, response. Increased alcohol consumption resulting from this pattern of reinforcement may, at least in theory, lead on to the development of alcoholism.

It is worth noting that there are particular problems in interpreting the direction of causality in this field. Subjects are prone to a 'search after meaning' which may well lead to respondent bias in retrospective studies. Heavy drinking may also generate its own, secondary, life events such as unemployment, divorce, accidents and illness. Retrospective eliciting and interpretation of a history of whether drinking increased before or after such life events can be difficult in the extreme. Unfortunately, there are very few good prospective studies.

Studies of normal people following major disasters (e.g. the Buffalo Creek flood in west Virginia (Gleser *et al*, 1981) and the Mount St Helen's eruption in Washington, USA (Adams & Adams, 1984)) show evidence of increased alcohol consumption or increased alcohol misuse in the period following the event. Retrospective and prospective research involving more commonplace forms of stress (marital disharmony, job related, etc) has contributed similar findings. Unfortunately contrary, negative (or at least non-significant) findings are also reported.

Findings are a little more clear cut among alcoholic subjects. Linsky *et al* (1987) in a major retrospective study found that both stressful life events and more chronic forms of stress were positively correlated with all studied indices of alcoholism. (These correlations were strongest in the context of strong social support for the use of alcohol, thus supporting Bales' (1946) theory.) Tatossian *et al* (1983) found that the frequency of life events was elevated in the year before alcohol abuse commenced, and was maintained at an elevated level for the subsequent 5 years. Other prospective studies have also linked alcohol consumption in alcoholics with stress, but even here negative findings have also been reported (Morrisey & Schuckit, 1978).

There is good evidence then, that stress of various sorts increases alcohol consumption, and that this may lead to the development of alcoholism. Possibly this effect occurs only in certain populations, or in circumstances of combination with other environmental (and perhaps genetic) vulnerability factors.

Summary

The aetiology of alcoholism is clearly not fully explained by any one theory or area of research. Availability must rank as contender for the single most important factor, based upon extensive epidemiological research (Chapter 5). However, even taking account of social and subcultural variations within a population, availability alone does not explain why some individuals drink heavily or develop 'alcoholism', while others do not. Genetic factors arguably offer the most convincing explanation for this inter-individual variation in vulnerability. Alcohol misuse and dependence are of multifactorial origin, determined by a complex interplay of constitutional and environmental factors each of which may be more or less important in any particular case.

Within any given population, there is a distribution of individual liability to the development of alcoholism, with a threshold above which alcoholism will be manifest. In any individual case, different environmental and constitutional factors may contribute, to a greater or lesser extent, to that liability (Cloninger *et al*, 1978; see Fig. 6.4). In fact, different liability distributions may exist for heavy drinking, dependence and other alcohol-related complications. For example, an individual may be strongly predisposed to heavy alcohol consumption, but be relatively invulnerable to dependence and other alcohol related complications. Alternatively, he or she may remain a light drinker for cultural and religious reasons, yet be at high risk of developing cirrhosis should his or her level of consumption ever increase.

In summary then, the aetiology of alcoholism is multifactorial and heterogeneous. Liability to develop alcoholism is strongly influenced by environmental, but also by individual factors. These factors appear to operate at three levels, influencing liability to heavy alcohol consumption, complications of alcohol consumption and physical dependence respectively.

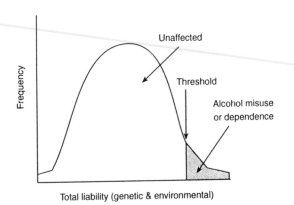

Fig. 6.4   Distribution of liability to alcoholism.

To conclude, our current understanding of the aetiology of alcoholism has been well summarised by Mulford (quoted in Institute of Medicine 1990, p. 35):

> "This way of thinking views every drinker as being at some stage of a dynamic lifelong process influenced by a multitude of weak, interacting, social, psychological, and physical forces with no single factor, except alcohol, being necessary, and none at all being sufficient to cause advancement in the process to the point of being labelled 'alcoholic' or 'problem drinker'. From this viewpoint the alcohologist's task of identifying the forces influencing the alcoholic process and untangling their complex interrelationships is much like that of the meteorologist's attempts to understand the process called 'the weather'."

Recommended reading

Agarwal, D. P. & Goedde, H. W. (1991) The role of alcohol metabolising enzymes in alcohol sensitivity, alcohol drinking habits, and incidence of alcoholism in Orientals. In *The Molecular Pathology of Alcoholism* (ed. T. N. Palmer), pp. 211-237. Oxford: Oxford University Press.

Chaudron, C. D. & Wilkinson, D. A. (eds) (1988) *Theories on Alcoholism*. Toronto: Addiction Research Foundation.

Cook, C. C. H. & Gurling, H. M. D. (1990) The genetic aspects of alcoholism and substance abuse: a review. In *The Nature of Drug Dependence* (eds G. Edwards & M. Lader), pp. 75-111. Oxford: Oxford University Press.

O'Doherty, F. & Davies, J. B. (1987) Life events and addiction: a critical review. *British Journal of Addiction*, **82**, 127-137.

Pohorecky, L. A. (1991) Stress and alcohol interaction: an update of human research. *Alcoholism: Clinical and Experimental Research*, **15**, 438-459.

Stockwell, T. & Bolderston, B. (1987) Alcohol and phobias. *British Journal of Addiction*, **82**, 971-979.

Sutton, S. (1987) Social-psychological approaches to understanding addictive behaviours: attitude behaviour and decision-making models. *British Journal of Addiction*, **82**, 355-370.

Windle, M. & Searles, J. S. (eds) (1990) *Children of Alcoholics*. New York: Guilford.

See also: Institute of Medicine, 1990; Schuckit, 1986; Wilson, 1987; Wilson, 1988.

References

Adams, P. R. & Adams, G. R. (1984) Mount St Helen's ashfall: evidence for a disaster stress reaction. *American Psychologist*, **39**, 252-260.

American Psychiatric Association (1980) *Diagnostic and Statistical Manual of Mental Disorders* (3rd edn) (DSM-III). Washington, DC: APA.

Bales, R. F. (1946) Cultural differences in rates of alcoholism. *Quarterly Journal of Studies on Alcohol*, **6**, 489-499.

Barry, H. (1988) Psychoanalytic theory of alcoholism. In *Theories on Alcoholism* (eds C. D. Chaudron & D. A. Wilkinson), pp. 103–141. Toronto: Addiction Research Foundation.

Bennett, L. A. & Wolin, S. J. (1986) Daughters and sons of alcoholics: developmental paths in transmission. *Alcoholism*, **22**, 3–15.

Blass, J. P. & Gibson, G. E. (1977) Abnormality of a thiamine requiring enzyme in patients with Wernicke-Korsakoff syndrome. *New England Journal of Medicine*, **297**, 1367–1370.

Blum, K., Noble, E. P., Sheridan, P. J., *et al* (1990) Allelic association of human dopamine D2 receptor gene in alcoholism. *Journal of the American Medical Association*, **263**, 2055–2060.

Bohman, M. (1978) Some genetic aspects of alcoholism and criminality. *Archives of General Psychiatry*, **35**, 269–276.

Brown, G. R. & Anderson, B. (1991) Psychiatric morbidity in adult in-patients with childhood histories of sexual and physical abuse. *American Journal of Psychiatry*, **148**, 55–61.

Cadoret, R. J. & Gath, A. (1978) Inheritance of alcoholism in adoptees. *British Journal of Psychiatry*, **132**, 252–258.

——, O'Gorman, T. W., Troughton, E., *et al* (1985) Alcoholism and antisocial personality. Interrelationships, genetic and environmental factors. *Archives of General Psychiatry*, **42**, 161–167.

——, Troughton, E. & O'Gorman, T. W. (1987) Genetic and environmental factors in alcohol abuse and antisocial personality. *Journal of Studies on Alcohol*, **48**, 1–8.

Caldwell, C. R. & Gottesman, I. I. (1991) Sex differences in the risk for alcoholism: a twin study. *Behaviour Genetics*, **21**, 563.

Clifford, C. A. (1982) *Twin Studies of Drinking Behaviour and Obsessionality, PhD Thesis.* London: University of London.

——, Fulker, D. W. & Murray, R. M. (1984) Genetic and environmental influences on drinking patterns in normal twins. In *Alcohol Related Problems* (eds N. Krasner, *et al*), pp. 115–126. New York: Wiley.

Cloninger, C. R. (1987) Neurogenetic adaptive mechanisms in alcoholism. *Science*, **236**, 410–416.

——, Christiansen, K. O., Reich, T., *et al* (1978) Implications of sex differences in the prevalences of antisocial personality, alcoholism, and criminality for familial transmission. *Archives of General Psychiatry*, **35**, 941–951.

——, Bohman, M. & Sigvardsson, S. (1981) Inheritance of alcohol abuse: cross fostering analysis of adopted men. *Archives of General Psychiatry*, **38**, 861–868.

Conger, J. J. (1956) Reinforcement theory and the dynamics of alcoholism. *Quarterly Journal of Studies in Alcoholism*, **17**, 296–305.

Cotton, N. S. (1979) The familial incidence of alcoholism. *Journal of Studies on Alcohol*, **40**, 89–116.

Enomoto, N., Takase, S., Takada, N., *et al* (1991) Alcoholic liver disease in heterozygotes of mutant and normal aldehyde dehydrogenase-2 genes. *Hepatology*, **13**, 1071–1075.

Gleser, G. C., Green, B. L. & Winget, C. (1981) *Prolonged Psychosocial Effects of Disaster: a Study of Buffalo Creek.* New York: Academic Press.

Goodwin, D. W., Hermansen, L., Guze, S. B., *et al* (1973) Alcohol problems in adoptees raised apart from alcoholic biological parents. *Archives of General Psychiatry*, **28**, 238–243.

——, Schulsinger, F., Moller, N., *et al* (1974) Drinking problems in adopted and non-adopted sons of alcoholics. *Archives of General Psychiatry*, **31**, 164–169.

——, ——, Knop, J., *et al* (1977) Psychopathology in adopted and non-adopted daughters of alcoholics. *Archives of General Psychiatry*, **34**, 1005–1009.

Gurling, H. M. D. (1989) *The Genetic Predisposition to Alcoholism and the Effects of Alcoholism on Brain Structure and Function. MD Thesis.* London: London University.

——, Clifford, C. A. & Murray, R. M. (1981) Investigations into the genetics of alcohol dependence and into its effects on brain function. In *Twin Research 3: Epidemiological and Clinical Studies* (eds L. Goedda, *et al*), pp. 77–87. New York: Alan R. Liss.

Horton, D. (1943) The functions of alcohol in primitive societies: a cross-cultural study. *Quarterly Journal of Studies on Alcohol*, **4**, 199–320.

Hrubec, Z. & Omenn, G. S. (1981) Evidence of genetic predisposition to alcoholic psychosis and cirrhosis: twin concordances for alcoholism and its biological end points by zygosity among male veterans. *Alcoholism: Clinical & Experimental Research*, **5**, 207–215.

Institute of Medicine (1990) *Broadening the Base of Treatment for Alcohol Problems.* Washington, DC: National Academy Press.

Jones, M. C. (1968) Personality correlates and antecedents of drinking patterns in adult males. *Journal of Consulting and Clinical Psychology*, **32**, 2–12.

Jones, E. E. & Berglas, S. (1978) Control of attributions about the self through self-handicapping strategies: the appeal of alcohol and the role of underachievement. *Personal and Social Psychology Bulletin*, **4**, 200–206.

Kaij, L. (1960) *Alcoholism in Twins.* Stockholm: Almqvist & Wiksell.

Kammeier, M. L., Hoffmann, H. & Loper, R. G. (1973) Personality characteristics of alcoholics as college freshmen and at time of treatment. *Quarterly Journal of Studies on Alcohol*, **34**, 390–399.

Kendler, S. K. (1985) A twin study of individuals with both schizophrenia and alcoholism. *British Journal of Psychiatry*, **147**, 48–53.

Kent, T. A., Campbell, J. L., Pazdernick, T. L., *et al* (1985) Blood platelet uptake of serotonin in men alcoholics. *Journal of Studies on Alcohol*, **46**, 357–359.

Knight, R. P. (1937) The psychodynamics of chronic alcoholism. *Journal of Nervous and Mental Disorders*, **86**, 538–548.

—— (1938) The psychoanalytic treatment in a sanatorium of chronic addiction to alcohol. *Journal of the American Medical Association*, **111**, 1443–1448.

Koskenvuo, M., Langinvainio, H., Kaprio, J., *et al* (1984) Psychiatric hospitalisation in twins. *Acta Geneticae Medicae et Gemellologiae*, **33**, 321–332.

Levine, H. G. (1978) The discovery of addiction: changing conceptions of habitual drunkenness in America. *Journal of Studies on Alcohol*, **39**, 143–174.

Linsky, A. S., Colby, J. P. & Straus, M. A. (1987) Social stress, normative constraints and alcohol problems in American states. *Social Science and Medicine*, **24**, 875–883.

Littleton, J. M. (1991) Alcohol and the central nervous system. In *The Molecular Pathology of Alcoholism* (ed. T. N. Palmer), pp. 238–253. Oxford: Oxford University Press.

Loranger, A. W. & Tulis, E. H. (1985) Family history of alcoholism in borderline personality disorder. *Archives of General Psychiatry*, **42**, 153–157.

Ludwig, A. M. & Wikler, A. (1974) "Craving" and relapse to drink. *Quarterly Journal of Studies on Alcohol*, **35**, 108–130.

McCord, W. & McCord, J. (1960) *Origins of Alcoholism*. Stanford: Stanford University Press.

Menninger, K. A. (1938) *Man Against Himself*. New York: Harcourt Brace.

Modell, J. G., Mountz, J. M. & Beresford, T. P. (1990) Basal ganglia/limbic striatal and thalamocortical involvement in craving and loss of control in alcoholism. *Journal of Neuropsychiatry*, **2**, 123-144.

Morrisey, E. R. & Schuckit, M. A. (1978) Stressful life events and alcohol problems among women seen at a detoxification centre. *Journal of Studies on Alcohol*, **38**, 1559-1576.

Mullan, M. J., Gurling, H. M. D., Oppenheim, B. E., *et al* (1986) The relationship between alcoholism and neurosis. *British Journal of Psychiatry*, **148**, 435-441.

Murray, R. M., Clifford, C. A. & Gurling, H. M. (1983) Twin and adoption studies. How good is the evidence for a genetic role? *Recent Developments in Alcoholism*, **1**, 25-48.

Myers, R. D. (1989) Isoquinolines, beta-carbolines, and alcohol drinking: involvement of opioid and dopaminergic mechanisms. *Experientia*, **45**, 436-443.

Naranjo, C. A., Kadlec, K. E., Sanhueza, P., *et al* (1990) Fluoxetine differentially alters alcohol intake and other consummatory behaviours in problem drinkers. *Clinical Pharmacology and Therapeutics*, **47**, 490-498.

O'Connor, J. (1975) Social and cultural factors influencing drinking behaviour. *Irish Journal of Medical Science* (Suppl), 65-71.

Orford, J. (1985) *Excessive Appetites*. Chichester: Wiley.

Pickens, R. W., Svikis, D. S., McGue, M., *et al* (1991) Heterogeneity in the inheritance of alcoholism. *Archives of General Psychiatry*, **48**, 19-28.

Pittman, D. (1967) *Alcoholism*. New York: Harper & Row.

Plant, M. A. (1979) *Drinking Careers*. London: Tavistock.

Polich, J., Burns, T. & Bloom, F. E. (1988) P300 and the risk for alcoholism: family history, task difficulty, and gender. *Alcoholism: Clinical and Experimental Research*, **12**, 248-254.

Reich, T., Cloninger, C. R., Lewis, C., *et al* (1981) Some recent findings in the study of genotype-environment interaction in alcoholism. In *Evaluation of the Alcoholics* (eds R. Meyer, *et al*), pp. 145-165. Rockville: US Drug Abuse & Mental Health Administration.

Robins, L. N. (1966) *Deviant Children Grown Up: A Sociological and Psychiatric Study of Sociopathic Personality*. Baltimore: Williams & Wilkins.

Roe, A. (1944) The adult adjustment of children of alcoholic parents raised in foster-homes. *Quarterly Journal of Studies on Alcohol*, **5**, 378-393.

Room, R. (1976) Ambivalence as a sociological explanation: the case of cultural explanations of alcohol problems. *American Sociology Review*, **41**, 1047-1065.

Schuckit, M. A. (1984) Differences in plasma cortisol after ingestion of ethanol in relatives of alcoholics and controls: preliminary results. *Journal of Clinical Psychiatry*, **45**, 374-376.

—— (1986) Genetic and clinical implications of alcoholism and affective disorder. *American Journal of Psychiatry*, **143**, 140-147.

——, Goodwin, D. W. & Winokur, G. (1972) A study of alcoholism in half-siblings. *American Journal of Psychiatry*, **128**, 1132-1136.

——, Parker, D. C. & Rossman, L. R. (1983) Ethanol-related prolactin responses and risk for alcoholism. *Biological Psychiatry*, **18**, 1153-1159.

Shaw, G. K., Majumdar, S. K., Waller, S., *et al* (1987) Tiapride in the long-term management of alcoholics of anxious or depressive temperament. *British Journal of Psychiatry*, **150**, 164-168.

Stacey, B. & Davies, J. (1970) Drinking behaviour in childhood and adolescence: an evaluative review. *British Journal of Addiction*, **65**, 203-212.

Steiner, C. (1974) *Games Alcoholics Play: the Analysis of Life Scripts*. New York: Ballantine.

Steinglass, P., Bennett, L. A., Wolin, S. J., *et al* (1987) *The Alcoholic Family*. London: Hutchinson.

Tatossian, A., Charpy, J. P., Remy, M., *et al* (1983) Events in the lives of 120 chronic alcoholics: preliminary study. *Annales Médico Psychologigues (Paris)*, **141**, 824-841.

Tollefson, G. D. (1989) Serotonin and alcohol: interrelationships. *Psychopathology*, **22**, 37-48.

Vaillant, G. E. (1980) Natural history of male psychological health: VIII antecedents of alcoholism and orality. *American Journal of Psychiatry*, **137**, 181-186.

—— (1983) *The Natural History of Alcoholism*. London: Harvard.

Wikler, A. (1961) On the nature of addiction and habituation. *British Journal of Addiction*, **57**, 73-79.

Wilson, G. T. (1987) Cognitive processes in addiction. *British Journal of Addiction*, **82**, 343-353.

—— (1988) Alcohol and anxiety. *Behaviour Research and Therapy*, **26**, 369-381.

Windle, M. (1990) Temperament and personality attributes of children of alcoholics. In *Children of Alcoholics* (eds M. Windle & J. S. Searles), pp. 129-167. New York: Guilford.

Winokur, G., Rimmer, J. & Reich, T. (1971) Alcoholism IV: is there more than one type of alcoholism? *British Journal of Psychiatry*, **118**, 525-531.

Wolin, S. J., Bennett, L. A. & Noonan, D. L. (1979) Family rituals and the recurrence of alcoholism over generations. *American Journal of Psychiatry*, **136**, 589-593.

World Health Organization (1965) *International Classification of Diseases. Manual of the International Statistical Classification of Diseases, Injuries and Causes of Death* (8th edn). Geneva: WHO.

—— (1977) *International Classification of Diseases. Manual of the International Statistical Classification of Diseases, Injuries and Causes of Death* (9th edn). Geneva: WHO.

7 Alcohol misuse: clinical features and treatment

Roch Cantwell and Jonathan Chick

Assessment of alcohol misuse ● Treatment of alcohol misuse ● Acute intervention ● Rehabilitation ● Maintenance ● Co-morbidity ● Conclusion

Assessment of alcohol misuse

Since Jellinek's original definition of 'alcoholism' as "any use of alcohol beverages that causes any damage to the individual or society or both" (Jellinek, 1960), attempts have been made to refine how we describe the interaction between alcohol and the individual. Jellinek identified subgroups of alcoholism based on drinking pattern. He recognised that patterns of drinking may evolve from one subgroup to another over time. For example, when regular drinkers, who become physically dependent, commence abstinence, they may have relapses which, though short, are marked by severe 'loss of control' and withdrawal symptoms (gamma alcoholism). This classification was not to be seen as exhaustive and Jellinek emphasised that the rest of the Greek alphabet "and if necessary other alphabets" could be employed to describe more patterns. While these subgroups have gained wide recognition, other ways of defining what we mean by alcoholism may utilise the quantity of alcohol drunk, the presence of related problems or, as described in Chapter 1, the

---

Box 7.1 Jellinek's typology

Alpha alcoholism: a psychological dependence on alcohol not leading to loss of control or physical dependence. It describes 'undisciplined' but not progressive drinking. Withdrawal symptoms do not occur and the main disability lies in interpersonal relationships

Beta alcoholism: heavy drinking complicated by physical damage without either physical or psychological dependence

Gamma alcoholism: that which involves 'loss of control' drinking and physical dependence. Withdrawal symptoms occur. The earlier stages of this form may resemble alpha alcoholism. Gamma alcoholism results in the most severe damage, both physical and social. It is the commonest form seen in Anglo-Saxon countries

Delta alcoholism: differs subtly from the gamma variety in that, instead of 'loss of control' there is 'inability to abstain'. Jellinek suggests that this form is more common in countries such as France where a high daily intake of alcohol is socially acceptable. It does not therefore result in disapproval or interpersonal difficulties

Epsilon alcoholism: bout drinking or 'dipsomania'

---

concept of dependence. Quantity consumed, severity of dependence and alcohol-related problems are not straightforwardly related to one another and when taking a history where alcohol misuse is suspected, it is helpful to structure the assessment around each of these three concepts.

History taking

Taking a history in suspected alcohol misuse requires sensitivity and a non-judgemental attitude. Accurate information gathering may be hindered by embarrassment on the part of patient or doctor but is not helped either by encouragement or admiration of alcoholic bravura. The scheme described below should be flexible and adapted to suit the needs of both assessor and patient.

The early part of the interview is concerned with *amount and pattern of consumption*. It should be kept in mind that the elderly, adolescents and women all have increased susceptibility to the effects of alcohol, as do those with low body weight. Certain occupations are regarded as high-risk for alcohol misuse – mostly those in which there is ease of access to alcohol such as with barworkers, chefs and brewery employees. Traditionally, doctors have also been viewed as a susceptible group and thought to be particularly difficult to help. This has recently been questioned (Lloyd, 1990; Chick, 1992a). Current drinking should be described in terms of quantity, daily/weekly pattern, usual place of drinking and whether alone or in company. Length of periods of abstinence should be noted. It is useful to ask patients to describe their typical day's drinking. It is claimed that drinkers frequently underestimate their intake. However, the need to impress or desperation to receive treatment can equally result in exaggeration of amount drunk.

Amount of alcohol consumed may give some indication as to future health risks. The Royal Colleges of Physicians (1987) and Psychiatrists (1986) have laid down guidelines for safe, hazardous and harmful levels. Safe levels are those up to 21 units per week for men and 14 units per week for women (with the proviso that intake is not all at one time and there are occasional drink-free days). Hazardous levels lie between 21–49 units per week for men and 14–35 units per week for women. Above these levels one enters the realm of harmful drinking. These guidelines are based on the epidemiology of alcohol-related problems and of alcoholic liver cirrhosis and indicate the levels at which the risk of development of alcohol dependence and damage to health commences.

When evaluating the degree of dependence on alcohol, Edwards & Gross's (1976) grouping together of features that comprise the alcohol dependence syndrome may form a basis for assessment:

(1) Narrowing of repertoire: drinking routine may become more fixed as the individual succumbs to the need to maintain sufficiently high blood alcohol levels and as cues to drinking become ingrained in daily life

(2) Salience of drinking: with increasing dependence, alcohol takes precedence over all else. Financial hardships are accepted as money is diverted to buy drink. Less time is invested in family, recreation and work. Previous high moral standards are compromised in the quest for alcohol

(3) Increased tolerance: individuals find that they need more alcohol to gain the same effects. Everyday activities can be carried out (albeit less effectively) even with high blood levels. Some patients may brag about their drinking capacity but in the late stages of dependence tolerance decreases

(4) Repeated withdrawal symptoms: these are often the most recognisable feature of the dependence syndrome. They occur as blood alcohol levels fall after brief periods of abstinence or reduction of intake. Characteristically they occur on waking and can disturb the person from sleep. Common symptoms include tremor, sweating, nausea and anxiety. Depressed mood may be present. In more severe withdrawal states illusions and hallucinations may give way to full blown delirium tremens. Withdrawal seizures occur in between 4% and 11% of withdrawal states, depending on the severity of the population studied

(5) Drinking to avoid or relieve withdrawal symptoms: at first, a lunch-time or early afternoon drink may be used to 'calm the nerves' or ease restlessness. As dependence progresses, a regular morning 'cure' is needed and individuals may keep a supply of alcohol within easy reach. In advanced dependence 'top up' drinks are required throughout the day

(6) Subjective compulsion to drink: the drinker finds it impossible to avoid alcohol and experiences a strong craving to drink. The fear of being unable to stop once started is summed up in the well-known Alcoholics Anonymous (AA) adage – 'one drink, one drunk'

(7) Reinstatement after abstinence: although there may be a loss of tolerance after a period of abstinence, the alcohol misuser may become as heavily dependent as before after only a few days drinking again.

The classification of alcohol dependence in ICD-10 is based on the Edwards & Gross description and, together with its comparison to DSM-III-R, is detailed in Chapter 1.

Assessment of *alcohol-related problems* can be subdivided into several different categories:

(1) Physical problems include symptoms of withdrawal but alcohol misusers may present with gastrointestinal disturbance or features of anaemia. Trauma or peripheral neuropathy may sometimes be the first indication of an alcohol problem. The alcoholic 'blackout' usually refers to an episode of amnesia during which the individual has been fully conscious but is unable to recall subsequently what had happened. Common among episodic heavy drinkers characteristically unable to recall how

they got home, such amnesia may occur in dependent drinkers with high tolerance for alcohol, even when they have not appeared intoxicated. In taking the history, the term 'blackout' should be used cautiously – not also to include drinking until passing out, or seizure

(2) Psychological problems are common in alcohol misuse, usually manifested as depression, anxiety or personality change. It is important to remember that withdrawal symptoms mimic anxiety and early morning symptoms may occasionally be mistaken for major depressive illness

(3) Social problems are all but inevitable. Family and friends will have been affected by the drinking and there are usually accompanying marital/relationship difficulties. Marital violence or child abuse may be present. Debts may have built up as money is siphoned off to pay for alcohol

(4) Forensic problems include drink-driving offences and breach of the peace. Stealing may be used to sustain the supply of alcohol. Disinhibition caused by alcohol increases the risk of violent and sexual crime

(5) Employment problems may be the spur to first presentation for help. Characteristically, Monday morning absences and poor afternoon performance caused by lunch-time drinking can result in warnings and ultimately dismissal.

A sequential history of the development of alcohol problems should be obtained. Other important areas include the presence of associated psychiatric syndromes, family history of alcoholism and evidence of cognitive impairment. Always check the internal consistency of the information gained and an interview with spouse or other informant is often invaluable. The question of why this person is seeking help now is important in the understanding and assessment of motivation for change. Motivation, however, is not static and can be fostered by the interviewer. Empathy, optimism and an active interest in the patient's welfare are vital therapist attributes. Whether intentionally or not, this meeting has a large therapeutic component and the relationship established with the patient may well determine whether he or she returns again or accepts recommendations for change. Lastly, ask about the patient's expectations of treatment. This can often give an important insight into their view of the nature of their condition.

Physical examination forms an essential part of the assessment. Signs of alcohol withdrawal may be obvious during the interview. Physical concomitants of long-standing misuse most commonly include weight loss, signs of nutritional deficiency and stigmata of liver disease but all organ systems may be involved. A blood alcohol level (by breathalyser) may give an indication, if compared against signs of intoxication, of severity of dependence.

Two further assessment methods – laboratory indicators and standardised questionnaires – are often used. Laboratory indicators include gamma-

Table 7.1 Screening instruments and markers of heavy drinking

	% +ve (in men admitting to problems and/or admitting to over 80 g ethanol/day)	% false +ve*	Normalisation with abstinence
CAGE	80	20	no
MAST	25–70[†]	0	
AUDIT[‡]	92	7	yes (in part)
GGT	50–60	10–15	1–3 weeks
CDT	80	<5	1–3 weeks
MCV (>98 fl)	30–40	5–10	2–10 weeks

*Other clinically evident causes of blood test evaluations having been excluded.
[†]Varies according to how sample is recruited.
[‡]Detection of problem drinkers in hospital, primary care and outpatients.
(see Chick *et al*, 1993).

glutamyltransferase (GGT), aspartate aminotransaminase (AST), mean cell volume (MCV) and blood alcohol concentration (BAC). Carbohydrate-deficient transferrin (CDT) is a promising marker with high specificity and sensitivity for heavy drinking, although in the detection of very early cases it may not have an advantage over GGT (Stibler, 1991). Questionnaires in common use include CAGE (comprising four simple questions) (Ewing, 1984), the Michigan Alcohol Screening Test (MAST) (Selzer, 1971) and the Severity of Alcohol Dependence Questionnaire (SADQ) (Stockwell *et al*, 1983). There are also combined assessment instruments such as the Alcohol Use Disorders Identification Test (AUDIT) devised for the WHO (Babor *et al*, 1989). In medical practice, where patients are more prepared to admit to alcohol problems, standardised questionnaires, or simply a few well-judged questions at interview, are more sensitive and, of course, more specific than biological markers.

Treatment of alcohol misuse

Throughout history, the treatment of alcohol problems has reflected society's attitude to alcoholism. In the widest sense, management has included complete prohibition (as in America of the 1920s) and cultures vary in the sanctions they place on individuals in relation to alcohol consumption. Prevailing treatments have often been influenced more by moral and political persuasion than scientific inquiry. Current approaches to treatment however tend to emphasise a 'biopsychosocial' model where alcohol problems are seen as having physiological, psychological and sociocultural dimensions. The balance of difficulties may be skewed toward one or other area for any particular individual but all factors must be considered when planning treatment.

Box 7.2 Stages of treatment

Stage 1: Acute intervention
  Emergency treatment – immediate resolution of symptoms
  Detoxification – management of acute intoxication and withdrawal
  Screening – identification of problem drinkers and their referral for
  treatment
Stage 2: Rehabilitation
  Evaluation and assessment – development of individualised treatment
  strategies based on assessment of problems
  Primary care – treatment to reduce drinking and associated problems
  (including both brief and intensive interventions)
  Extended care (stabilisation) – consolidation of achievements made
  through primary care
Stage 3: Maintenance
  Aftercare – longer-term continued support to maintain changes
  achieved
  Relapse prevention – therapy directed at avoiding return to previous
  patterns of drinking
  Domiciliary care – provision of ongoing support to those too impaired
  by alcohol use to return to independent living

(modified from Institute of Medicine, 1990)

In its comprehensive report, the United States Institute of Medicine delineates three major stages in the management of individual patients and their families (Institute of Medicine, 1990) (see Box 7.2). This overview emphasises the recognition of "both the acute and chronic care needs of persons with alcohol problems" in overall management. In devising treatment strategies, there is a need to redress the emphasis often placed on acute treatments to the detriment of follow-up and community support, while at the same time recognising the growing wealth of evidence which supports the efficacy of brief interventions for the less severely affected. This chapter will focus on strategies for the individual and those immediately affected by his or her drinking. Cognitive–behavioural aspects of treatment are reviewed more extensively in Chapter 8.

Acute intervention

Management of acute intoxication

Simple intoxication rarely requires specific treatment. In comatose patients, general measures to counteract respiratory depression and cardiovascular collapse may be necessary. Acute hypoglycaemia occasionally complicates severe intoxication and alcoholic coma and must be looked for. Significant respiratory depression may occur at blood alcohol levels as low as 400 mg%, though alcohol-dependent individuals with a high tolerance are more resistant. There are no compounds approved currently which specifically reverse the effects of alcohol. The most promising is flumazenil, a benzodiazepine antagonist, which has been reported to produce improved levels of consciousness in comatose patients in one controlled study (Lheureux *et al*, 1991) and reversal of alcohol-induced ataxia and anxiety in others. Analogous drugs under investigation include lithium and naloxone.

Treatment of alcohol withdrawal states

Who requires detoxification?

The majority of patients withdrawing from alcohol do not require medication - up to 85% in one randomised study of emergency department patients (Naranjo *et al*, 1983). An explanation of the symptoms, reassurance and, if necessary, advice on relaxation techniques and dealing with insomnia will suffice. Severe symptoms, a history of withdrawal fits, malnutrition or other physical illness which might be exacerbated by withdrawal are all indications for administration of appropriate medication. A patient presenting with mild symptoms of withdrawal but with a high blood alcohol level (>150 mg%) is likely to go on to develop severe symptoms if he or she has stopped drinking. It must be remembered also that withdrawal symptoms do not only occur on cessation of drinking but also if intake is reduced from a previously high average. In routine assessment, a hand-held breathalyser gives a good measure of blood alcohol concentration and is both convenient and very useful.

Setting for detoxification

Since most patients do not experience serious complications during withdrawal, in-patient detoxification is not routinely required. Out-patient or home detoxification is often sufficient and has a good outcome in over two-thirds of patients with moderate alcohol withdrawal syndrome (Hayashida *et al*, 1989). Those likely to need admission include patients who have severe symptoms, medical or psychiatric complications, a history of withdrawal fits or delirium tremens, and those with few social supports.

What drug to use

Benzodiazepines are the drugs of choice in alcohol withdrawal. Long-acting substances such as chlordiazepoxide and diazepam (t½ 30–60 hours) are most commonly used, a typical regime beginning with oral chlordiazepoxide 20 mg qds (diazepam 5–10 mg qds) plus prn, depending on the severity of withdrawal. In in-patients, oral doses up to 400 mg per day of chlordiazepoxide may be required. Dosage is then reduced daily in stepwise fashion (approximately 20% decrements) and stopped usually after a period of five to seven days. Parenteral administration may be required if nausea and vomiting are severe (sublingual lorazepam has been suggested as an alternative) and a centrally-acting antiemetic can also be given. If moderate or severe liver damage is suspected, then oxazepam or lorazepam (which are not hydroxylated by the liver) are more appropriate.

Chlormethiazole is becoming less popular as an alternative to the benzodiazepines. It has no particular advantages over the benzodiazepines but has a greater potential for dependence and, in combination with alcohol, for respiratory depression. It should be administered cautiously, if at all, to out-patients (Committee on Safety of Medicines, 1987). Other drugs which have been proposed in withdrawal states include the beta-blockers atenolol and propranolol, clonidine, bromocriptine, lithium, the calcium channel blocker verapamil and anticonvulsants such as carbamazepine and sodium valproate. None have the combined sedative and antiepileptic potential of the benzodiazepines. Many are still under investigation. Antipsychotics are not recommended as they may lower the fit threshold.

Use of vitamins

Thiamine has been implicated for some time in the aetiology of Wernicke's encephalopathy and, with less certainty, in Korsakoff's psychosis and peripheral neuropathy. It is used in treatment of these conditions. The practice of thiamine supplementation prophylactically during moderate to severe withdrawal is well established. Other vitamin deficiencies may occur in alcoholism, in particular of nicotinic and folic acid, and vitamin E. Magnesium depletion also occurs. Parenteral replacement therapies such as Pabrinex contain multiple vitamins but the possibility of deficiencies other than thiamine needs to be considered when oral replacements are used.

Oral supplementation is appropriate in withdrawal states if symptoms are moderate to severe and/or the patient has not been eating regularly. A comprehensive regime should include thiamine 100–200 mg/day and multivitamins. In severe withdrawal (including delirium tremens), marked physical debility or if there are any signs of Wernicke's encephalopathy, parenteral vitamins (i.m. or i.v.) should be used. Anaphylactic reactions can occur with parenteral administration and these should only be given in hospital where supervision and emergency measures are at hand.

Management of complications

A history of seizures requires that adequate prophylaxis is used. Benzodiazepines remain the agents of choice. With oral administration, peak blood levels are achieved more rapidly than with phenytoin and there is evidence to suggest that diazepam is more effective than phenytoin in alcohol withdrawal convulsions. If withdrawal signs are severe and there is a risk of seizures then a loading oral dose of chlordiazepoxide 80-100 mg or diazepam 20 mg can be given and subsequent doses raised accordingly. Convulsions during detoxification are best treated with diazepam 10 mg i.v. administered slowly over one to two minutes and repeated as necessary.

Delirium tremens is heralded by the development of confusion often with illusions, hallucinations and poorly formed delusional beliefs. It has a mortality rate of up to 10% and requires urgent treatment. Medical management is again with benzodiazepines in doses adequate to control agitation and produce sedation. They may need to be administered i.m. or, slowly, i.v. Absorption of i.m. preparations can however be unpredictable. Vitamin supplementation should always be given to help prevent the development of the Wernicke-Korsakoff syndrome. General measures such as nursing in a well-lit room, regular orientation and reassurance are important. Physical complications such as hypoglycaemia, dehydration, infection and electrolyte imbalance may supervene and require corrective treatment. A reduced consciousness level or the presence of neurological signs should alert the physician to the possibility of head injury. Intracranial haemorrhage may be misdiagnosed as simple intoxication or delirium tremens and appropriate investigation and treatment thereby delayed.

With increasing frequency, patients are presenting with multiple dependencies. If detoxification is appropriate then it is best to tackle the alcohol withdrawal first. The standard reducing benzodiazepine regime can be modified by more gradual reduction (e.g. by 10% of the dose per day). Higher initial doses may be required if there is co-dependency with the minor tranquillisers.

Rehabilitation

Even in untreated samples there is evidence of improvement with time. Perhaps one in ten alcoholics will achieve abstinence unaided and a further 10-30% experience attenuation of their problems. In long-term studies 'spontaneous remissions' are often preceded by a major change in life circumstances (such as the development of a new relationship or change of job) and such changes may also influence the course of those in treatment. The literature on natural history is scanty however and still compares poorly with average estimates of between 50% and 80% experiencing some improvement across a broad range of interventions.

Stopping drinking is generally seen as the first step in tackling alcohol misuse. Even for those who intend to return to some form of controlled drinking, an initial period of abstinence is often recommended. The first goal however must be to keep the patient in useful therapy. If a rigid and inflexible approach is used, the patient may feel alienated and default from treatment. The result is a frustrated therapist and an unchanged drinking problem. Some degree of compromise may be required.

There is no one treatment that is consistently superior to all others. Alcoholism is a diverse label, encompassing all of the concepts discussed in the first part of this chapter, and so it seems intuitively correct to suppose that a range of treatments should be made available. Rather than ask which treatment works best for alcoholics, we should investigate which treatment works best for what type of individual with alcohol problems. Reflecting this, there has been some breakdown in the traditional format of specialist services providing one favoured model of care. The newer 'smorgasbord approach' offers a range of options for the patient. One danger of this lies in the means by which patients avail themselves of the choices. Treatment plans may be sampled in small amounts and choice may relate more to the patient's perception of the ease of therapy. Against this, there is evidence that people are more likely to comply with a course of action they have chosen for themselves, and compliance is a good predictor of positive outcome. The patient must, however, be able to make an informed choice.

Techniques for assessing suitability for individual treatments are essential. Matching may be based on severity of problem, degree of dependence, social stability, personality type and a host of other factors. Selection can be by the therapist, patient or following on completion of assessment questionnaires. Usually it is by combination of two or more methods and after some degree of negotiation. It is only by standardising and adequately describing these methods that meaningful research will emerge on comparisons between therapies. Matching patients to therapies will be considered further in the section describing types of treatment. Miller (1989) provides a comprehensive review.

The presence of alcohol-induced cognitive impairment may influence choice of therapy (Wilkinson & Sanchez-Craig, 1981). Up to 70% of those entering treatment have some specific deficits in problem solving, abstract thinking and memory. Cognitive impairment may interfere with comprehension and retention of information in educational based programmes, especially within the first month of abstinence (Sanchez-Craig & Walker, 1982; Goldman, 1986). There is now evidence that cognitive functioning may recover with abstinence over a period of time and this should be taken into account when planning treatment.

The relationship established between patient and therapist has already been alluded to. Therapist's accurate empathy, Carl Rogers' concept, has been shown repeatedly to be associated with improved outcome at up to two years. Sanchez-Craig *et al* (1991) found, in a brief intervention, that improved outcome was associated with having a more experienced therapist. Other important qualities include a belief in the treatment model, fluency in counselling, a readiness to accept the patient's views as valid and a non-judgemental, non-confrontational approach (Sanchez-Craig, 1990).

While few would dispute that patient motivation is vital for successful therapy, motivation is often erroneously viewed as static and fully formed (or absent) at the time of first contact. Motivation depends on what advantages there are, in the patient's view, in doing something about their drinking, compared to the benefits perceived from continuing in the same pattern. Patients attending only at the behest of others, or coming with little hope that treatment will help, are less motivated. However, the therapist can enhance the desire for change. Motivation may be measured by compliance with treatment and good compliance is closely associated wth good outcome across a wide range of treatments. Simple feedback by the therapist to the patient about the risk of harm from drinking is an effective way of enhancing their compliance. This may be augmented by discussing serial changes in GGT. Techniques for increasing patient motivation are comprehensively reviewed by Miller (1985) (see also Chapter 8).

Before examining individual treatment approaches in detail it is useful to review two of the controversies that have excited those involved in treatment over the past three decades. These concern the overall philosophy of care of individuals with alcohol problems – should abstinence always be the goal of treatment and, as alcoholism is often regarded as a chronic condition, does it follow that treatment must also be of a prolonged and intensive nature?

Controlled drinking versus abstinence

Amid the many debates exercising the minds of alcohol specialists, none, in recent times, has stirred the emotions more than that for and against controlled drinking. The view of abstinence as the only option for recovering alcohol misusers was challenged in 1962 by Davies in a seminal paper. He described seven alcoholics who returned to moderate alcohol consumption and had maintained this up to 11 years after discharge. Several subsequent studies, including a 4 year follow-up to the influential RAND report (Polich *et al*, 1981) confirmed these findings for a small number of dependent drinkers. Heather & Robertson, in 1981, suggested a radical new approach might be appropriate, where abstinence is advised only in "exceptional circumstances in which a return to normal drinking is not possible". A common criticism of these findings is that those achieving control were not alcoholic in the first place. Davies (and subsequent followers) have refuted this, showing that a small but definite group had symptoms of severe dependence. A more serious challenge results from studies which show that the proportion of drinkers successfully returning to moderate consumption varies inversely with duration of follow-up and period over which drinking behaviour is evaluated. When Davies' original seven were retraced only two had stayed clear of serious alcohol problems two decades on (Edwards, 1985). However, abstinent drinkers also relapse and long-term controlled drinking with good social adjustment has been found in one 12–22 year follow-up of alcoholics treated at a Swedish hospital (Nordstrom & Berglund, 1987).

The debate is sterile unless it takes account of individual differences between patients. When matching variables are examined, it is those who are less dependent, have a shorter drinking history and fewer associated problems

Table 7.2 Guidelines for controlled drinking versus abstinence

Controlled drinking	Abstinence
< 40 years old	> 40 years old
Early detection	Long duration
No/minimal signs of dependence	Evident dependence
No major medical complications	Medical problems/abnormal liver functioning
No psychiatric comorbidity	Dual psychiatric diagnoses
No impulsive traits	Impulsive personality
Social stability	Poor social supports
Good compliance with treatment	Poor attendance, disagrees with monitoring
Patient's clear preference for control	Patient desires abstinence
Partner agrees with non-abstinent goal	

None of the above is an *absolute* criterion for control or abstinence (see Chick, 1992*b*).

that do best with controlled drinking (Table 7.2). When less severe problem drinkers were assigned randomly to controlled drinking or abstinence groups, both receiving additional behavioural therapy, outcome was improved in the two groups, with no significant differences (Sanchez-Craig *et al*, 1984). In the long-term Swedish follow-up, patients who at the time were socially stable and not highly impulsive were most likely to be among those who had successfully controlled their drinking. Severe dependence did not, however, preclude future controlled drinking. In the general population, problem drinking is much more common than severe dependence and many who would refuse to consider abstinence may still be helped by techniques to control intake.

Intensive therapy versus brief

In 1977, Edwards *et al* challenged traditional wisdom on alcoholism treatment. Their study examined the outcome of 100 married male alcoholics, seen consecutively at an out-patient clinic, and allocated randomly to either treatment or control groups. This followed an initial assessment and counselling session. The former was offered a broad range of treatment, including regular out-patient care, deterrent drugs and six-week admission if appropriate. The control group received no further treatment. At one year follow-up there were no overall differences in terms of outcome between the two groups. A suggestion that those with more severe problems did better with a more intensive approach and those with less severe problems were helped more by simple advice has not been borne out in a recent reanalysis.

Subsequent randomised controlled studies have demonstrated the value of brief approaches over no intervention. Kristenson *et al* (1983) showed that in heavy drinkers, regular out-patient monitoring of GGT coupled with advice, resulted in a significant improvement in terms of absenteeism, hospitalisation and mortality, compared with controls. In Edinburgh (Chick *et al*, 1985), male in-patients in a general hospital were identified as problem drinkers by means of a screening interview. Severely dependent and socially unsupported patients were excluded. Randomly assigned to no treatment or brief intervention (consisting of 30–60 minutes of nurse counselling), the intervention group showed a significant reduction in alcohol-related problems and GGT in comparison to controls. A further study of general hospital patients (Elvy *et al*, 1988) had similar results. In all these studies, the control groups also showed improvements over time and, in the first two, there was no significant difference between groups in mean reduction in intake. This may not only reflect the natural history of the condition but also the difficulty in designing truly 'no-intervention' control groups.

An attempt to repeat some of the findings of Edwards *et al*'s 1977 report was made in Edinburgh some 11 years later (Chick *et al*, 1988). Again, 'extended treatment' showed no advantage over 'advice only' at two year follow-up in terms of achievement of stable abstinence or problem-free drinking. However, cumulative overall harm associated with excessive drinking was reduced to a greater degree in the extended treatment group. The message from this and other similar studies seems to be that even the briefest of contacts between services and patients is an impetus toward improvement.

The original study of Edwards *et al* included the provision of in-patient care, if required, for the treatment group. In-patient alcohol treatment units were then and still largely remain the mainstay of specialist intervention in the UK, North America and much of Europe. While the reader is referred to Chapter 11 for a comprehensive review of the organisation of treatment services, it is relevant to the understanding of how individual treatments are integrated into an overall plan of care to look in greater detail at how these in-patient units have evolved.

These first appeared in the 1950s and became known in the UK as the Minnesota model of care. The model's primary components include detoxification, education about the effects of alcohol and attendance at Alcoholics Anonymous meetings, usually within a four week in-patient stay, although some clinics ask patients to stay much longer. Extended rehabilitation and aftercare in out-patient and residential settings are included in the programme of care. A modification of the Minnesota model developed at the Hazelden Foundation incorporates a highly structured regime of group meetings and individual counselling. Ex-alcohol misusers play an important part as therapists. The aim of both the Minnesota and Hazelden models is complete abstinence, in line with AA philosophy.

The Minnesota and Hazelden models have been criticised for their inflexibility and their overreliance on untrained counsellors. Most UK NHS alcohol treatment units have made considerable adaptations to these forms, introducing a degree of eclecticism, altering the emphasis on contact with AA, sometimes offering deterrent drugs, and extending the range and type of psychotherapy, both behavioural and dynamic, depending on local treatment beliefs. Much of the day-to-day treatment occurs within groups which serve multiple purposes including patient assessment, education, social skills training and relapse prevention. Just as in the Hazelden method, constructive confrontation by fellow patients to help the drinker face reality is an important therapeutic ingredient. The groups also provide an opportunity for airing issues about daily life in the unit from which patients can learn. The aim is to blend all models of treatment philosophy, including medical, social and psychological approaches. A multidisciplinary approach is essential, usually including psychiatrists, nurses, psychologists and social workers.

When the Hazelden model was compared with a traditional Finnish psychiatric approach with considerably less treatment time, significantly more patients achieved total abstinence at one year with the former (14% v. 1.9%). If those achieving controlled drinking were included, any significant difference disappeared (Salaspuro & Keso, 1990). Evidence favouring in-patient care over briefer interventions is scant, although in a Boston study random allocation of alcoholic employees to compulsory in-patient care, AA only, or a choice of either found that after two years follow-up, more achieved continuous abstinence in the compulsory in-patient group (37%) than in either of the other two groups (17% and 16% respectively). There was however, no advantage on measures of work performance, symptoms, or problem drinking (Walsh *et al* , 1991). Day or out-patient care was not offered in this study.

In part these two dilemmas, control v. abstinence and intensive v. brief, arise from the 'either/or' insistence of many of their advocates. It should be clear by now that both intensive and brief therapies may each be of benefit for different patient groups. Current evidence suggests that those with more social problems and personality disturbance are more likely to benefit from intensive/extended therapy whereas brief interventions, perhaps permitting moderation as a goal, are sufficient for the non-dependent socially-stable drinker (Ojehagen & Berglund, 1986; Chick, 1992*b*).

Specific therapies

The specific therapies below reflect those either in common usage or for which there are encouraging signs of usefulness. The list is not exhaustive and each is rarely used in isolation. Furthermore, while all forms should involve the patient assuming responsibility for making changes in his or her own daily life, practical assistance in effecting these changes may often be appropriate.

Psychotherapies

Brief interventions

Brief intervention is most suited to that group of drinkers whose intake is within the 'hazardous' range (i.e. above recommended limits but without evidence of dependence or current alcohol-related problems). Heather (1989) has identified two other groups, in addition, that may be targeted: (i) low/moderately dependent drinkers and (ii) highly dependent drinkers who are not reached by conventional treatment services.

By their very nature, brief strategies are less time-consuming and potentially allow a greater number of people to be helped than do more traditional methods. Their goal is frequently (though not invariably) a return to problem-free drinking. Techniques can often be learned by non-specialists, also increasing availability of treatment, and at a lower cost to service providers. Two levels have been described.

(1) Minimal intervention   At their simplest, brief interventions with a primarily educative and motivational function may consist of one session of advice with or without follow-up. The principle is to take advantage of a medical contact. This provides the opportunity for screening using a few simple questions, and a brief counselling intervention. Further strategies may include feedback of laboratory indicators. The setting may be among general hospital patients, casualty or general practice attenders. Selection might also be based on occupational risk or targeted at specific age groups. Meta-analysis of several large randomised controlled studies, mainly in primary care, with one year follow-up, shows on average that a minimal intervention leads to a reduction in reported alcohol consumption of one-quarter (Freemantle *et al* , 1993). A wider ranging review which includes brief interventions in non-medical settings (such as in response to newspaper advertisements) found a mean reduction in consumption 38% greater than in controls (Bien *et al*, 1993). In this research, however, severely dependent and socially unsupported patients have usually been excluded. The essential ingredients of such interventions can be summarised under the acronym FRAMES (Table 7.3). The cost-effectiveness of these procedures is increasingly recognised (Chick, 1993). More work needs to be done to identify which components of these interventions are therapeutic but they go some way toward tackling the 'preventive paradox' (Kreitman, 1986), which suggests that by focusing on that middle range of drinkers who are much more numerous, more damage to society can be prevented, than by attending only to 'alcoholics' (Chick, 1992b).

Table 7.3   FRAMES – ingredients of minimal interventions for alcohol misuse

---

Feedback about personal risk or impairment
Responsibility – emphasis on personal responsibility for change
Advice to cut down or, if indicated because of severe dependence or harm, to abstain
Menu of alternative options for changing drinking pattern
Empathic interviewing
Self-efficacy – an interviewing style which enhances this

(See Bien *et al*, 1993).

(2) Brief therapy   The second type may more properly be called brief therapy. Although the emphasis shifts in different styles, these have in common the use of behavioural and cognitive approaches whose aim is to reduce (or occasionally eliminate) alcohol consumption and so prevent or reduce alcohol related problems. As with all behavioural techniques, a detailed assessment is first obtained, goals of treatment agreed and a treatment contract entered with review and modification as therapy progresses. Specific techniques commonly employed include self-monitoring, rehearsal of drink-reducing strategies and identification of 'high-risk' situations. Brief therapy is generally out-patient based and time-limited. It is more likely to be administered by specialists within the field of alcohol treatment.

Behavioural Self-Control Training (BSCT), one well-described form of brief therapy in alcoholism, has the advantage of being adaptable, in problem drinkers, to moderation or abstinence-orientated goals with equal efficacy (Sanchez-Craig *et al*, 1984). It is not suited, however, to those who are severely dependent. Beneficial effects have been noted with both therapist and self-administered forms. Briefly, BSCT draws together several cognitive–behavioural strategies which are undertaken in progression. They include:

(1) Setting limits on number of drinks (and on peak breath alcohol concentrations) per day
(2) Self-monitoring of drinking behaviour
(3) Altering rate of drinking
(4) Developing assertiveness in refusing drinks
(5) Setting up a reward system for achieving goals
(6) Becoming aware of antecedents to overdrinking
(7) Learning coping skills other than drinking.

Treatment may be carried out in out-patient groups and usually runs for approximately 7 weeks with subsequent periodic follow-up (see Sanchez-Craig, 1984).

Not all forms of brief therapy are designed to be administered by specialist agencies. The DRAMS (Drinking Reasonably And Moderately with Self-control) scheme (Heather, 1987) was devised on behalf of the Scottish Health Education Group for use in general practice. It consists of a drinking diary and self-help manual for the client with a guide, laboratory indicators record sheet and screening checklist for the GP. If a problem is suspected by the GP, the checklist is administered and, if indicated, a blood sample obtained. A strategy is agreed on reduction of intake if tests and the patient's diary confirm a problem. Self-monitoring and feedback of further blood tests then ensue. The scheme has found acceptance although there is some doubt as to its superiority over simple advice.

Simple behavioural techniques can be incorporated into most forms of counselling and are readily understood by patients. They can be tailored easily to individual situations and help patients regain a sense of mastery over

---

Box 7.3 Strategies to aid controlled drinking

Practise techniques for coping with triggers
Avoid high risk settings
Set limits e.g.
    for occasional drinkers: "never more than six units on a single
    occasion"; "never drink before 6pm"; "only drink at weekends"
    for daily drinkers: "never more than four units per day"; "no spirits"
Keep a drinking diary
Avoid round drinking
Have a non-alcoholic spacer between drinks
Pace drinking
Eat food before or during drinking
Avoid heavy drinking acquaintances
"Don't drink to solve problems"

---

their drinking. Examples of commonly used strategies are given in Box 7.3. Cognitive–behavioural approaches are dealt with in more detail in Chapter 8.

Individual and group psychotherapy

Working with the individual forms the basis for most out-patient services. Much would fit under the rubric of supportive psychotherapy and counselling, where the therapist's role is one of education, monitoring and encouragement. Individual dynamic or insight-oriented therapy risks deflecting attention away from the problem, i.e. the drinking. While a patient continues to drink in an uncontrolled manner, exploration of underlying conflicts is unlikely to be fruitful and, if judged suitable for therapy, a period of stability or abstinence is desirable initially.

Group therapy comes in many guises – insight-oriented, behavioural, supportive and educative. Often, individual programmes will create groups to serve the particular demands of their patients – for example women's groups – or the expertise of their staff. They may run for a fixed length of time or be open-ended with patients entering and leaving depending on their stage of treatment. Some explorative groups may last for a number of years and become self-running. The sharing of experiences and mutual support offered in groups explains their popularity in many programmes. They are also regarded as a cost-effective way of servicing a large number of sufferers.

There is little evidence either to support or refute the value of dynamic therapy in alcoholism. Based on clinical experience however, it would seem prudent to ensure that careful selection procedures are adhered to if it is to prove beneficial. In general, people with good self-esteem will respond best to the confrontational nature of group dynamic therapy. Because of the heterogeneous nature of groups within the traditional treatment setting, research on which components prove helpful to whom is needed. A recent study, comparing interactional group therapies with coping skills training, did suggest that those with higher measures of sociopathy were better served by introduction to coping skills. Patients with cognitive impairment had better outcomes with interactional therapies, perhaps because the training methods and homework tasks necessary for coping skills training required some intellectual effort (Cooney *et al*, 1991).

Couple therapy

The spouse and family can have an important influence on the alcohol abuser, and also are often greatly affected by the drinking. They have found support in organisations such as AlAnon, Al Ateen and in groups for COAs (children of alcoholics). Traditional specialist services have also included partners in their programmes. Sometimes it is as an 'informant' to aid in diagnosis and assessment. On occasions the primary purpose has been to aid recovery in the drinker (often involving the spouse in supervised disulfiram administration) and to educate the spouse about the nature and effects of alcohol. Many units, acknowledging the inevitable detrimental effect of drinking on close relationships, provide conjoint therapy. Finally, individual or group support may be offered to the partner or children in their own right, in recognition of their need to deal with intense feelings of guilt, anger and resentment. The style of intervention may be similarly wide-ranging, encompassing supportive, behavioural or psychodynamic principles.

There is a link between good marital and family adjustment and improved outcome after treatment (Moos & Moos, 1984). Involving the spouse in therapy increases compliance in the drinker. Once abstinence or control has been achieved, marital disharmony may be implicated in the development of relapse. Enhancing the marital relationship can have a beneficial effect in consolidating outcome and spouse involvement in therapy can improve the relationship both in the short and long-term. O'Farrell (1989) in a review of marital and family therapy in alcoholism agrees that attempts to involve the spouse, and any adult family members living with the patient, should be the norm in all assessment procedures.

Aversion therapy

Aversion therapy for alcohol dependence is rarely used in the UK nowadays. Based on the principles of classical conditioning, an unpleasant stimulus is paired with alcohol consumption. Chemical aversion using emetine hydrochloride or apomorphine is still offered. Evidence for its efficacy is controversial. Persistent conditioned aversion to alcohol has been produced and there is evidence of individual variation, with strength of conditioning being related to successful treatment outcome (Cannon *et al*, 1986). Older, more stable male alcoholics may respond best and Thurber (1985) in a meta-analysis of controlled studies claims "moderate support" for the procedure. Most studies are of case reports or uncontrolled groups and controlled trials suggest equal effectiveness of non-aversive techniques and a strong placebo action.

Covert sensitisation is a form of aversion therapy using imagery alone. First described in 1970, it has enjoyed a recent revival in popularity (Elkins, 1980). Nausea is induced by use of suggestion, occasionally augmented by the presence of a noxious odour (valeric acid). Conditioning does occur and again strength of conditioning is predictive of outcome. While there are fewer ethical dilemmas associated with its use, conclusive evidence of its efficacy is awaited.

Pharmacotherapy

Alcohol-sensitising (deterrent) medications

Disulfiram ("Antabuse") and citrated calcium carbimide ("Abstem" in the UK) are deterrent drugs. They are not intended as forms of aversion therapy. They may be best regarded as a form of exposure/response prevention therapy (Brewer, 1990). Disulfiram is the most widely used, carbimide being available in the UK only on a named patient basis. Both compounds act by inhibiting aldehyde dehydrogenase (ALDH) (Fig. 7.1). Inhibition caused by disulfiram is irreversible, several days needing to elapse having stopped the drug before ALDH function is restored to normal. The effects of carbimide wear off after approximately 24 hours. It is the accumulation of acetaldehyde that is primarily responsible for the drug–alcohol reaction, which is proportional in severity to the dose of drug and the dose of alcohol. However, disulfiram may inhibit other enzyme systems, e.g. dopamine beta-hydroxylase (DBH). Symptoms of

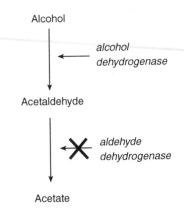

Fig. 7.1 Disulfiram inhibits the enzyme aldehyde dehydrogenase (aldehyde-NAD oxireductase, ALDH), preventing the oxidation of acetaldehyde to acetate.

the reaction include flushing, nausea, vomiting, dyspnoea, palpitations, dizziness, headache and apprehensiveness. Marked hypotension may occur. That associated with carbimide tends to be shorter-lasting and has a more rapid onset. Severity of the reaction with either compound, although dose related, shows much individual variation. On rare occasions it may be life-threatening.

Disulfiram should not be commenced within 24 hours of alcohol consumption unless a breath test shows blood alcohol levels to be zero. The patient and, if possible, his or her partner should be fully informed of the nature of the drug–alcohol interaction and to seek medical advice if they suspect a reaction is occurring. Time spent emphasising the need to avoid alcohol (both while taking the drug and for at least 7 days after discontinuation) and exploring any anxieties about treatment is essential. Since patients often unilaterally decide to stop taking the drug after a few weeks, a decision should be made as to whether or not the administration of disulfiram is to be supervised, and if so, by whom. Supervision may be within the family, by a close acquaintance, at an out-patient clinic or in the workplace. At the usual recommended dose of 200 mg daily, side-effects of disulfiram are uncommon (with the possible exception of somnolence when it should be taken at bedtime) and the majority of patients are liable to develop an alcohol reaction. Occasionally a patient tests this and if the reaction is not aversive, an increased dose may be required. Some clinics have considerable experience of prescribing higher doses, such as 300 mg or 400 mg daily (Brewer, 1986). The patient should carry a card identifying the medication and be warned to avoid foods and proprietary medicines which contain alcohol. The practice, previously commonplace, of inducing an initial 'test reaction' with deterrent drugs has now been abandoned. Carbimide is usually administered in a dose of 50 mg twice daily, and 48 hours after the last dose there may be no alcohol reaction. With disulfiram the sensitisation lasts for several days so that the drug can be taken on alternate days if a supervision regime makes that more convenient than daily dosing.

Patients often raise objections to alcohol-sensitising drugs. Most commonly, there is a reluctance to take something seen as a 'crutch'. This can be countered by emphasising that disulfiram only introduces a time-delay into their fight against alcohol and responsibility remains with them to build up strategies to deal with the urge to drink. Others may be fearful of the risks associated with the drug–alcohol reaction. Patients' uncertainty about the need for abstinence may be a further reason for reluctance. Once commenced, there is no absolute consensus regarding how long a patient should remain on medication. Most clinics would agree however that, for the majority of patients, a minimum time of between six months and a year is recommended if the treatment is proving beneficial. At that stage, patient and therapist may agree to a trial period off medication with a return to disulfiram should relapse occur.

Contraindications to disulfiram (Box 7.4) arise from the possible seriousness of the drug–alcohol reaction in certain vulnerable groups (most commonly

---

Box 7.4   Contraindications to deterrent drugs

Disulfiram
    cardiovascular and cerebrovascular disease
    severe pulmonary disease
    chronic renal failure
    severe liver disease
    diabetes mellitus
    psychosis
    organic brain disease
    epilepsy
    neuropathy
    pregnancy
    anticonvulsant, anticoagulant and antihypertensive medication

Calcium carbimide
    thyroid disease

---

those with cardiovascular disease) and from its effect on those with accompanying psychotic illness, which may be exacerbated by disulfiram's inhibition of DBH. In this case, carbimide, which has no effect on DBH, may be used. Disulfiram's safety in liver disease is uncertain though it should be avoided if there is evidence of portal hypertension. Very rarely disulfiram can itself cause an idiosyncratic, life-threatening hepatotoxicity and liver function tests should be monitored during the first three months' treatment. It has also been associated infrequently with peripheral neuropathy and is to be avoided in patients with pre-existing neuropathy.

The effectiveness of the alcohol-sensitising drugs has been most closely investigated in regard to disulfiram. Early uncontrolled studies, following its introduction in 1948, were enthusiastic about its successes, though some cautioned that it was not effective in 'skid-row' alcoholics (Gallant *et al*, 1968). Recent controlled trials have not shown consistent benefits. In the largest study to date (Fuller *et al*, 1986) 605 subjects were assigned to one of three groups (disulfiram 250 mg, 1 mg or vitamin tablet). At one year no overall differences were found between groups in terms of abstinence but those who received disulfiram 250 mg reported significantly fewer drinking days. Those who drank less in the disulfiram group tended to be older and socially stable.

In Fuller's study, those who improved in all three groups had complied best with treatment. Attempts have been made, therefore, to improve compliance with disulfiram. One method is to arrange supervision of drug-taking. Discontinuation rates are high in those who are unsupervised (Brewer, 1986) and voluntary supervision has been associated in some randomised controlled studies with excellent outcome at six months (Chick *et al*, 1992) and two years (Azrin *et al*, 1982). Long-acting, surgical implants of disulfiram have now mostly been discontinued because of inefficacy and local inflammation.

In summary then, deterrent drugs may be effective if the patient sees real benefits from abstinence and agrees to supervision. This should, however, be seen as one aspect only of a treatment package of support and re-education.

Other drug therapies

The 1980s saw the first appearance of reports claiming a beneficial effect for the selective serotonin reuptake inhibitors (SSRI) in heavy drinkers (Naranjo *et al*, 1986). A reduction in amount drunk or number of drinking days in heavy drinkers has been reported for zimeledine, citalopram, viqualine and fluoxetine. The dose required is in excess of that at which an antidepressant effect is noticeable. This effect appears independent of antidepressant action or of the known nausea and reduction in appetite associated with SSRIs. It has been proposed that SSRIs may redress altered brain 5-HT activity associated with chronic alcohol consumption (Tollefson, 1989). A refinement of this argument suggests that a subgroup of alcoholics may have a pre-existing serotonergic deficit and that these resemble that group described by Cloninger as Type II, characterised by early onset, high genetic loading and antisocial behaviour (Buydens-Branchey *et al*, 1989). Some reports have now emerged concerning their efficacy in dependent drinkers and large scale trials are underway. It has also been claimed that SSRIs reduce memory impairment in alcohol amnesic disorder (Martin *et al*, 1989). This merits further investigation.

Several other compounds have also been proposed as long-term treatments for alcoholism, although none is of proven efficacy. Lithium has been investigated, but the most careful studies have not shown improved drinking outcome in non-depressed alcoholics (Dorus *et al*, 1989). Acamprosate (calcium acetyl homotaurinate), a synthetic analogue of GABA, has been shown to decrease relapse rates and reduce intake (as measured by GGT) in abstinent alcohol dependent subjects (Lhuintre *et al*, 1990). Further studies are examining its possible benefits. Naltrexone, an opiate antagonist, has been found to reduce relapse in newly detoxified alcohol dependent patients (O'Malley *et al*, 1992; Volpicelli *et al*, 1992). This is an exciting time in the development of new pharmacological approaches to alcoholism and rapid changes may be expected over the coming years. Medication alone, however, is unlikely to be a complete solution for a disorder in which psychological, biological and social factors are so intertwined.

Drug treatments may also, of course, be appropriate in the management of co-morbidity in alcoholism (see below).

Maintenance

Relapse prevention

By its nature, alcoholism is a chronic condition, prone to relapse. Should relapse occur, then the therapist's skills often lie in turning an experience of failure and defeat into an opportunity for education and a means for future planning. Acknowledging the risk of relapse allows patients to voice their unspoken fears and may enable them to develop confidence in plans for recovery. Techniques are described which focus on reducing that risk once abstinence or controlled drinking has been achieved. Most concentrate on the identification of high risk situations and how to tackle them. The self-efficacy model (Annis, 1986) relies on cognitive–behavioural techniques to help patients review and enhance their ability to cope in risky situations. An initial analysis of high risk settings leads on to the formulation of a hierarchical arrangement according to the patient's perceived degree of confidence in each situation. Homework assignments are designed to progress through the hierarchy with the patient gaining in confidence and self-efficacy at each stage. Strategies for tackling assignments include rehearsals during treatment sessions and cognitive techniques to increase the sense of mastery.

Other components of relapse prevention attempt to reduce concomitant symptoms or social disabilities that perpetuate drinking. These may include stress management to reduce anxiety (using progressive relaxation, systematic desensitisation or biofeedback) and social skills and assertiveness training. Yet further methods are based on behavioural approaches that decrease the patient's responsiveness to environmental cues which can heighten craving for alcohol. Cue therapy involves repeated exposure to situations where drink is available and craving increased. Sights, smells and sounds of drinking environments are recreated both in imagination and *in vivo*. Non-reinforcement (by not drinking) results in extinction of the desire to drink. In practice, methods are usually combined with other forms of long-term therapy such as deterrent medications.

Evidence to support relapse prevention therapies above other forms of treatment is not yet conclusive. People who can identify only certain situations as giving rise to a high risk of drinking, as opposed to those for whom a wide range of settings in daily life pose risks, may benefit most. Relapse prevention models based on developing new coping skills may be superior to interactional group therapy for patients who have other psychiatric problems (Cooney *et al*, 1991). Cue therapy can decrease subjective desire to drink but, as yet, support for its efficacy comes mainly from case reports. However, new therapies which recognise the need to deal practically with day to day challenges in patients' lives are a welcome development.

Alcoholics Anonymous

Founded in the USA in 1935, the development and expansion of AA is one of the greatest success stories in the field of self-help organisations. There are now more than 73 000 groups worldwide (Makela, 1991) and from it has evolved complementary organisations such as AlAnon and Al Ateen. Its principles include the anonymity of its members, mutual support and the belief that the alcoholic is ill. This last conviction is central to AA philosophy. The alcoholic is "powerless over alcohol" but is also responsible for regaining control of his or her life. This is achieved through acceptance of AA beliefs, acknowledgement of the need for help and complete abstinence from alcohol. Several of these principles are enshrined in AA's 'Twelve Steps', providing a framework through which the recovering alcoholic progresses.

Criticisms levelled at AA usually focus on its inflexible concept of alcoholism and its insistence on complete abstinence. As against this, the new member gains acceptance and considerable support, often in the form of a 'sponsor' - another member who, in the early stages, can offer advice and encouragement and is readily available. Frequent attendances at meetings ("90 meetings in the first 90 days" is recommended) provide an alternative to a daily routine dominated by alcohol. And members are welcomed back, time and again, should they relapse. Psychiatrists in training are also welcomed at 'open' meetings of AA locally. Links can be made to help future patients attend their first meeting.

Box 7.5   The twelve steps of Alcoholics Anonymous

Step 1   We admitted we were powerless over alcohol - that our lives had become unmanageable.

Step 2   Came to believe that a Power greater than ourselves could restore us to sanity.

Step 3   Made a decision to turn our will and our lives over to the care of God *as we understood Him.*

Step 4   Made a searching and fearless moral inventory of ourselves.

Step 5   Admitted to God, to ourselves and to another human being the exact nature of our wrongs.

Step 6   Were entirely ready to have God remove all these defects of character.

Step 7   Humbly asked Him to remove our shortcomings.

Step 8   Made a list of all persons we had harmed, and became willing to make amends to them all.

Step 9   Made direct amends to such people wherever possible, except when to do so would injure them or others.

Step 10   Continued to take personal inventory and when we were wrong promptly to admit it.

Step 11   Sought through prayer and meditation to improve our conscious contact with God *as we understood Him,* praying only for knowledge of His will for us and the power to carry that out.

Step 12   Having had a spiritual awakening as a result of these steps, we tried to carry this message to alcoholics and to practise these principles in all our affairs.

Despite its worldwide appeal and fervent belief in its success there have been few comprehensive evaluations of AA as a treatment modality. The small number of randomised controlled trials that have been carried out have used populations such as court-referrals and methadone-maintenance patients, which make results difficult to generalise to populations seen in the community at large. Many studies show an association between abstinence and AA attendance (Alford, 1980; Polich *et al*, 1980) though it is unlikely that those wishing only to reduce their intake would want to join AA in the first place. There are some pointers to those patients who may derive most benefit from AA affiliation. Older patients are more accepting of the disease concept and of AA principles. Those who believe they have lost control and who accept that they are 'powerless' over alcohol may embrace AA more readily and gain most benefit (Ogborne & Glaser, 1981). Patients who are most seriously impaired make poor use of AA (Boscarino, 1980). If those with high levels of dependence do attend regularly however, they are more likely to achieve abstinence and improved health when compared to infrequent attenders (Edwards *et al*, 1987). Emrick (1987) provides a review of studies into AA effectiveness.

Co-morbidity

The dual diagnosis of alcoholism with other psychiatric conditions is increasingly recognised. (See also Chapter 9). Figures from the Epidemiological Catchment Area studies suggest that 37% of those with alcoholism also suffer a second mental disorder (Regier *et al*, 1990). Other substance abuse and sociopathy are common. Also increased are depression, anxiety and panic disorders, phobias and mania. Although people with dual diagnoses are greater users of medical facilities, they do not always disclose their drinking, and alcohol abuse among both general medical and psychiatric patients often remains undiagnosed. The converse is also true. Other diagnoses may not be sought and can remain untreated in alcohol misusers. These findings have important implications for the treatment and outcome of alcoholism. Associated psychiatric disorders and, in particular, depression are predictors of early relapse and poorer prognosis. Suicide is also commoner in alcoholism, though recent estimates have revised the risk downward (2–4% rather than 11–15%) and it is likely that those most at risk will have an associated psychiatric disorder. Figures vary but depression is probably implicated in between a half and three-quarters of alcoholic suicides.

The greatest difficulty lies in making a diagnosis in the presence of heavy drinking. Mood state is altered by alcohol. Social problems linked to drinking may increase anxiety and depression. Withdrawal symptoms may mimic anxiety and panic. A careful history can help establish the primacy of depression or other disorders if symptoms clearly predate increased drinking. More commonly however, the patient needs to stop drinking in order to confirm an underlying disorder. Anxiety and depressive symptoms may take several weeks to diminish. Because of this, it is wise to avoid specific treatments until some three to six weeks have elapsed following detoxification. This may not be possible if there is a substantial risk to the patient through waiting, but the majority of depressive and anxiety symptoms will resolve during this time.

If an underlying disorder is present, then treatment takes place as indicated by the condition. There are no psychiatric treatments contraindicated by the presence of alcohol problems but the risk of relapse should always be borne in mind. Medications that may prove a means of self-harm should be given only when adequate precautions have been taken; alcohol causes disinhibition and may increase the risk of impulsive self-injury in those already contemplating such action. Treatment may be sequential (treatment of one disorder followed by the other), parallel (concurrent but separate treatment) or integrated, where both disorders are managed in the one setting (Ries, 1993). The skills mix of the service and particular needs of the patient determine which model of treatment is most appropriate.

Conclusion

The therapist today has perhaps more to offer the patient suffering from drink-related problems than ever before. Developments in the understanding of the genesis of this destructive condition have engendered a tempered optimism. The possibility of more effective treatments, particularly cognitive–behavioural and pharmacotherapeutic, gives encouragement to patients and therapists. The strength and wisdom of AA is still there for those able and willing to avail themselves of it. In psychiatry, the therapeutic relationship remains a significant force for change. The determination to go to the first AA meeting, or follow an agreed therapy, often follows if empathy and informed understanding is felt by the patient through that relationship.

References

Alford, G. S. (1980) Alcoholics Anonymous: An empirical outcome study. *Addictive Behaviours*, **5**, 359–370.

Annis, H. M. (1986) A relapse prevention model for treatment of alcoholics. In *Treating Addictive Behaviours: Processes of Change* (eds Miller & Heather). New York: Plenum.

Azrin, N. H., Sisson, R. W., Meyers, R., *et al* (1982) Alcoholism treatment by disulfiram and community reinforcement therapy. *Journal of Behavioural Therapy and Experimental Psychiatry*, **13**, 105–112.

Babor, T. F., de la Fuente, J. R. & Saunders, J. (1989) *AUDIT: The Alcohol Use Disorders Identification Test: Guidelines for Use in Primary Care*. Geneva: World Health Organization.

Bien, T. H., Miller, W. R. & Tonigan, J. S. (1993) Brief interventions for alcohol problems: a review. *Addiction*, **88**, 315–336.

Boscarino, J. (1980) Factors related to "stable" and "unstable" affiliation with Alcoholics Anonymous. *International Journal of the Addictions*, **15**, 839-848.

Brewer, C. (1986) Patterns of compliance and evasion in treatment programmes which include supervised disulfiram. *Alcohol and Alcoholism*, **21**, 385-388.

—— (1990) Combining pharmacological antagonists and behavioural psychotherapy in treating addictions: why it is effective but unpopular. *British Journal of Psychiatry*, **157**, 34-40.

Buydens-Branchey, L., Branchey, M. H., Noumair, D., *et al* (1989) Age of alcoholism onset. II. Relationship to susceptibility to serotonin precursor availability. *Archives of General Psychiatry*, **46**, 231-236.

Cannon, D. S., Baker, T. B., Gino, A., *et al* (1986) Alcohol aversion therapy: relation between strength of aversion and abstinence. *Journal of Consulting and Clinical Psychology*, **54**, 825-830.

Chick, J. (1992*a*) Doctors with emotional problems: how can they be helped? In *Practical Problems in Clinical Psychiatry* (eds K. Hawton & P. Cowen), pp. 242-253. Oxford: Oxford University Press.

—— (1992*b*) Emergent treatment concepts. In *Annual Review of Addictions Research and Treatment, Vol. II* (eds P. E. Nathan, J. W. Langenbucher, B. S. McCrady & W. Frankenstein), pp. 297-312. New York: Pergamon Press.

—— (1993) Brief interventions for alcohol misuse: effective but not for all alcohol misusers. *British Medical Journal*, **307**, 1374.

——, Badawy, A. & Borg, S. (1993) Identification of excessive drinking and alcohol problems. *Alcohol and Alcoholism*, (Suppl. 2), 121-125.

——, Gough, K., Falkowski, W., *et al* (1992) Disulfiram treatment of alcoholism. *British Journal of Psychiatry*, **161**, 84-89.

——, Lloyd, G. & Crombie, E. (1985) Counselling problem drinkers in medical wards: a controlled study. *British Medical Journal*, **290**, 965-967.

——, Ritson, B., Connaughton, J., *et al* (1988) Advice versus extended treatment for alcoholism: a controlled study. *British Journal of Addiction*, **83**, 159-170.

Committee on Safety of Medicines (1987) Fatal interaction between Heminevrin (chlormethiazole) and alcohol. *Current Problems*, **20**, 2.

Cook, C. C. H., Walden, R. J., Graham, B. R., *et al* (1991) Trace elements and vitamin deficiency in alcoholic and control subjects. *Alcohol and Alcoholism*, **26**, 514-548.

Cooney, N. L., Kadden, R. M., Litt, M. D., *et al* (1991) Matching alcoholics to coping skills or interactional therapies: two-year follow-up results. *Journal of Consulting and Clinical Psychology*, **59**, 598-601.

Davies, D. L. (1962) Normal drinking in recovered alcohol addicts. *Quarterly Journal of Studies on Alcohol*, **23**, 94-104.

Dorus, W., Ostrow, D. G., Anton, R., *et al* (1989) Lithium treatment of depressed and nondepressed alcoholics. *Journal of the American Medical Association*, **262**, 1646-1652.

Edwards, G. (1985) A late follow-up of a classic case series: D. L. Davies' 1962 report and its significance for the present. *Journal of Studies on Alcohol*, **46**, 181-190.

——, Brown, D., Duckitt, A., *et al* (1987) Outcome of alcoholism: The structure of patient attributions as to what causes change. *British Journal of Addiction*, **82**, 533-545.

—— & Gross, M. (1976) Alcohol dependence: provisional description of a clinical syndrome. *British Medical Journal*, **1**, 1058-1061.

——, Orford, J., Egert, S., *et al* (1977) Alcoholism: a controlled trial of 'treatment' and 'advice'. *Journal of Studies on Alcohol*, **38**, 1004-1031.

Elkins, R. L. (1980) Covert sensitisation treatment of alcoholism: contributions of successful conditioning to subsequent abstinence maintenance. *Addictive Behaviours*, **5**, 67–89.

Elvy, G. A., Wells, J. E. & Baird, K. A. (1988) Attempted referral as intervention for problem drinking in the general hospital. *British Journal of Addiction*, **83**, 83–89.

Emrick, C. (1987) Alcoholics Anonymous: Affiliation processes and effectiveness as treatment. *Alcoholism: Clinical and Experimental Research*, **11**, 416–423.

Ewing, J. A. (1984) Detecting alcoholism: The CAGE questionnaire. *Journal of the American Medical Association*, **252**, 1905–1907.

Freemantle, N., Gill, P., Godfrey, C., Long, A., *et al* (1993) Brief interventions and alcohol use – are brief interventions effective in reducing harm associated with alcohol consumption? *Effective Health Care*, No. 7.

Fuller, R. K., Branchey, L., Brightwell, D. R., *et al* (1986) Disulfiram treatment of alcoholism: a Veterans Administration cooperative study. *Journal of the American Medical Society*, **256**, 1449–1455.

Gallant, D. M., Bishop, M. P., Falkner, M. A., *et al* (1968) A comparative evaluation of compulsory group therapy and/or Antabuse and voluntary treatment of the chronic alcoholic municipal court offender. *Psychosomatics*, **9**, 306–310.

Goldman, M. S. (1986) Neuropsychological recovery in alcoholics: endogenous and exogenous processes. *Alcoholism: Clinical and Experimental Research*, **10**, 135–144.

Hayashida, M., Alterman, A. I., McLellan, A. T., *et al* (1989) Comparative effectiveness and costs of in-patient and out-patient detoxification of patients with mild to moderate alcohol withdrawal syndrome. *New England Journal of Medicine*, **320**, 358–365.

Heather, N. (1987) DRAMS for problem drinkers: the potential of a brief intervention by general practitioners and some evidence of its effectiveness. In *Helping the Problem Drinker* (eds Stockwell & Clement), pp. 83–104. London: Croom Helm.

—— (1989) Brief intervention strategies. In *Handbook of Alcoholism Treatment Approaches* (eds R. Hester & W. Miller), pp. 93–116. New York: Pergamon Press.

—— & Robertson, I. (1981) *Controlled Drinking*. London: Methuen.

Institute of Medicine (1990) *Broadening the Base of Treatment for Alcohol Problems*. Washington: National Academic Press.

Jellinek, E. M. (1960) *The Disease Concept of Alcoholism*. New Haven: Hillhouse.

Kreitman, N. (1986) Alcohol consumption and the preventive paradox. *British Journal of Addiction*, **81**, 353–365.

Kristenson, H., Ohlin, H., Hulten-Nosslin, M. B., *et al* (1983) Identification and intervention of heavy drinking in middle-aged men: results and follow up of 24–60 months of long-term study with randomized controls. *Alcoholism: Clinical and Experimental Research*, **7**, 203–209.

Lheureux, P. & Askenasi, R. (1991) Efficacy of flumazenil in acute alcohol intoxication: a double blind placebo-controlled evaluation. *Human and Experimental Toxicology*, **10**, 235–239.

Lhuintre, J. P., Moore, N., Tran, G., *et al* (1990) Acamprosate appears to decrease alcohol intake in weaned alcoholics. *Alcohol and Alcoholism*, **25**, 613–622.

Lloyd, G. (1990) Alcoholic doctors can recover. *British Medical Journal*, **300**, 728–730.

Makela, K. (1991) Social and cultural preconditions of Alcoholics Anonymous (AA) and factors associated with the strength of AA. *British Journal of Addiction*, **86**, 1405–1413.

Martin, P. R., Adinoff, B., Eckardt, M. J., *et al* (1989) Effective pharmacotherapy of alcoholic amnestic disorder with fluvoxamine. *Archives of General Psychiatry*, **46**, 617–621.

Miller, W. R. (1985) Motivation for treatment: a review with special emphasis on alcoholism. *Psychological Bulletin*, **98**, 84–107.

—— (1989) Matching individuals with interventions. In *Handbook of Alcoholism Treatment Approaches* (eds Hester & Miller), pp. 261–271. New York: Pergamon Press.

Moos, R. H. & Moos, B. S. (1984) The process of recovery from alcoholism. III. Comparing functioning in families of alcoholics and matched control families. *Journal of Studies on Alcohol*, **45**, 111–118.

Naranjo, C. A., Sellers, M., Chater, K., *et al* (1983) Nonpharmacologic intervention in acute alcohol withdrawal. *Clinical Pharmacology and Therapeutics*, **34**, 214–219.

——, Sellers, E. M. & Lawrin, M. O. (1986) Modulation of ethanol intake by serotonin uptake inhibitors. *Journal of Clinical Psychiatry*, **47**, 16–22.

Nordstrom, G. & Berglund, M. (1987) A prospective study of successful long-term adjustment in alcohol dependence – social drinking versus abstinence. *Journal of Studies on Alcohol*, **48**, 95–103.

O'Farrell, T. J. (1989) Marital and family therapy in alcoholism treatment. *Journal of Substance Abuse Treatment*, **6**, 23–29.

Ogborne, A. C. & Glaser, F. B. (1981) Characteristics of affiliates of Alcoholics Anonymous: A review of the literature. *Journal of Studies on Alcohol*, **42**, 661–675.

Ojehagen, A. & Berglund, M. (1986) Early and late improvement in a 2-year outpatient alcoholic treatment programme. *Acta Psychiatrica Scandinavica*, **74**, 129–136.

O'Malley, S., Jaffe, A. J., Chang, G., *et al* (1992) Naltrexone and coping skills therapy for alcohol dependence. *Archives of General Psychiatry*, **49**, 881–887.

Polich, J. M., Armor, D. J., Braiker, H. B. (1980) *The Course of Alcoholism: Four Years After Treatment*. New York: Wiley.

Powell, B. J., Penick, E. C., Rahaim, S., *et al* (1986) The dropout in alcoholism research: a brief report. *International Journal of the Addictions*, **22**, 283–287.

Regier, D. A., Farmer, M. E., Rae, D. S., *et al* (1990) Comorbidity of mental disorders with alcohol and other drug abuse. Results from the Epidemiological Catchment Area (ECA) study. *Journal of the American Medical Association*, **264**, 2511–2518.

Ries, R. (1993) Clinical treatment matching models for dually diagnosed patients. *Psychiatric Clinics of North America*, **16**, 167–175.

Royal College of Physicians (1987) *Medical Consequences of Alcohol Abuse: a Great and Growing Evil*. London: Tavistock.

Royal College of Psychiatrists (1986) *Alcohol: Our Favourite Drug*. London: Tavistock.

Salaspuro, M. & Keso, L. (1990) In-patient treatment of employed alcoholics: a randomized clinical trial of Hazelden-type and traditional treatment. *Alcoholism: Clinical and Experimental Research*, **14**, 584–589.

Sanchez-Craig, M. (1984) *Therapist's Manual for Secondary Prevention of Alcohol Problems: Procedures for Teaching Moderate Drinking and Abstinence*. Toronto: Addiction Research Foundation.

—— (1990) Brief didactive treatment for alcohol and drug-related problems – an approach based on client choice. *British Journal of Addiction*, **85**, 169–177.

——, Annis, H. M., Bornet, A. R., *et al* (1984) Random assignment to abstinence and controlled drinking: evaluation of a cognitive–behavioural program for problem drinkers. *Journal of Consulting and Clinical Psychology*, **52**, 390–403.

——, Spivak, K. & Davila, R. (1991) Superior outcome of females over males after brief treatment for reduction of heavy drinking: replication and report of therapist effects. *British Journal of Addiction*, **86**, 867–876.

—— & Walker, K. (1982) Teaching coping skills to chronic alcoholics in a coeducational halfway house. I. Assessment of programme effects. *British Journal of Addiction,* **77**, 35–50.

Selzer, M. L. (1971) The Michigan Alcoholism Screening Test: The quest for a new diagnostic instrument. *American Journal of Psychiatry,* **127**, 1653–1658.

Stibler, H. (1991) Carbohydrate-deficient transferrin in serum: a new marker of potentially harmful alcohol consumption reviewed. *Clinical Chemistry,* **37**, 2029–2037.

Stockwell, T., Murphy, D. & Hodgson, R. (1983) The Severity of Alcoholism Dependence Questionnaire: Its use, reliability, and validity. *British Journal of Addiction,* **78**, 145–155.

Thurber, S. (1985) Effect size estimates in chemical aversion treatments of alcoholism. *Journal of Clinical Psychology,* **41**, 285–287.

Tollefson, G. D. (1989) Serotonin and alcohol: interrelationships. *Psychopathology,* **22**, 37–48.

Volpicelli, J. R., Alterman, A. J., Hayashida, M., *et al* (1992) Naltrexone in the treatment of alcohol dependence. *Archives of General Psychiatry,* **49**, 880–896.

Walsh, D. C., Hingson, R., Merrigan, D., *et al* (1991) A randomised trial of treatment options for alcohol-abusing workers. *New England Journal of Medicine,* **325**, 775–782.

Wilkinson, D. A. & Sanchez-Craig, M. (1981) Relevance of brain dysfunction to treatment objectives: should alcohol-related cognitive deficits influence the way we think about treatment? *Addictive Behaviours,* **6**, 253–260.

8 The cognitive-behavioural approach to the management of addictive behaviour

Bill Saunders

Cognitive-behavioural understanding of addictive behaviour ● A framework for intervention ● Cognitive-behavioural strategies ● Conclusion

---

Cognitive-behavioural understanding of addictive behaviour

The term cognitive–behavioural refers to a psychotherapeutic approach that covers a range of strategies and techniques based on conditioning and operant learning principles, extended to include the impact of cognitive processes on the development and modification of behaviour. These cognitive processes include thinking, self-efficacy, imagery, outcome expectancies, self-talk and fantasy. The premise is that what people believe about the things they do, and the reasons for doing them, are important components of behaviour (Ellis, 1982).

As noted by Wilson (1984) a characteristic of the cognitive–behavioural approach is its reliance on experiment, at both the individual case level and in the justification of clinical procedures. A further defining characteristic of this approach is the focus on the 'here and now' rather than the past. This is not to deny past experience, which is of importance in the development of habits and the framing of attitudes, but intervention is predicated on the assessment and modification of current behaviour. It is this preoccupation with behaviour that gives the approach its name, albeit with the acknowledgement that behaviour is cognitively mediated.

As probably needs no mention, the behaviourist approach has been in conflict with other, more traditional, psychotherapeutic approaches. It has been somewhat wryly noted that whereas in most psychotherapeutic practice people are encouraged to think their way into new ways of acting, the behaviourist aphorism is to get people to act their way into new ways of thinking (Meyer & Chesser, 1971). The good cognitive–behavioural practitioner acknowledges the interrelationship of thinking and behaviour and deploys a range of strategies that enhance adaptive thinking and behaviour.

While the cognitive–behavioural model may be seen as a recent and distinct psychotherapeutic approach, some of the strategies and techniques subsumed within the theory pre-date the formal framing of cognitive-behaviourism. This is particularly so in the addictions arena where, for example, some of the strategies advised by Alcoholics Anonymous (AA) or Narcotics Anonymous (NA) are clearly cognitive–behavioural in nature. The admonition to stop drinking 'a day at a time' (Alcoholics Anonymous, 1988) equates well with short-term goal setting and the AA requirement that individuals undertake a 'fearless moral inventory' (Alcoholics Anonymous, 1983) is not dissimilar to the cognitive–reappraisal strategies included in the cognitive–behavioural counselling strategy known as motivational interviewing (Miller & Rollnick, 1991).

Axioms of the approach

In the cognitive–behavioural approach to addictive behaviour a number of ideas about the nature of addiction are assumed. It is relevant to acknowledge the existence of these assumptions because in the main, they run counter to disease models of addiction.

(1) Addictive behaviour is a learned phenomenon which is open to modification. This may include the use of modelling or self-monitoring strategies to induce less harmful drinking behaviours; the enhancement of clients' awareness of the antecedents of heavy use; or learning, via exposure to high risk situations, that resisting temptation is possible.

(2) While it is agreed that excessive drinking causes disorders such as liver cirrhosis, peripheral neuropathy and brain damage, the behaviour of excessive drinking, or any other excessive drug consumption, is not considered a disease in its own right, but as a behaviour no different in principle from any other. That is, it is learned and is influenced by a range of factors.

(3) Anyone who uses drugs can experience drug-related problems and such problems are diverse. A useful way of conceptualising drug problems is to disaggregate drug-related problems into those relating to intoxication (single session excessive use), regular use (problems generated by daily, or near daily use over some years) and problems of dependence (by which is implied difficulty in resisting drug use or experiencing negative affect when not using) (Thorley, 1982). The importance of this type of understanding is that common notions of there being two groups of users, those that are 'addicts' and those that are harm-free 'social' users, can be discarded for a more fluid understanding that at any time some of the pool of users may be experiencing problems (of different types) and some are not, but that demarcation is fluid. Today's problem drinker can very well be tomorrow's sober citizen and vice versa. Both for alcohol and other drugs people are known from general population studies to move in and out of periods where they have problems (Cahalan, 1970; Wille, 1980; Lichtenstein & Weiss, 1986). 'Once an addict always an addict' is not a tenet of the cognitive–behavioural model, although it is acknowledged that some behaviours which have become overlearned and automated, are easily activated (or re-activated) by internal or external cues.

(4) There is no single cause of problem drug use. Any given individual's relationship with any drug will be determined by a wide range of factors, which vary from individual to individual (see Chapters 2 and 6). Within a cognitive–behavioural model the presentation of problematic drug use

is individually coloured and thus considerable care is taken in the assessment of the individual and in the formulation of an individual management plan. No two problem drinkers or drug users are deemed to be the same.

(5) The individual, while influenced by his or her social milieu and past learning, is the agent of change. The assumption within a cognitive-behavioural model is that problem drug users not only determine when they will use, but importantly, when they will not.

Dependence in the cognitive-behavioural approach

Given that the majority of drug problems coming to the attention of psychiatrists are likely to present problems of dependence, as opposed to, for example, the Accident and Emergency specialist who will more frequently encounter the consequences of acute intoxication, particularly from alcohol use, it is relevant to consider how dependence is perceived within the framework of a cognitive-behavioural approach. There are differences of opinion within the cognitive-behavioural school. Some practitioners accept the notion of the Alcohol or Drug Dependence Syndrome (Hodgson & Stockwell, 1985) while others believe that dependence can more usefully be perceived as a general psychological state which is not, of itself, problematic (Peele, 1985). The term addictive behaviour is often used to denote the escalation of a state of non-problematic dependence into a troublesome behaviour.

A cognitive-behavioural account of dependence has been given by Orford (1985) in his authoritative book *Excessive Appetites*. Orford has argued that addictive behaviour is characterised by an initially rewarding behaviour being altered, via 'modest encouragement' and the lack of either individual or societal restraint, into an habitual behaviour. While reliance upon any particular behaviour may not be troublesome, what characterises an addiction is the elevation of the behaviour from one over which the individual has a sense of balance into one of conflict. The person engages in the behaviour to such a degree that contraindications accrue and he or she is confronted with the choice of either continuing with the behaviour and experiencing increased costs, or giving up the behaviour and losing some of the benefits of use.

The individual has therefore to decide about a behaviour which is highly overlearned, enjoyed, valued and relied upon, but which is also increasingly 'costly' in that it engenders a range of legal, medical, social and familial problems. Orford has stated that it is the conflict between wanting to do something very much and simultaneously knowing that one should not, which is the hallmark feature of addictive behaviour. An interesting aspect of Orford's model is that rather than being unaware of the adverse consequences of their behaviour, problem drug users are considered to be only too aware of the costs of their actions and this knowledge further escalates the behaviour.

Orford has also written that many of the supposed personality characteristics of 'alcoholics' or 'addicts' (such as being unreliable, untrustworthy, ambivalent and dishonest) are in fact the consequences of being over-involved in any behaviour. For Orford it is the cognitive conflict experienced by excessive users which results in them not knowing their own minds. They thereby oscillate between abstention and excess, and between heartfelt, but vulnerable, resolutions to quit.

Contained within the Orford model are a number of key implications for counselling problem drug users. The first is that the vexed issue of motivation can be understood as a battle between the perceived costs and benefits of the behaviour. A second implication is that having made a decision to quit or curtail drug use the individual is then confronted with another equally difficult decision – whether to persevere with that decision or to revert to the old, troublesome, but rewarding behaviour.

Understanding the process of behaviour change

Also relevant to cognitive-behavioural counselling for addiction behaviours is the research of Prochaska & DiClemente (1993) who have identified five stages in the process of behaviour change (Fig. 8.1). In the first, *pre-contemplation*, individuals are relatively content with their behaviour and are unlikely to express any need to change. In the *contemplation* stage individuals are beginning to realise that the behaviour in which they are involved has both costs and benefits and they are beginning to feel 'two-ways' about their behaviour. In the third stage, *preparation for change* (also called '*ready for action*') individuals are involved in the planning of behavioural change, goal setting and in assessing past successes and failures. In addition to this, individuals make a firm resolution to change. *Action* involves the initial attempt at modifying the problematic behaviour whereas *maintenance* is the final stage in the process of change. Sustaining change is often very difficult. Maintaining a resolution over time may require not merely the modification of habits but

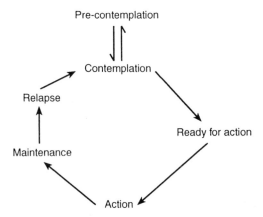

Fig. 8.1   Stages of change, after Prochaska & DiClemente (1993).

change in the way one lives. New relationships, new jobs, a change of friends, perhaps even a change of country, are sometimes necessary to sustain behaviour change. Relapse may occur.

As the model suggests, not everyone who arrives at counselling agencies is at the same stage of change. Different behavioural strategies are appropriate at different stages and clinicians should adapt their intervention accordingly.

A framework for intervention

Cognitive-behavioural interventions are predicated on a detailed and thorough assessment. When working with problem drug users such assessment is an on-going process and the case history approach, as elegantly and comprehensively outlined by Edwards (1987), is recommended as an integral part of management. However, the emphasis within a cognitive-behavioural approach is also very much on current behaviour, since it is behaviour change which is usually the focus of therapeutic endeavour. Specificity is a key feature of this type of assessment which is known as a *functional analysis*, an important aspect of which is the taking of a detailed drinking or drug taking history. Of particular interest to the cognitive-behaviourist is the determination of the circumstances – the when, the where, the who, the how and the why – which influence drug use. Of critical concern is determining those factors that result in the client subjectively experiencing 'loss of control' and the circumstances when 'control' is deemed to have been maintained. Similarly, past relapses are scrutinised for common underpinning processes.

A vexed issue in the management of addictive behaviours is the inter-relationships between the client's drug use history, their psychological state and their social-familial functioning. The role of assessment is to tease out, as far as is ever possible, these inter-correlations. For example, in the management of problem drinking, is the excessive alcohol use generated by pre-morbid personality characteristics or is the current free-floating anxiety a consequence of excessive alcohol use? Concomitantly, what is the role of the spouse, or social factors such as job or housing, in maintaining or changing the status quo? The traditional belief is that if the excessive behaviour is curtailed or stopped, other spheres of the individual's life will fall into place. Clinical experience shows this is only sometimes the case. For many problem drug users a change in drug use can expose a plethora of other problems that require attention. As part of clinical work the author has found it useful to encapsulate the interrelationships between drug history, family life and psychological functioning in a simple three circle model (Fig. 8.2).

One circle involves the client's drink or drug taking history with particular reference to the degree of dependence experienced by the client. It is argued that as the degree of dependence increases this circle figuratively spins more rapidly and has greater influence on the two related circles. The second circle, the client's psychological status, is, as the excessive behaviour develops,

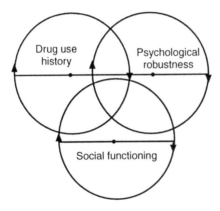

Fig. 8.2 A clinical model for client assessment.

increasingly influenced by that development. Thus pre-existing levels of psychological distress (such as anxiety, depression, low-self esteem) will be exacerbated. This in turn feeds back into the drinking/drug taking cycle adding additional impetus to substance use. It is contended that whether psychological distress 'caused' the original drug use or is a consequence of drug use is a moot point, and that what matters is that the two interact and have the potential to synergistically accelerate drug taking. Simultaneously, the third circle, that of social functioning (family, friends, work) is influenced by and influences the other two circles. Thus the unhappy relationship, the unrewarding job, the deterioration of family life are further eroded by drug use and this deterioration pushes drug use along further. The important implication of this model, which is well accepted and appreciated by clients, is that in order to stop the maelstrom of addictive behaviour all circles need, in some way, to be addressed. Just stopping the drug use is seldom enough.

Assessment is, therefore, a key issue in the management of addictive behaviour. A careful assessment will indicate what, in addition to the first task of responding to the excessive drug use, will also need attention. Failure to consider these other aspects of human functioning can often result in any attempt at change being short-lived.

Cognitive-behavioural strategies

Saunders & Allsop (1991*a*), using Prochaska and DiClemente's framework coupled with Orford's understanding of addictive behaviour, have proposed that 'giving up' addiction behaviour should be understood as a process in which different cognitive-behavioural strategies need to be deployed at different stages. They have argued that it is useful to plan intervention in four steps – *resolution, commitment, action* and *maintenance*. These stages and the relevant cognitive-behavioural interventions that can be applied at each stage

Clinical strategies

Resolution →	Commitment →	Action →	Maintenance
Motivational interventions	Assessment of high risk situations	Problem solving skills training	Job counselling
Assessment of stage of change	Goal setting	Resolution enhancement exercises	Marital therapy
Brief neuropsychological assessment →	Assessment of self-efficacy →	Monitoring of progress →	Family therapy
			Social environment changes →

	Resolution →	Commitment →	Action →	Maintenance
Client prognostic attributes	Decision making skills	Short-term goal setting skills	Avoidance and coping skills	Plasticity of lifestyle
	Robust resolution to change	Knowledge of high risk situations	Familial support	Lifestyle changes
	'Ready for action' or 'Actioner' change status	Planning	Rewards for change	Relationship enhancement
	Intact cognitive functioning	Appropriate confidence	Alternative behaviours	Life satisfaction

| Relapse ↕↑ | ↕↑ | ↕↑ | ↕↑ | Survival |

Fig. 8.3 Clinical strategies and planned interventions.

are described below. It is believed that these strategies enhance the development of attributes which are linked to good outcome. For example, the use of motivational interventions encourages the making of robust resolutions to change whereas the teaching of problem solving facilitates the development of coping skills. The suggested interaction of clinical strategies and prognostic indicators are outlined in Fig. 8.3.

Robust resolutions

The first stage of behaviour change is deciding that change is necessary. A robust decision to quit or curtail drug use is vital if change in drug taking behaviour is to be sustained. Effort needs to be directed toward ensuring that clients embark on the change process with well thought out and established reasons for making such attempts. One strategy designed to facilitate the establishment of a robust resolution to change is motivational interviewing. As outined by Miller (1983) motivational interviewing presupposes that drug use involves both costs and benefits for the individual. The emphasis within motivational intervention is to encourage a cognitive (and an emotional) self-appraisal of current problems and concerns, allowing the client to appreciate for him or herself the need for change.

The importance of this process of review has been noted by Stimson & Oppenheimer (1982, p. 160) who in reporting the results of a 10 year follow-up of 128 heroin users, wrote that:

> "at any time there are some advantages in continuing as an addict and some in ceasing. The conflict between reasons for continuing and reasons for stopping is a source of tension. In retrospectively assessing their lives, many (addicts) saw a shift in the balance between advantages and disadvantages as having led them to make decisions to stop using drugs."

Detailed clinical examples of motivational interviewing in practice are available and the technique has been usefully applied in the management of heroin and alcohol dependence, youth drug problems (Miller & Rollnick, 1991), and helping patients with behaviour change in general medical practice (Rollnick *et al*, 1993). Miller & Rollnick (1991) have argued that motivational interviewing is a distinct style of counselling based on a number of therapeutic strategies. These include the deliberate expression of empathy, the avoidance

---

Box 8.1 Motivational interviewing

Express empathy
Avoid arguing
Detect and "roll with" client resistance
Highlight discrepancies in clients' history
Draw out clients' discomfort about the behaviour

of arguments, the need to detect and 'roll with' client resistance, the highlighting of discrepancies in the client's history and the ability to draw out the client's own discomfort about the behaviour. A central tenet of motivational interviewing is that the more help clients are given to express their concerns about a problem, the more likely they are to decide for themselves that change is necessary. One of the liberating aspects of a motivational interviewing stance is that the counsellor is freed from having to make clients see the error of their ways. Instead good counselling is about facilitating the enunciation of ambivalence that clients feel and permitting them to decide for themselves what their future conduct will be.

It is necessary to note that while motivational interviewing has been widely acclaimed as a valuable counselling strategy for addictive behaviour, direct evidence of its effectiveness is limited. To date there is only one published controlled study demonstrating the value of motivational intervention (Saunders *et al*, 1994). Heroin addicts attending a methadone clinic who received a motivational intervention out-performed a control group in terms of their commitment to abstention and their compliance with treatment, and also reported fewer problems at six months follow-up. Despite the lack to date of replicated evidence regarding the effectiveness of motivational interviewing, the popularity and acceptance of this approach (Davidson *et al*, 1991; Miller & Rollnick, 1991) rests on its intuitive appeal and the thoroughness with which Miller *et al* have presented its rationale.

Motivational interviewing aims to enhance an individual's resolution to change, and to increase the likelihood that the resolution is sustained. In AA the use of members' stories and the repetition of past drinking related disasters serves a similar function. As the work of Litman *et al* (1983*b*) on relapse has shown, being able to recall vividly past alcohol-related adverse consequences is associated with on-going abstinence. When counselling problem drug users one skill is the imparting of beneficial, selective, recall. Clients need to be prompted to recall the pain while forgetting, or at least minimising, the contemporaneous pleasures. Many manage to do the exact opposite thereby facilitating a slide back into drug use.

Commitment

Having accepted the need for change, clients are confronted with the task of planning how to carry out that resolution. This commitment or planning stage involves negotiation with the client of what will be attempted. What are the goals, immediate, short-term and long, that the client hopes to achieve? The client needs to consider whether cutting alcohol consumption down or out is the goal of treatment. Similarly, is total abstinence from illicit substances the goal of intervention or is harm minimisation the focus of counselling? While 'controlled drinking' can still cause considerable furore in some clinics, for most cognitive–behaviourist alcohol specialists this is now passé. What matters is what the client wants to do and what the assessment indicates is the optimum clinical choice. Clinical experience is that most clients set their own goals anyway and the best clinical results are achieved by invitation not imposition – self-selection of goal has been demonstrated to be associated with better outcome (Orford & Keddie, 1986) and with high treatment retention rates (Ojehagen & Berglund, 1989). Clear criteria for the selection of abstinence or controlled drinking goals have been reported by Heather & Robertson (1981) (see Chapter 7).

Also important at the planning stage is the recognition of future threats to the resolution to change, the identification of areas of vulnerability and, if possible, the generation of appropriate degrees of confidence. Confidence (self-efficacy) has been repeatedly demonstrated as a prognostic factor of change: the greater the individual's confidence the greater the likelihood of success (Annis, 1986). However, care needs to be taken with regard to alcohol-related problems. For some clients cognitive impairment may result in undue optimism about their capacity to resist temptation and their high confidence may not be matched by the skills or mental ability to abstain (Allsop *et al*, 1992).

Clinicians should attempt to gauge both self-efficacy and anticipated high risk situations in preparing clients. In this regard measures developed by Annis & Davis (1988) which tap both confidence and perceived high risk situations have been found to be useful clinical tools, as is the Relapse Precipitants Inventory developed by Litman *et al* (1983a). The latter authors also found that the higher the perceived number of challenging situations, the worse the prognosis.

A 12-item questionnaire (Rollnick *et al*, 1992) based on the Prochaska and DiClemente Stage of Change model locates where clients are in the giving up process. Clinical use suggests it is a useful tool that prompts discussion about the change process and the client's current intentions. It can assist in the important task of setting appropriate goals for the intervention – tailoring the clinical response to the individual's needs is paramount. For example, a 'pre-contemplator' will be better served by harm minimisation work than advice on how to stop. Conversely an 'actioner' will probably benefit from a focus on coping skills rather than the detailed appraisal of the benefits of change. Successful intervention need not mean the achievement of prolonged abstinence, but could rather be the nudging of a contemplator into less harmful drug taking practices or the instilling of an enhanced appreciation of the costs of drug use in a pre-contemplator.

Whatever the negotiated goal(s) of intervention it is valuable to temper any enthusiasm for total, lifelong, change by establishing a series of short-term, practical goals. For example, negotiating and agreeing that for the next week, weekend or Friday night, the client will attempt not to drink or use drugs, and then planning how this may be achieved, may be a major achievement for the client. One obese person, agreeing to survive a weekend without eating chocolate or fast food, revealed she had not done so for over 30 years.

A key idea of short-term goal setting is that small successes are the breeding ground of long-term change. One successful self-changer lost over 50 kilos of weight by embarking on a 7 day programme in which he lost just under 2 ounces a day. Heartened by losing 12 ounces in the first week he set himself progressively tougher daily assignments. Clients proving to themselves that behaviour change is possible is a critical step in long-term behaviour change.

Furthermore, experiences of success reinforce the original change resolution, enhance self-efficacy and teach the client coping skills. As is demonstrated in the literature on smoking, those individuals who attempt to quit, even if they relapse, are aided by the experience. Indeed, Lichtenstein & Weiss (1986) found that relapsed quitters were, in comparison to non-attempters, more committed to future change attempts and more confident in their ability to succeed. Similarly, DiClemente *et al* (1991) found that smokers in the 'ready for action' category reported significantly more attempts at quitting in the past year (five as against one or two for 'contemplators') and were more confident about their next attempt to quit. Ready for actioners outperformed the contemplators (in terms of achieving abstinence) by a factor of almost three.

The emphasis within this commitment phase is on forewarning and thereby forearming. Clinical experience is that a not insignificant proportion of clients leap off into behaviour change without being properly prepared for the challenge of the change they are proposing.

Taking action

As relapse rates show only too clearly, making a resolution and keeping it is difficult. Shiffman (1986) found that 80% of smokers returned to use within one year of quitting, a figure not dissimilar to that reported for opiate users, where 76% of a treatment sample re-used within six months (Gossop *et al*, 1990). The figures are no better for alcohol with 93% of clinic attenders relapsing into some use over four years (Polich *et al*, 1981).

Relapse is not only a problem for excessive drug users. Norcross & Vangarelli (1989), in an innovative and presageful study, discovered that of some 200 New Yorkers who made New Year's resolutions to change specific behaviours, 45% had given up their resolution after one month, a figure which rose to 60% at six months and 81% at two year follow-up. These resolution decay curves are identical to relapse curves frequently cited in the alcohol and drug literature (Marlatt & Gordon, 1985).

Relapse is not an exotic condition of problem drug users; it is a common part of human behaviour. We need to appreciate that our resolutions flounder for similar reasons to those of our clients. If this is accepted then relapse is de-mystified and addiction counselling is less bewildering.

It is clear from the literature that a range of factors contribute to an individual deciding to quit and then reversing that decision. A central idea in the well accepted relapse model proposed by Marlatt & Gordon (1985) is that relapse is often caused by individuals encountering high risk situations with which they are unable to cope. While this emphasis on high risk situations has been criticised as being overstated (Saunders & Allsop, 1987) there is no doubt that some relapses are precipitated by individuals being overwhelmed by adverse circumstances. There has been considerable interest in training people in coping strategies which include refusal skills, assertive training, social skills, relaxation training, stress management, problem solving, criticism skills, negotiation skills, and relationship enhancement. Monti *et al* (1989) have produced a useful clinical guide of such methods. Research shows that coping skill acquisition improves overall outcome (Heather & Tebbutt, 1989), although only if utilised in the management of clients with assessed deficits. The tendency to offer all clients coping skills training needs to be avoided, since clinical experience is that many people have these skills, but just choose not to use them.

Additionally, the wide range of 'at risk' situations reported by clients makes training in appropriate skills for all circumstances virtually impossible. An alternative is to teach clients a generic coping response, such as problem solving (D'Zurilla & Goldfried, 1971), which can be applied to the management of a broad range of high risk situations. It is also relevant to note that recent research indicates that people are not accurate predictors of why they will relapse. Baily *et al* (1991) in a prospective study of 94 attenders at an alcohol clinic found that the self-reported anticipated reasons for relapse were inconsistent with the later reported actual reasons. Thus training people to cope with situations they believe will be problematic is of limited value. Also it has been found that some clients relapse in circumstances in which they had previously managed to cope (Allsop, 1990).

Thus, while some relapses are generated by clients encountering situations with which they are unable to cope, others (possibly the majority) entail clients choosing to expose themselves to some temptation and then being 'overwhelmed'. This is practically equivalent to deciding to re-use, but it is more comfortable for the client to attribute relapse to external, omnipotent, forces, than to acknowledge that they deliberately chose a risky (but in the short-term enjoyable) option. The question: "Do relapses happen to people or do people decide to make relapses happen?" merits close consideration; the latter entails a failure of resolution more than a failure of coping.

Such failures in resolution are of considerable interest particularly because of certain aspects of thinking which clients appear to engage in prior to relapse. In psychological terms this concerns self-talk, or in more evocative terms, 'The Beast' (Trimpey, 1989). Many clients report that before resuming drug use they are troubled by a voice in their heads which suggests, variously and somewhat covertly, that: "one wouldn't hurt"; "you've been good you deserve a little one"; "he doesn't appreciate your efforts" or "see if you can control it". While such inner voices are simply representations of the ambivalence that many clients feel about stopping, personifying such thoughts as the Beast (or as one female client decided 'the Demoness') can be a useful strategy in highlighting almost subliminal internal messages and giving clients something to fight against. "Watch out for the Beast" or "that's the Beast speaking" can alert clients to potentially inimical thinking and be a rallying cry of support. Beast beating strategies can be brainstormed by group members and much humour deployed to counteract the Beast's insidious messages. Encouraging clients to verbally berate the Beast, such as shouting out loud pithy slogans to chase the Beast away, is a useful strategy to reinforce the notion that much temptation comes from within but nonetheless can be resisted.

The prevention of relapse should therefore attend to enhancing clients' resolutions and to the instilling of cognitive strategies that support change as well as fostering clients' behavioural coping skills.

From this perspective Saunders & Allsop (1991*b*) reported a clinical trial in which severely dependent problem drinkers were randomly allocated to one of two experimental relapse prevention interventions or to a supportive counselling control group. On follow-up at six and 12 months it was found that one group performed significantly better than the comparison groups. Participants in this group (who were counselled in pairs) received eight, 90 minute counselling sessions, which included motivational interviewing, problem solving skills training, rôle play and active, real-life, rehearsal of coping with high risk situations. Participants in this group remained abstinent four times longer than the no-relapse treatment control and three times as long as the other experimental group – a discussion based relapse prevention group. Also the successful group, on average, took between four and seven times longer to return to 'heavy' drinking than did the comparison groups. The conclusion from this study is that an amalgam of cognitive procedures (motivational interviewing) and coping skills (problem solving and *in vivo* exposure) is a potent relapse prevention endeavour.

Of current experimental interest are attempts to investigate cue exposure as a treatment to reduce the incidence of relapse. The cognitive basis of this approach is that since 'impaired control' can be considered a central symptom of addictive behaviour, it is necessary to train addicts in how to improve their control. The successful use of cue exposure and response prevention in the management of obsessive compulsive behaviours suggests that if severely dependent alcohol users are exposed to a powerful cue for further drinking (such as the consumption of three or four drinks) and are then encouraged to resist the strong urge to drink more, they will learn, over time, that resistance or some control is possible. Or, in conditioning theory, the conditioned response i.e. drug-taking, will be extinguished. Cues may be internal such as feelings of anxiety, or external such as the sight of drug or injecting apparatus known to be powerful in heroin and cocaine addicts, or a group of drug-using acquaintances. Cue exposure as a treatment requires development and evaluation, but may have potential (Drummond *et al*, 1990).

Maintaining resolutions; the importance of social processes

Norcross & Vangarelli (1989) in their study of American New Year resolution makers found that those who maintained their resolutions, when compared to the 'relapsers', used more stimulus control procedures (i.e. avoided or reduced their exposure to cues) and also reported that they received greater levels of social support.

The importance of social factors was also reported by Prochaska & DiClemente (1986). They found that while cognitive–behavioural factors were critical at the initiation and implementation stages of change, social factors such as quality of familial support, employment conditions and marital functioning, were vital in the maintenance of change. Prochaska & DiClemente also noted that 'giving-up' is a long haul, with the maintenance phase lasting from around six months to five years.

Social factors in the maintenance process were also demonstrated by Billings & Moos (1983). They compared problem drinkers who succeeded in their resolutions to quit with those who relapsed. They found that 'survivors' when compared to their less successful counterparts, reported significantly higher levels of family support, job satisfaction, fewer adverse life events and more effective coping skills. But clinicians should see these factors as interlocking and reciprocal, rather than separate. For example, a relatively stable social environment facilitating good quality familial interaction, in turn reinforces the original decision to abstain thereby prompting determination to cope with challenges. Such coping is thus reinforced, which further increases familial support, job performance, social stability and determination to succeed. It is easier to resist temptation if there are benefits for doing so. Poor quality relationships, boredom, unemployment, and a denuded daily existence are infertile ground for sustaining resolutions to change drug use.

Similarly, Havassy *et al* (1991) in a study of some 200 people attempting to give up smoking, alcohol consumption or opiate use, found that structural social support (e.g. presence of close friends, significant partner and group affiliations) was significantly associated with good outcome. Continuing contact with drug using social networks was linked to relapse. The latter is not a surprising finding; being perhaps research confirmation of the AA or NA line that attendance at meetings and association with sober people is a prerequisite of success.

Cognitive–behavioural approaches are based on the notion that human behaviour is socially influenced. Hence cognitive–behaviourally oriented clinicians do have an ideological responsibility, at least, to focus some of their attention onto the social, as well as the psychological, functioning of their clients. One of the most successful series of treatment studies, those reported by Azrin (1976) and Sisson & Azrin (1988), directly involved manipulating social, rather than psychological, variables. Thus participants in what is known as the Community Reinforcement Approach received advice and practical help in such matters as housing, jobs, interpersonal relationships, leisure activities and financial support. As a group they far exceeded in outcome a comparison, conventionally treated, group.

Such work is consistent with the spontaneous remission literature (Tuchfeld, 1981; Sobell *et al*, 1991) and treatment studies that have enquired of successful participants why they succeeded. For example Orford & Edwards (1977) found that rather than attributing success to counselling, 'survivors' tended to report improved marital relationships, positive changes in their external realities – such as work and housing – plus enhanced psychological wellbeing, as the factors that maintained their efforts. Perhaps to overstate the case, cognitive-behavioural approaches are based on the notion of the individual acting in a social world. It is unfortunate that, at times, some clinicians (including cognitive-behaviourally oriented ones) forget this and retire into the ever increasing fine tuning of relatively ineffective, individually-oriented, counselling.

Conclusion

It is possible that the addictions field is on the verge of a third generation of treatments. The first generation, that of intensive, in-patient, psycho-therapeutically based programmes is past. The second, a rebound into brief intervention for less chronic and less severe clients, while of considerable benefit (see Chapter 7) risks resulting in the 'tough cases' being relatively ignored. However, with the increasing acceptance of the cognitive-behavioural approach to the cost-effective management of addictive behaviours, there may be a renewed interest in the intensive and long-term management of difficult cases.

Importantly, the public acceptance of cognitive–behavioural methods has now reached the stage that a self-help group, known as Rational Recovery (RR), has spontaneously appeared in the USA and offers a viable, cognitive – behavioural, and non-spiritual, alternative to AA. If this movement is sustainable, and there are already over one hundred RR groups operating in the USA and the RR text *The Small Book* (Trimpey, 1989) is now in its third edition and seventh print run, then the groundwork may well have been established for a synergistic relationship between clinics and the communities they serve. Certainly one aspect previously absent from the cognitive-behavioural approach was a compatible community based support group. It may well be that the combination of proven, professionally delivered programmes augmented by accessible community support, will result in the addictions field being able to throw off the finding that client characteristics, rather than treatment characteristics, are the best predictors of outcome (Armor *et al*, 1978).

References

Alcoholics Anonymous (1983) *Twelve Steps and Twelve Traditions.* New York: Alcoholics Anonymous World Services.
—— (1988) *Living Sober.* Australia: General Service Office of Alcoholics Anonymous, Australia.

Allsop, S. (1990) Relapse prevention and management. *Drug and Alcohol Review*, **9**, 114-154.

—— & Saunders, B. (1991) Reinforcing robust resolutions: motivation in relapse prevention with severely dependent problem drinkers. In *Motivational Interviewing: Preparing People to Change Addictive Behaviour* (eds W. Miller & S. Rollnick), pp. 236-247. New York: Guilford Press.

Annis, H. (1986) A relapse prevention model for the treatment of alcoholics. In *Treating Addictive Behaviour* (eds W. Miller & N. Heather), pp. 407-431. New York: Plenum.

—— & Davis, C. (1988). Assessment of expectancies. In *Assessment of Addictive Behaviours* (eds D. Donovan & G. Marlatt), pp. 84-111. New York: Hutchinson.

Armor, D., Polich, J. & Stambul, H. (1978) *Alcoholism and Treatment*. New York: Wiley.

Azrin, N. (1976) Improvements in the community of reinforcement approach to alcoholism. *Behaviour Research and Therapy*, **14**, 339-348.

Baily, S., Saunders, B., Phillips, M., *et al* (1991) *Pathways to Survival: The Influence of Gender in Alcohol Relapse*. Technical Report prepared for the Research into Drug Abuse Advisory Committee. Perth: Addiction Studies Unit, Curtin University of Technology.

Billings, A. & Moos, R. (1983) Psychosocial processes of recovery among alcoholics and their families: implications for clinicians and program evaluators. *Addictive Behaviours*, **8**, 205-218.

Cahalan, D. (1970) *Problem Drinkers*. San Francisco: Fossey-Bass.

Davidson, R., Rollnick, S. & McEwan, I. (1991) *Counselling Problem Drinkers*. London: Routledge.

DiClemente, C., Prochaska, J., Fairhurst, S., *et al* (1991). The process of smoking cessation: an analysis of precontemplation, contemplation and preparation stages of change. *Journal of Consulting and Clinical Psychology*, **59**, 2.

Drummond, C., Cooper, T. & Glautier, S. (1990) Conditioned learning in alcohol dependence: implications for cue exposure treatment. *British Journal of Addiction*, **85**, 725-743.

D'Zurilla, T. & Goldfried, M. (1971) Problem solving and behaviour modification. *Journal of Abnormal Psychology*, **78**, 107-126.

Edwards, G. (1987) Case history as initiation of therapy. In *The Treatment of Drinking Problems: A Guide for the Helping Professions* (2nd edn) (Edwards, G.), pp. 167-189. Oxford: Blackwell Scientific.

Ellis, A. (1982) *Rational Emotive Therapy and Cognitive Behaviour Therapy*. New York: Springer.

Gossop, M., Green, L., Phillips, G., *et al* (1990) Factors predicting outcome amongst opiate addicts after treatment. *British Journal of Clinical Psychology*, **29**, 209-216.

Havassy, B., Hall, S. & Wasserman, D. (1991) Social support and relapse: commonalities among alcoholics, opiate users, and cigarette smokers. *Addictive Behaviours*, **16**, 235-246.

Heather, N. & Robertson, I. (1981) *Controlled Drinking*. London: Methuen.

—— & Tebbutt, J. (1989) *The Effectiveness of Treatment for Alcohol and Drug Problems: An Overview*. Monograph Series No. 11. National Campaign Against Drug Abuse. Canberra: Australian Government Publishing Service.

Hodgson, R. & Stockwell, T. (1985) The theoretical and empirical basis of the alcohol dependence model: a social learning perspective. In *The Misuse of Alcohol: Crucial Issues in Dependence Treatment and Prevention* (eds N. Heather, I. Robertson & P. Davies), pp. 17-34. London: Croom Helm.

Lichtenstein, E. & Weiss, S. (1986) Task Force 3: patterns of smoking relapse. *Health Psychology*, **5** (Suppl.), 19–40.

Litman, G., Stapleton, J., Openheim, A., *et al* (1983*a*). An instrument for measuring coping behaviours in hospitalized alcoholics: implications for relapse prevention treatment. *British Journal of Addiction*, **78**, 269–276.

——, ——, ——, *et al* (1983*b*) Situations related to alcoholism relapse. *British Journal of Addiction*, **78**, 381–389.

Marlatt, G. & Gordon, J. (1985) *Relapse Prevention*. New York: Guilford Press.

Miller, W. (1983) Motivational interviewing with problem drinkers. *Behaviour Psychotherapy*, **11**, 147–172.

—— & Rollnick, S. (1991) *Motivational Interviewing: Preparing People to Change Addictive Behaviour*. New York: Guilford Press.

Meyer, V. & Chesser, E. (1971) *Behaviour Therapy in Clinical Psychiatry*. London: Penguin.

Monti, P., Abrams, D., Kadden, R., *et al* (1989) *Treating Alcohol Dependence*. London: Cassell.

Norcross, J. & Vangarelli, D. (1989) The resolution solution: longitudinal examination of New Year's change attempts. *Journal of Substance Abuse*, **1**, 127–134.

Ojehagen, A. & Berglund, M. (1989) Changes of drinking goals in a two-year out-patient alcoholic program. *Addictive Behaviours*, **14**, 1–9.

Orford, J. (1985) *Excessive Appetites: A Psychological View of Addiction*. Chichester: Wiley.

—— & Edwards, G. (1977) *Alcoholism*. Oxford: Oxford University Press.

—— & Keddie, A. (1986) Abstinence or controlled drinking in clinical practice: a test of the dependence and persuasion hypotheses. *British Journal of Addiction*, **81**, 495–504.

Peele, S. (1985) *The Meaning of Addiction*. New York: Lexington Books.

Polich, J., Armor, D. & Braiker, H. (1981) *The Course of Alcoholism: Four Years After Treatment*. New York: Wiley.

Prochaska, J. & DiClemente, C. (1986) Toward a comprehensive model of change. In *Treating Addictive Behaviours* (eds W. Miller & N. Heather), pp. 3–27. New York: Plenum.

—— & —— (1992) Stages of change in the modification of problem behaviors. In *Progress in Behavior Modification* Vol. 28 (eds M. Hersen, R. Eisler, & P. Miller), pp. 183–218. Sycamore, IL: Sycamore Publishing.

Rollnick, S., Heather, N., Gold, R., *et al* (1992) Development of a short 'readiness to change' questionnaire for use in brief opportunistic interventions among excessive drinkers. *British Journal of Addiction*, **87**, 743–754.

——, Kinnersley, P. & Stott, N. (1993) Methods of helping patients with behaviour change. *British Medical Journal*, **307**, 188–190.

Saunders, B. & Allsop, S. (1987) Relapse: a psychological perspective. *British Journal of Addiction*, **82**, 417–429.

—— & —— (1991*a*) Incentives and restraints: clinical research into problem drug use and self-control. In *Self-Control and the Addictive Behaviours* (eds N. Heather, W. Miller & J. Greeley), pp. 283–303. Sydney: Pergamon Press.

—— & —— (1991*b*) Alcohol problems and relapse: can the clinic combat the community? *Journal of Community and Applied Social Psychology*, **1**, 213–221.

——, Wilkinson, C., Phillips, M., *et al* (1994) *Motivational Interviewing: A Controlled Trial of an Innovative Therapeutic Approach for the Counselling of Problem Heroin Users*. Technical Report to the Research into Drug Abuse Advisory Committee. Perth: Addiction Studies Unit, Curtin University of Technology.

Shiffman, S. (1986) Task Force 2: models of smoking relapse. *Health Psychology*, **5** (Suppl.), 13-27.

Sisson, R. & Azrin, N. (1988) The Community reinforcement approach. In *Handbook of Alcoholism Treatment Approaches* (eds R. Hester & W. Miller), pp. 242-258. New York: Pergamon Press.

Sobell, L., Sobell, M. & Toneatto, T. (1991). Recovery from alcohol problems without treatment. In *Self-Control and Addictive Behaviours* (eds N. Heather, W. Miller & J. Greeley), pp. 198-235. Sydney: Pergamon.

Stimson, G. & Oppenheimer, E. (1982) *Heroin Addiction: Treatment and Control in Britain*. London: Tavistock.

Thorley, A. (1982) Medical responses to problem drinking. *Medicine*, Third Series, **35**, 1816.

Trimpey, J. (1989) *Rational Recovery from Alcoholism: The Small Book* (3rd edn). Lotus CA: Lotus Press.

Tuchfeld, B. (1981) Spontaneous remission in alcoholics: empirical observations and theoretical implications. *Journal of Studies on Alcohol*, **42**, 626-641.

Wille, R. (1980) Processes of recovery among heroin users. In *Drug Problems in the Sociocultural Context* (eds G. Edwards & A. Arif), pp. 103-113. Geneva: World Health Organization.

Wilson, G. (1984) Behaviour therapy. In *Current Psychotherapies* (3rd edn) (ed R. Corsini), pp. 239-278. Illinois: Peacock Publishers.

9 Psychiatric syndromes associated with alcohol and substance misuse

J. Spencer Madden

Abstinence syndromes • Toxic states and psychoses • Cerebral damage • Disorders of mood • Alcohol and eating disorders • Personality disorders • Further aspects of comorbidity • Classification

---

Psychiatric disorders frequently accompany the misuse of alcohol or other drugs (Helzer *et al*, 1990; Regier *et al*, 1990). The disorders generally result from substance usage, but may precede and lead to harmful substance consumption, or can share causative factors with psychoactive drug intake. Although clinical and conceptual difficulties exist it is usually possible to disentangle the psychiatric effects of substance misuse or dependence from pre-existent or concomitant mental disorder.

Abstinence syndromes

Delirium tremens

Alcohol withdrawal features though well described are still sometimes misdiagnosed, especially in general hospitals. The most florid is delirium tremens. Historically there was debate whether the syndrome is precipitated simply by alcohol withdrawal or by infection, other types of illness or trauma in persons who are debilitated by alcohol consumption. It is now recognised that the condition is a severe form of the alcohol withdrawal syndrome; illness or injury can arrest drinking and so provoke the disorder.

Delirium tremens (DT) supervenes during the second or third day of alcohol cessation. The anxiety and insomnia that are found when chronic high intake of alcohol ceases become accentuated. Clouding of consciousness develops, with disorientation. Frequent nightmares progress to hypnagogic and hypnopompic hallucinations, and then to hallucinations in the waking state. As is usual with hallucinations that follow a clear organic cause the false perceptions are predominantly visual. The hallucinated images are generally alarming to the patient, and can be of any size, but are typically small, or are reduced considerably from their real dimensions as Lilliputian hallucinations. Small animals may move ominously (hence the term 'the rats'); pink elephants are of course rare but objects of this nature are usually perceived as no more than 40 cm in height, and often less. There is also a tendency for visual hallucinations to appear as lengthy objects such as lines of light. Hallucinations may occur in other modalities, especially in hearing. The sounds can synchronise with visual imagery; for example, playing movements of a group of little musicians appear in time with their music.

Mood fluctuates from a predominant fear or anxiousness to phases of alcoholic joy. The patient's imagination can engage in his or her usual activity; this 'occupational delirium' is sometimes focused on drinking.

Tremors are prominent and greatly aid diagnosis. Initially present in the hand they spread to the lips, tongue and in severe instances to the whole body. When marked they prevent shaving or the fastening of clothes buttons. Additional to tremors are jerking movements or jactitations which are subjectively distressing. Withdrawal convulsions are a dramatic feature. Pulse rate and blood pressure are raised; there is mild pyrexia. Electrolyte deficiencies may arise of sodium, potassium and magnesium.

The usual course of DT is to recovery. Improvement commences around the fourth day. By the end of the first week of abstinence the patient is considerably better. Milder cases occur, taking the form of one or two nights troubled by hallucinations. In the early decades of the 20th century DT had a high death rate of about 30%; the disorder was also more common. Nowadays, at least in the UK, the disorder is infrequent and deaths are rare. Explanations of these twin changes are conjectural. The factors might include earlier treatment, more efficient treatment of DT and of associated illnesses such as infections, and a better standard of underlying health for alcoholics as well as for the general population.

Box 9.1 Features of delirium tremens

Tremor
Autonomic overarousal
Clouding of consciousness
Disorientation
Altered motor activity
Mood instability
Illusions
Hallucinations
Delusions
Convulsions

Treatment centres on provision of a drug that is cross-dependent with alcohol, that is, a compound which in adequate dose suppresses alcohol withdrawal features. Benzodiazepines are preferred to chlormethiazole (Heminevrin) since they are less likely to be misused by patients. Also, chlormethiazole can cause respiratory depression in overdose. Of the benzodiazepines chlordiazepoxide (Librium) is preferred because it is least likely to be misused; 100–180 mg a day by mouth in divided doses usually suffice; occasionally a larger amount can be titrated over the course of a day. Withdrawal fits may require a temporary rise of dosage, or the addition of phenytoin (Epanutin) or carbamazepine (Tegretol). Since benzodiazepines themselves induce physical dependence they must not be stopped abruptly. When given for alcohol withdrawal they are discontinued in stages over a period of 7 to 14 days; anticonvulsants should also be removed after this phase.

Treatment additionally requires attention to the general physical status. Sometimes though not always deficiencies of water and electrolytes need correction. Since DT is classically a disease of the night when reality stimuli are minimal the patient is not kept in darkened surroundings or in isolation.

General sedative withdrawal

Similar reactions to delirium tremens can follow the sudden cessation of general sedatives such as benzodiazepines or chlormethiazole, and were formerly encountered from barbiturate withdrawal. Convulsions are more common than from alcohol withdrawal. Severe abstinence states from cessation of a general sedative are treated (in hospital) with gradually decreasing amounts of the preparation that was taken by the patient. Alternatively tapering doses of chlordiazepoxide or diazepam are given in quantities sufficient to suppress marked abstinence features. The prolonged withdrawal features that are sometimes associated with benzodiazepine withdrawal are described on p. 193 (and see Chapter 4).

Stimulant withdrawal

The cessation of a high level of amphetamine or cocaine intake induces dysphoria, with depression, lassitude and drug craving. Depression is more likely to follow the extensive use of cocaine but a depressive mood, with suicidal ideation or actions, can supervene when amphetamine consumption ceases. It is incorrect to prescribe stimulants in relief, but an antidepressant may be required.

Opioid and cannabis withdrawal

The withdrawal syndromes from opioids and cannabis (Jones *et al*, 1975) are not accompanied by clouding of consciousness, delirium or convulsions (see Chapter 3).

Toxic states and psychoses

Pronounced mental changes often amounting to psychosis may arise from drug or alcohol intake. The anomalies may be brief and attributable to a single episode of substance use. For example, the mental effects of lysergic acid diethylamide (LSD), of 'magic mushrooms' or sometimes of volatile inhalants include transient hallucinations and illusions. The effects of volatile inhalants tend to last only for 30 minutes unless renewed by further intake. The acute results of the other psychotomimetic agents generally subside within several hours. The psychotic effects of an inordinately high amount of an amphetamine-like drug taken in a single episode can endure for a couple of days; they are similar to but briefer than the longer lasting psychosis that follows chronic amphetamine usage. Cocaine produces a delirious condition that can be fatal, as well as a more prolonged psychosis.

The presence of a more prolonged psychosis in a patient with a history of drug misuse does not necessarily imply a drug-induced disorder. The drug consumption needs to have been of sufficient extent and recency to justify a role in causation. Moderate intake of cannabis on weekend evenings, or amphetamine usage that ceased some months before the onset of psychotic features, do not point to a drug psychosis. If the psychosis and drug intake overlap close enquiry may show that the psychotic illness preceded the drug usage and led to the latter as a form of self-medication. Careful analysis of the extent and time of drug use is required in diagnosis.

Amphetamine psychosis

There is a wide range of compounds similar in structure and activity to amphetamine. Their chemical conformation resembles that of the naturally occurring neurotransmitters dopamine and noradrenaline. Acute toxicity from amphetamine-like drugs produces an excited state with hallucinations, delusions, anxiety, restlessness, hypertension and tachycardia. The patient usually recovers within a day or two although convulsions, unconsciousness and death can supervene.

A longer lasting psychosis follows the prolonged consumption of large amounts of drug. Delusions are present, generally of a paranoid nature. Hallucinations develop, usually auditory but also visual or tactile. Anxiety or fear are frequent, as is overactivity of thought, speech and movement. Aggression may occur. Stereotypical movements are common; the stereotypy may involve repetitive movements of the tongue and mouth or include more complex activities such as the repeated performance of a physical task. Although thought disorder is not prominent (Bell, 1965) the presentation resembles schizophrenia (Connell, 1958; Janowsky & Risch, 1979).

As with other prolonged psychoses that have behavioural manifestations amphetamine psychosis requires management in hospital. Admission allows drug cessation, protection of the patients and others, reassurance in a stable environment, and tranquilliser administration. Recovery usually ensues within a few days of removal from the stimulant compound.

Khat psychosis

Khat is a shrub grown in the Yemen countries and adjacent parts of Africa. The leaves, which are chewed for their psychoactive effect, contain cathinone and allied compounds that are similar to amphetamine in chemical structure and results. Occasionally khat leaves are smuggled into other countries, including the UK, for consumption by immigrants from areas of khat growth. The overconsumption of khat induces a temporary amphetamine-like psychosis (Madden, 1990).

Cocaine psychosis

Medical emergencies are precipitated by cocaine. Convulsions with respiratory failure are the most frequent. Cardiovascular stimulation with hypertension, tachycardia, cardiac arrhythmias, myocardial infarction or intracerebral bleeding comprise another pattern. A third form has psychiatric over-tones, presenting as a delirious state with paranoid ideas and clouding of consciousness; like the other medical crises sudden death can ensue.

A more prolonged psychosis, which has similarities to that provoked by amphetamines, follows the repeated use of cocaine in high quantities. As with amphetamines, enhancement of catecholamine activity in the brain is implicated in the pathogenesis. Clinically, suspiciousness in the patient moves towards delusions of a paranoid aspect, with a resemblance to paranoid schizophrenia.

Hallucinations are found of auditory, visual or tactile natures. The feature of 'formication', in which the patient hallucinates by touch (that is sometimes supported by sight) insects on the skin is not prominent in modern accounts of the disorder. Violence is sometimes a feature of heavy cocaine intake (Brower *et al*, 1988) and can be aggravated by psychosis.

Hallucinogen psychosis

Hallucinogens such as lysergic acid diethylamide (LSD), mescaline and certain fungi produce short-lived effects which resemble psychosis. The features include hallucinations, delusions, and alterations of affect. The psychotomimetic changes are interesting to the user and sometimes pleasant; that is why the substances are taken. The effects usually subside within a matter of hours; when the experiences are unpleasant the alarmed subject can usually be quietened by reassurance without admission to hospital.

Occasionally the psychotic-like changes persist. A long-term psychosis is more likely if the user has been taking the preparation frequently over a sustained period of days or weeks. A prolonged psychosis has been noted after LSD intake and (more rarely) following consumption of hallucinogenic mushrooms. The illness requires hospital admission and a major tranquilliser, although phenothiazines are reported to aggravate the psychosis produced by some less common hallucinogens used in USA, such as phencyclidine (PCP). The prognosis is satisfactory, with recovery taking place over an interval of a few days to a few weeks.

Ecstasy (3,4 methylenedioxymethyl-amphetamine, MDMA), a stimulant and hallucinogenic tablet widely used in recent years at 'dance raves', has caused chronic paranoid psychosis (McGuire & Fahy, 1991).

Cannabis psychosis

A brief toxic reaction can develop to a high amount of cannabis taken on a single episode. The clinical aspects centre on hallucinations and agitation. More prolonged psychotic features sometimes accompany the extensive use of cannabis. The features include paranoid delusions that may be poorly formed, auditory hallucinations, and imprecision of thought with rambling speech. Such aspects are indistinguishable from those found in schizophrenia though manic symptoms can also occur. It is accepted that cannabis exacerbates pre-existent schizophrenia (Chopra & Smith, 1974; Treffert, 1978). There are also numerous case reports which attribute psychotic changes among cannabis users to the drug (Carney & Bacelle, 1984).

Yet there is a debate whether cannabis produces a psychotic illness. The association of psychosis and cannabis may be coincidental or result from self-medication with the drug by patients who are already psychotic.

It must be emphasised that there are cases where there is a clear temporal link between phases of heavy cannabis intake and psychosis, with the psychotic features waxing and waning in step with the intensity of drug consumption (reviewed by Chaudry *et al*, 1991). Some of the prolonged recoveries which ensue on cannabis cessation may fall within the category of episodes of schizophrenia that are followed by sustained remission but the close timing between drug usage and psychosis is impressive. Cannabis products remain in fatty tissues for over 30 days (Hunt & Jones, 1980). It is postulated therefore that cannabis psychosis occurs as a form of chronic intoxication that persists until drug metabolites are gradually depleted from body fat (Ghodse, 1986). The relevant issues require further exploration. The review by Thornicroft (1990) is recommended.

Amotivational syndrome from cannabis

The regular heavy use of cannabis is sometimes accompanied by a state of low drive, indifference to conventional requirements or rewards, and poor concentration. Contented lethargy and diffuse thinking are acute results of the drug; possibly therefore a prolonged amotivational condition arises as a form of cannabis toxicity.

On the other hand individuals who do not accept the usual conventions of society can include extensive cannabis usage as part of their life style. The causative role, if any, of cannabis in providing an amotivational syndrome is uncertain (Edwards, 1982), but it is probably significant that the subject is not a feature of recent investigations.

Alcoholic hallucinosis

This intriguing condition is characterised by a prolonged state of auditory hallucinations and delusions, with preservation or only slight clouding of consciousness, and the absence of distinct schizophrenic features such as thought disorder. The hallucinations usually refer to the patient in the third person; third person hallucinations, of course, are not a Schneiderian first rank symptom if alcohol is implicated (Schneider, 1959). The delusions are not bizarre; often they take the form of secondary delusions that attempt to explain the hallucinations. The syndrome does not have a clear link with alcohol withdrawal.

Management requires an initial period in hospital. The patient is detoxified from alcohol in the usual manner and given a major tranquilliser. Recovery is usual within weeks or months. A small number of patients develop a chronic hallucinatory illness, in some instances after repeated recurrences.

A follow-up study of patients who had undergone alcoholic hallucinosis showed that 27% remained well, 19% became diagnosed as schizophrenic and, surprisingly, 21% underwent an affective illness of the depressive or manic type (Cutting, 1978a). Other studies have uncovered a small proportion of subjects who developed dementia.

Alcoholic hallucinosis has been described as a variant of schizophrenia or of delirium tremens. Neither tenet carries conviction. Glass (1989a,b) has outlined the perplexities concerning the nature of the syndrome. She noted that previous reports varied in their methods of data collection, especially with regard to the operational criteria for the demarcation of alcoholic hallucinosis, schizophrenia and affective disorder. The illness can be viewed as a response of a brain that, for genetic and environmental reasons, is predisposed to react in this particular way to heavy drinking. Further work is needed on familial loading for psychosis, on psychosocial stresses and on the temporal relationship to alcohol consumption.

Alcoholic paranoia

The distinctive feature of this disorder is the combination of paranoid delusions with high alcohol consumption. Auditory hallucinations may be present. The personality is well preserved.

Descriptions of paranoid states in alcohol dependence tend to concentrate on morbid sexual jealousy. Yet it should be noted that delusions of a non-sexual or non-jealous nature can arise in excessive drinkers. Ideas of reference progress to delusional thinking. Similarly, jealous suspicions of the marital or other sexual partner can advance to the false conviction that the partner is unfaithful. In fact, fleeting ideas of a jealous nature, expressed as accusations when intoxicated, are not uncommon (Glatt, 1961; Madden, 1984).

Morbid jealousy/sexual dysfunction

The classical explanation for morbid jealousy in alcoholism was lucidly outlined by Eugen Bleuler (1916). Impotence is common in male alcoholics, both as an immediate effect of alcohol intake and as a long-term result of hypogonadism. The excessive drinker can suspect and then believe that his partner is finding solace with a lover. Furthermore, the same conviction can arise in a male or female alcoholic when the partner evinces a natural loss of interest in physical relationships with the intoxicated drinker. The interpretation may apply in some cases, but investigation has revealed a lack of a clear or consistent link between sexual dysfunction and sexual jealousy in alcoholics (Shrestha *et al*, 1985). More specifically, the association is indefinite between impotence (when the drinker is male), reduced libido of the partner, and sexual jealousy (Madden, 1984).

Fixed delusions in an alcohol dependent patient require abstention and a period of treatment with a major tranquilliser. These measures are best achieved by hospital admission. Prolonged delusions of jealousy in a male, especially if retained while sober, arouse concern for the safety of the partner. Homicide is a risk. The partner should be warned and a period of separation advised, as by taking the deluded patient into hospital for treatment. Therapy involves removal from alcohol and a major tranquilliser.

It should be noted that prolonged heavy drinking in males adversely affects the production and metabolism of testosterone, with testicular atrophy, oligospermia and erectile impotence. Gynaecomastia from excess oestrogens can also develop. Sexual problems associated with these features in alcoholics can prove intractable, but since the difficulties may be aggravated by or be entirely due to psychological and marital stresses counselling can be provided. Opioids reduce the release from the brain of gonadotrophic hormones in both sexes, with reduction of sexual drive and in women of reproductive function; tolerance to these effects can develop.

Cerebral damage

Cognitive deficits are uncommon among misusers of substances other than alcohol. There are theoretical suppositions that drug users might incur cerebral damage from injuries while intoxicated, from respiratory depression with anoxia, or from pre-existent brain lesions that helped to shape personalities prone to drug misuse. The expectations are not substantiated in practice, by psychometric or other signs of impairment. Moreover psychoactive drugs lack the neurotoxicity of alcohol and their usage is not accompanied by the nutritional deficiency that often accompanies alcohol dependence. Illicit drug users are younger as a group than alcoholics so apart from other considerations their brains perhaps have greater capacity to withstand noxious influences.

There are two possible exceptions. Patients dependent on benzodiazepines tend to be middle-aged or elderly. Memory deficits have been described in patients who have taken benzodiazepines for at least a year (Golombok *et al*, 1988). The benzodiazepine changes may be temporary. Impairments of attention, vigilance and speed of information processing were noted in a group of long-term benzodiazepine users but reverted to normal when the drugs were discontinued (Sakol & Power, 1988). The evidence is not definite that benzodiazepines induce long standing cognitive sequelae.

The other and more certain exception relates to the complications of HIV infection from drug injection. The human immunodeficiency virus invades microglial cells to produce a subacute encephalitis with dementia. Patients may be subjectively aware of their intellectual and memory impairments. Dementia or delirium can also arise from invasion of the central nervous system by opportunistic infections or by tumours. It does not appear that cognitive deficits arise in seropositive patients before the onset of immunological decline or the appearance of other symptoms (King, 1990).

Global cerebral damage in alcoholism

The clinical appearances of widespread brain impairment from alcoholism range in intensity from mild cognitive deficits found only on psychometric testing to obvious severe disability. The deficits and the underlying structural changes differ from those encountered with the more circumscribed lesions of Wernicke-Korsakoff psychosis. Generalised impairment is more common than Wernicke-Korsakoff although patients can show an admixture of the two syndromes.

The brain shrinkage which is found radiologically and pathologically in global damage is attributable to alterations of white rather than of grey matter (Harper *et al*, 1985; De la Monte, 1988). Changes of white matter, unlike lesions of cortical neurones, can be reversible. The concentration of changes within the former helps to explain the partial reversibility of the hemisphere shrinkage. There is a proposal, derived from animal experiments, that alcohol produces a retraction of the network of dendrites; the dendritic arbor is capable of expansion following lengthy abstention from alcohol (Harper, 1988). Shrinkage of white matter does not depend on altered water content though lipid alterations may play a role (Harper & Kril, 1989).

More permanent neuronal damage, located in the cerebral cortex, accounts for degeneration of axons with some irretrievable loss of white matter (Harper *et al*, 1987). Damage also occurs in the nucleus basalis of Meynert (Arendt *et al*, 1983; Akai & Akai, 1989). This basal area has been implicated in subcortical dementia. The concept of subcortical dementia is debatable (Brown & Marsden, 1988) but if accepted would help to explain some of the cognitive impairment in alcoholism.

Computed tomography (CT) reveals that about 40% of typical patients in alcoholic clinics have hemisphere shrinkage with ventricular dilatation.

Psychometric deficits are as common. When both CT and psychometry are administered some 60% of clinic attenders are shown as impaired. That there is little correlation between the two investigatory approaches may reflect a lack of sensitivity in the neuropsychological tests that are usually applied. The subjects are intact on neurological examination and do not usually exhibit obvious intellectual deficits at interview.

The radiological and psychological changes are partly reversible in the course of months of abstinence (Jacobson, 1988). Hence shrinkage is a preferable term to atrophy; the former term implies transience while the latter points to permanence. Even obvious dementia is not necessarily fixed or progressive. Alcoholic patients with clinically apparent dementia can gain substantial improvements of functioning.

The anomalies that are found on psychometric testing centre on impaired abstracting and problem solving functions, rigidity of mental set, difficulty in complex sensory-motor responses, reduced visual–spatial performance, and defective memory for recent events. General intelligence is little affected. Verbal ability is not shown as implicated, although here particularly the apparent normality may reflect an insensitivity of the usual tests.

There are three views of the cortical areas that are predominantly involved (Cutting, 1978*b*). Firstly, the frontal areas, because alcoholics are reputed to show specific features of frontal damage and because the frontal lobes are revealed as especially affected on radiological investigation. Secondly, the parietal lobe on the non-dominant side since the visuo-spatial deficits point to this region. Finally, overall cortical damage not concentrated to a specific area is postulated as the most appropriate consideration.

Social drinkers have been reported to show a mild degree of cognitive impairment and of radiologically apparent brain shrinkage (Parker & Noble, 1977; Cala *et al*, 1983). The psychological findings have not been replicated consistently. The discrepancies between studies arise because of differences in definition of social drinking, and because investigations do not always allow for the after-effects of recent alcohol ingestion (Bergman, 1991).

Alcohol itself as a neurotoxin is the principal culprit for the generalised brain damage of alcohol dependence. Nutritional deficiency, including thiamine depletion, is common in alcoholics, but its role here is uncertain. Liver disease, irrespective of its aetiology, is capable of producing cognitive deficits but neuropsychological impairment is found among alcoholic patients who are free from hepatic complications. As with other forms of brain damage age is a contributory factor, although of course age is usually correlated with length of excessive drinking. Female gender may comprise another risk factor (Harper & Kril, 1990). An accelerated vulnerability of females compared with males to alcoholic brain damage would accord with their more rapid progression into alcohol dependence and into the complication of cirrhosis. Pre-existent cerebral deficits that predispose to alcohol misuse, and head injuries while intoxicated, may also contribute to neuropsychological impairment.

Treatment centres on prolonged alcohol abstinence. Despite the lack of clear indications vitamin supplements, especially of thiamine, are given when generalised brain damage is apparent. Wernicke's encephalopathy is an acute condition that requires urgent intravenous thiamine to protect life and to prevent a long-standing amnesic (Korsakoff) state. In the absence of Wernicke's disease oral vitamins are sufficient for a number of reasons. Parenteral thiamine is painful to patients and possesses the risk of anaphylactic reaction; the brain damage has been chronically established so urgent restoration is not necessary; oral thiamine combined with abstinence restores tissue levels of thiamine to normal within a week (Baines *et al*, 1988). Alcohol reduces the absorption of thiamine and its hepatic transformation into an active coenzyme; these effects apparently revert to normal quickly with abstinence. Thiamine doses of 150–250 mg daily in divided amounts are appropriate. Although the rationale is unclear the vitamin is often given with other water-soluble vitamins of the B complex, namely riboflavin, nicotinamide and pyridoxine.

The cognitive deficits of alcoholism improve with psychological treatment techniques (Goldman *et al*, 1983). The measures strengthen memory capacity, augment the ability to understand new information and improve competence for the practical details of living.

Pharmacological treatments for the dementias in general are under development. Currently the measures are focused on correction of neuro-transmitter deficiencies such as brain cholinergic depletion. Their application to alcohol-induced damage is receiving investigation. Here the interest extends to the catecholamines dopamine and noradrenaline and to the indoleamine serotonin (McEntee & Mair, 1990).

Cognitive impairment can affect the ability of patients who are alcoholic to comply with or benefit from treatment of their drinking and allied difficulties (O'Leary *et al*, 1979; Guthrie & Elliott, 1980). Counselling is the central means of treatment in alcoholism. Abstinence is especially required therefore to allow time for an improvement of mental functioning consistent with active understanding of counselling. Computed tomography and psychometry are not routinely applied to alcohol patients so cerebral deficits are not always detected. There is an obvious implication for the choice of drinking goal for patients with severe dependence on alcohol.

Wernicke–Korsakoff syndrome

The eponymous disorders of Wernicke's encephalopathy and Korsakoff's psychosis are here viewed as manifestations of the same illness. The marked pathological and clinical overlap between the two states justifies a unitary concept (Victor *et al*, 1971, 1989).

The lesions are located in the medial areas of the base of the brain, around the third ventricle, Sylvian aqueduct and brain stem nuclei (Fig. 9.1). The mamillary bodies are always affected; the medial dorsal nucleus of the thalamus is also involved when memory loss occurs (Victor *et al*, 1989).

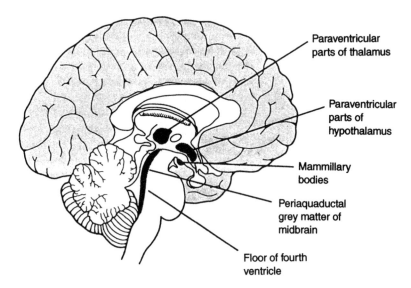

Paraventricular
parts of thalamus

Paraventricular
parts of
hypothalamus

Mammillary
bodies

Periaquaductal
grey matter of
midbrain

Floor of fourth
ventricle

Fig. 9.1 Parts of the brain implicated in Wernicke–Korsakoff syndrome.

Histologically, inflammatory cells, petechial haemorrhages and loss of neurones are found.

The full assemblage of Wernicke features involves mental changes, cerebellar ataxia and ophthalmoplegia. Not all aspects of the triad are inevitably present, or their clinical signs may be slight, transient and unrecognised. Psychological features predominate, taking the form of drowsiness, disorientation, amnesia, stupor or coma. Ataxia particularly affects the trunk. Oculomotor palsies are most evident with the sixth cranial nerve, leading to weakness or paralysis of the lateral rectus muscle. Paralyses of gaze can also occur.

The apathy or somnolence that are the most common presentations may be considered unremarkable in an ill patient newly admitted to hospital. Other mental features can be mistaken for delirium tremens. In fact autopsy studies show that the condition is often undiagnosed during life (Harper *et al*, 1986). A high level of clinical suspicion is therefore necessary.

The encephalopathy is undoubtedly due to thiamine deficiency. There are several mechanisms for the shortage. Dietary intake of alcoholics can be defective. Funds for a proper diet may be low; alcohol provides so-called 'empty calories' which substitute for a more varied diet; gastritis suppresses appetite. Thiamine is absorbed from the small intestine by two mechanisms, through passive absorption and through an active process involving energy transaction in the mucosa. Alcohol impairs the latter process of active transport of thiamine across the bowel membrane. The absorbed vitamin is transported to the liver as thiamine monophosphate where it is changed into thiamine pyrophosphate (TPP). The metabolically active form of the vitamin is TPP, which functions as a coenzyme for carbohydrate metabolism in the brain and elsewhere. Formation of TPP can be reduced by alcoholic liver disease.

Thiamine is required urgently as treatment of Wernicke's disorder, in order to protect life and to prevent a subsequent Korsakoff state with amnesia. Because of impairment of active bowel absorption the vitamin is given parenterally, at first intravenously. Divided daily doses of 150–250 mg or more are given, that are often combined with the B vitamins riboflavin, nicotinamide and pyidoxine. Equipment should be quickly accessible to treat a possible anaphylactic reaction to parenteral administration. The i.v. vitamin injections are administered slowly over 10 minutes to minimise the risk of anaphylaxis.

The leading feature of Korsakoff's psychosis is memory loss. The condition can follow as a long-standing sequel of Wernicke's disorder, ensue after delirium tremens, or develop insidiously. The amnesia involves events occurring before and after the onset of illness. The anterograde amnesia extends back in time over months or years. There is difficulty in the temporal ordering of events together with a failure of consolidation of material in memory. Consolidation is strengthened by spaced repetition and constant usage, hence there is preservation of long-practised abilities such as verbal performance and social skills. Incorrect accounts of events may be provided by patients which conceal forgetfulness. The false accounts rely to some extent on actual occurrences that are remembered in part or in a wrong sequence. The falsifications, known as 'confabulations', are not always encountered. Confabulations if present can arise spontaneously, when they are often far-fetched; more commonly they are responses to requirements placed on the memory. The two types of confabulation are known respectively as 'fantastic' and 'momentary' (Berlyne, 1972).

During recent decades psychiatric attention concerning organic mental states has concentrated almost exclusively on intellectual changes (Berrios, 1989). In the Korsakoff state consciousness and perception are unaltered, but there are disturbances of affect and volition. Apathy and placidity are found; these features continue the similar aspects of Wernicke's disorder. Patients are not distressed by memory loss. A degree of abulia exists: patients are content to spend their time virtually unoccupied or in passive compliance with requests and instructions.

As noted the pathological findings indicate the identity of the Wernicke and Korsakoff conditions, with the former as the acute and sometimes lethal stage. It has been suggested that the Korsakoff state may follow subclinical episodes of thiamine deficiency (Lishman, 1981). Unfortunately the Korsakoff disorder does not make a convincing response to thiamine treatment.

The pathological and clinical picture of the Wernicke–Korsakoff syndrome is often complicated by the effects of lesions elsewhere in the brain (Harper & Kril, 1989; Victor *et al*, 1989; Jacobson *et al*, 1990). The combination of WK and more generalised damage contributes to the nosological difficulties which have hampered understanding of the organic cerebral complications of alcohol misusers. Naturally the concurrence of WK and global impairment aggravates the disability of patients. Whether or not the Wernicke–Korsakoff syndrome and widespread cerebral damage occur singly or in combination presumably depends in part on nutritional status and perhaps on variations in the genetic susceptibility of brain regions (Lishman, 1990).

A degree of improvement with abstinence from alcohol is usual for both the amnesia defects of the Wernicke–Korsakoff state and, as already noted, for the more generalised deficits of global brain damage. The rate of recovery is most rapid within the first few weeks and slows thereafter. Progress can continue for as long as 2 years. It is not possible at the beginning to forecast the extent of recovery but patients do not usually require permanent institutional care.

Thiamine supplements to alcoholic beverages are proposed as a preventive means for the Wernicke–Korsakoff syndrome (Price, 1985). The measure resembles the prophylactic addition of thiamine to flour that for other reasons has been a long-standing practice in many countries. The vitamin can be added to beverages in a form that does not distort their taste or odour. Thiamine fortification of this kind has not as yet proved politically acceptable.

Subdural haematoma

Alcoholics are liable to develop subdural haematoma from head injury when intoxicated. The apparent injury may be slight. The symptoms can quickly follow trauma but more commonly there is a latent interval of weeks or months. Headache, memory impairment, drowsiness and impairment of consciousness develop, often in a fluctuating manner. Papilloedema can be absent. Focal symptoms and signs may be slight, but when present point to local pathology, which is frequently bilateral. The condition can be mistaken for prolonged intoxication, for delirium tremens, for the effects of drugs given during detoxification, for global cerebral damage or for WK. Neurological investigation is required, followed by surgery to remove the extravasated fluid. Early intervention protects life and prevents long standing cognitive deficit.

Investigative developments

Newer techniques for investigation of cerebral structure and function hold promise to deepen understanding of brain damage in alcoholism. They have already produced positive findings. Magnetic resonance imaging (MRI) reveals atrophy of the mamillary bodies in Wernicke's disease (Charness & DeLaPaz, 1987). Changes in water content of the brain, especially of the white matter, are shown by MRI which are probably due to alterations in the structuring of intracellular water (Besson, 1990).

Evoked potentials (also known as event-related or cognitive potentials) are a non-invasive assay of the electrical responses in the brain to specific stimuli which are auditory, visual or somatosensory. Anomalies of evoked potentials among alcoholics are repeatedly reported (see Chapter 6).

Positron emission tomography (PET) and single-photon emission tomography (SPET) allow evaluation of cerebral metabolism, cerebral blood flow and neuroreceptor systems. Alterations of regional blood flow have been identified by the latter technique in alcoholic patients (O'Carroll *et al*, 1991).

Finally, magnetic resonance spectroscopy (MRS) is a potentially powerful method for non-invasive exploration of tissue chemistry *in vivo*. An integrated examination using MRI and MRS unifies the anatomical and biochemical identification of abnormalities. MRS investigations for neurological disorders and for a few psychiatric conditions commenced in the 1980s. Anomalies have been found in conditions where neuronal loss is expected (Menon *et al*, 1991). The extension of MRS to the field of alcohol studies will deepen appreciation of the short and long-term effects of alcohol consumption on the brain.

Disorders of mood

Substance misusers are prone to mood disturbances of depression and anxiety. The alterations of affect may be coincidental, or can precede and contribute to alcohol or drug misuse. More commonly the affective changes follow the substance usage as understandable psychogenic reactions or as physical consequences. Depression varies with current substance use, being less prominent in abstinence and most marked with continuing dependence (Ross *et al*, 1988). Anxiety and depression are particularly prevalent among alcohol and cocaine users, where it is considered that both psychological and physical processes are implicated.

Affective changes in alcohol dependence

Depression

People dependent on alcohol are prone to depression (Tyndel, 1974; Nakamura *et al*, 1983). About a quarter attempt suicide; the suicide rate is at least seven times the expected rate. Comorbidity of depression and alcoholism is commoner in women than men. In the general population, criteria for depressive disorder at some time in life are met in half the females rated as having had an alcohol disorder, and in a third of the men (see Davidson & Ritson, 1993). The mood disorder is generally secondary to the excessive alcohol intake. Prospective studies suggest that the *onset of alcoholism* usually antedates the onset of depression and Schuckit (1986) concludes that "For about 90% of the men and women who have symptoms of alcoholism and depression together, the diagnosis is alcoholism, not affective disorder". Even in a study by O'Sullivan *et al* (1983) where as many as 34 out of 106 alcoholics with depression were found to have experienced prior onset of depression, the drinking histories of the two groups (and a third group with pure alcoholism) were similar. It may therefore be that even when alcoholism is secondary to an affective disorder, it develops an autonomous course independent of the 'underlying' disorder.

Observations of alcoholics during experimental drinking periods indicate that in the course of consumption they develop increasing anxiety and depression (Freed, 1978; Mendelson & Mello, 1979). The further development to suicidal ideation has also been observed experimentally in alcoholic subjects during phases of drinking (Tamerin & Mendelson, 1969).

Box 9.2   Reasons for coexistence of alcohol dependence and depression

Loss of social supports, unemployment, due to drinking
Pharmacological effects of alcohol
Primary depressive disorder (but secondary alcoholism may then have its own course)
Alcohol misusers more likely to attend clinics if depressed
Some genetic component in common - possibly
Both secondary to other conditions, e.g. antisocial personality disorder, drug misuse, characterological depression

---

The physical mechanisms by which alcohol induces depression are uncertain. Disturbance of neurotransmitter activity presumably occurs. Dopaminergic systems could be involved, while reduction of serotonin activity has also been implicated (Pietraszek *et al*, 1991).

Alcoholics are more likely to receive treatment if they develop a mood disorder.

Alcoholism and affective disorders have genetic components. It was formerly proposed that alcoholism (and sociopathy) in males could represent an inherited spectrum of illness that appears in females as depression (Winokur, 1971*a,b*). The depressive spectrum was challenged (Schuckit, 1986; Schuckit & Sweeney, 1987). Adoption studies have been equivocal about the possible genetic link. However, when 'alcoholism' (DSM-III-R, alcohol abuse and alcohol dependence) was identified in a population-based (rather than clinical) sample of female twins a genetic link with major depression (MD) emerged (Kendler *et al*, 1993), the cross-twin correlation for MD and alcoholism in monozygotic twins was 0.29, and in dizygotic twins 0.11. However it was also clear that genetic factors did not account for all of the observed correlation in liability between MD and alcoholism – shared family environment plays a part.

Schuckit (1986) draws attention to conditions in which both depression and alcoholism may develop as secondary features. These disorders include antisocial personality disorder, Briquet's syndrome, drug misuse and characterological depression. The prognosis in these conditions is considered to be that of the underlying disorder rather than that of alcoholism or depression.

Clinical In general the features of secondary depression in alcoholism resemble those of primary depression in non-alcoholics except that sleep disturbances and circadian rhythm are often altered by the immediate results of alcohol.

Depressive symptoms in alcoholics usually remit with continued abstinence (Pettinati *et al*, 1982). Management therefore relies on measures to terminate drinking. Antidepressants are not indicated when the depression is secondary to alcoholism. Their use has the potential drawback that patients and care givers divert their attention away from the underlying drinking.

When bipolar or unipolar affective disorder precedes alcohol misuse, current alcohol or drug misuse worsens the prognosis (O'Connell *et al*, 1991). Manic patients may drink, not always as is supposed from an exuberant diminution of self-restraint, but as self-medication for disagreeable symptoms such as tension and insomnia. Although many persons who are depressed notice a reduction of their enjoyment of alcohol and reduce its consumption depressed patients can of course drink to relieve their symptoms. When this occurs the depression continues despite abstinence and warrants treatment in its own right, together with measures to abate the alcohol intake.

Self-harm Self-harm by alcohol misusers generally occurs while drinking. Two mechanisms explain the link. First, the acute intoxication effect of alcohol unleashes self-injury by disinhibition and by release of feelings and ideas which are suppressed or repressed when sober. Second, the chronic intake of alcohol promotes a more sustained phase of depression, as a psychological reaction to problems and through physical processes.

The threat of suicide in an intoxicated alcoholic must be taken seriously, with observation of the patient until sober. If the suicidal phase remits with sobriety the opportunity should be seized to initiate a treatment programme, which need not take place within hospital. The occurrence of a more lengthy depressed state in an alcoholic patient calls for particular concern. A sense of hopelessness or a broken interpersonal relationship are predictors of continuing risk of suicide.

Anxiety

Anxiety is similarly common among alcoholic patients (Mullaney & Trippett, 1979). Several mechanisms are implicated. Alcohol is capable of inducing anxiety after an initial effect of tension reduction. The withdrawal syndrome for alcohol includes anxiety as a prominent feature; alcoholics repeatedly undergo at least partial withdrawal, in which anxiety is a symptom. Furthermore the subjective awareness of alcohol dependence promotes anxiety through impairment of self-esteem and of self-confidence. Excessive drinkers who are tense, clinically or subclinically, for these reasons can develop, through conditioning aided by kindling, the conditioned response of anxiety to associated stimuli (George *et al*, 1990). In contrast to the above processes anxiety, panic and phobias can precede alcohol misuse and lead to excessive drinking as a method of temporary alleviation. In summary, alcohol misuse produces anxiety symptoms and aggravates them when they already exist (Stockwell & Bolderston, 1987), but the former process of a primary alcoholic condition is more usual (Schuckit, 1985).

Attempts to treat anxiety symptoms while alcohol misuse continues are not successful. Therapy centres in the first place on the excessive drinking. Frequently abstinence or a considerable reduction of alcohol intake suffice to produce a substantial reduction of symptoms (Hamm *et al*, 1979). The persistence despite elimination of heavy drinking of fears or phobias that handicap the patient requires their usual treatment with behavioural psychotherapy. An antidepressant can also assist. Benzodiazepines are avoided because of the risk of additional substance misuse.

Anxious patients should in general receive a careful and sympathetic enquiry into their level of drinking. Equally the understanding and management of alcohol patients are aided by assessment of anxiety symptoms.

Affective changes and cocaine

An intensive period of cocaine consumption can promote during its course, in addition to euphoria, features of tension, anxiety, excitement, irritability, suspiciousness and aggressiveness. The paranoid changes sometimes progress to delusions and hallucinations, which may persist for days or weeks after drug cessation.

More commonly, pronounced affective changes develop during cocaine withdrawal. There is an immediate stage of anhedonia (the 'crash'), which lasts a few hours or days. Its symptoms involve lethargy, depression, agitation and hypersomnia. They may be succeeded by a prolonged phase of weeks or months during which depression is prominent; the subject experiences drug craving and is vulnerable to a recurrence of cocaine consumption. Symptoms that arise during withdrawal and the subsequent depressive phase are possibly caused by depletion of brain dopamine, though other neurotransmitter symptoms involving noradrenaline and serotonin may be involved. Additional to depression cocaine users are at increased risk of panic attacks (Anthony *et al*, 1988).

Pharmacological treatments are employed for the depression and associated craving that follow cocaine cessation (Gawin, 1988; Kleber, 1989). Amantadine and bromocriptine are compounds that are given. Amantadine releases dopamine from presynaptic terminals; bromocriptine is a direct agonist at dopamine receptor sites. The tricyclic antidepressants form another category of medication that is employed. Desipramine is the forerunner for this purpose, though there is scant evidence that it is more effective than other tricyclic compounds for cocaine users. Amantadine and bromocriptine act more quickly than antidepressants and are therefore more advantageous as initial treatments. Tricyclic drugs delay cardiac conduction, as can cocaine; the two preparations could affect the heart synergistically so caution is required with tricyclic medication if the patient is particularly likely to continue or resume taking cocaine. More modern antidepressants may be advantageous.

Affective changes and amphetamines

Cessation of the regular intake of an amphetamine-like substance leads to withdrawal symptoms of lassitude and depression. Stimulant drugs are not required as treatment. Instead, counselling, reassurance and support are provided. Occasionally the depression is severe or prolonged, when antidepressant medication and perhaps admission to hospital are required.

Affective changes and opioids

Opioid users can be depressed and anxious, with low self-esteem and inadequacy feelings. The features result from a psychological reaction to dependence and allied troubles, or from inherent personality problems. Sensitive treatment of the drug dependence and alleviation of associated psychosocial difficulties are required.

Opioid drugs are not considered to produce mood disorders as a direct biological sequel, except that temporary depression is sometimes a feature of the opioid withdrawal syndrome. Patients who have been chronically dependent on opioids may experience more prolonged depression when the abstinence symptoms have abated. The mood change can represent a period of mourning for the drug and former life style, as well as reflect confrontation with problems in the absence of a drug cushion. Counselling and support are provided in treatment. The aim is to promote new strategies which counteract unpleasant emotions and craving and to encourage alternative activities as replacement for drug-centred pursuits. Antidepressants are infrequently required as additional therapy.

Drug injectors who become aware that they are seropositive for HIV infection develop understandable distress. Uncertainty about the future, the prospect of premature death, excessive health rumination, concern over the attitudes of others, and guilt over previous practices are common themes. Counselling before and after antibody testing with informed consent for the investigation reduce the impact. Counselling before a test informs and prepares the patient concerning the implications of a positive result and gives the opportunity to advise on the avoidance of risk-taking behaviour. Afterwards, counselling for a seropositive patient indicates the lengthy period of well-being, discusses contacts whom the patient ought to inform, and explores other social issues. Counselling for a seropositive patient also involves the assessment of mood and of suicidal ideation, and the provision of advice on support organisations, on HIV clinics and an intercurrent illness. A prolonged period of counselling and psychological support is helpful (King, 1989).

Affective changes and benzodiazepines

Withdrawal of benzodiazepines in patients who have been taking this class of drug over a prolonged period can induce a variety of symptoms (see Chapter 4). The symptoms arise although the drug withdrawal is not abrupt. The patients have usually taken benzodiazepines regularly on prescription and do not evince the more fluctuating or intermittent pattern of intake that is adopted by illicit drug users.

The features include fatigue, drowsiness and insomnia. Gastrointestinal symptoms, sweating and lightheadedness can arise. Other aspects are unsteadiness of posture or gait, muscle twitching, paraesthesiae, and sensitivity to light, sound, taste or smell. Anxiety and depression are prominent, with the former including panic attacks and agoraphobia. The symptoms can break through during continued benzodiazepine intake; this is attributed to the development of tolerance to drug effects, including tolerance to drug suppression of withdrawal features. The symptoms are not manifestations of the original condition for which benzodiazepines were prescribed.

Treatment (and to a large extent prevention) depends on a gradual rather than a rapidly phased withdrawal of benzodiazepines. There is some disagreement over the appropriate length of the reduction regime, but drug discontinuation should take place over weeks or months (Lader & Morton, 1991). Lorazepam is the preparation most likely to produce difficulties, perhaps because of its potency. It is advantageous to change from lorazepam to diazepam during the withdrawal process. One mg of lorazepam is the pharmacological equivalent of 10 mg of diazepam.

Anxiety symptoms that remain disabling require treatment by behavioural and cognitive techniques. Depression may need antidepressant medication; antidepressants also exert an antianxiety effect. A period in hospital is sometimes required for severe anxiety or depression. In-patient treatment also allows the patient to continue benzodiazepine reduction if there is reluctance to reduce intake further in the community. In general, however, the management of benzodiazepine withdrawal should be conducted outside hospital.

Alcohol and eating disorders

There is an association between dietary disorders and alcohol misuse. Excessive drinking is unduly prevalent in patients with eating disorders who attend clinics; furthermore among female problem drinkers in treatment there is a higher than expected prevalence of dietary problems (Peveler & Fairburn,

1990). The association is particularly strong for bulimia. Eating disorders develop in patients before alcohol misuse.

The typical patient is a young adult woman who developed bulimia in her late teens or early twenties. Bulimia may have been preceded by anorexia nervosa. As the patient entered adult life her difficulties became complicated by excessive drinking which can amount to actual dependence on alcohol.

Patients with two disorders are more likely to receive treatment than subjects with one condition but there are deeper explanations for the association in clinical practice of dietary and alcohol problems. Bulimic subjects experience shame and low self-esteem; such feelings are temporarily suppressed although later aggravated by alcohol. Drinking temporarily inhibits the desire for food.

Pathological eating and drinking may both reflect personality difficulties. There are resemblances between the two forms of addictive behaviour. Impaired self-control, craving, conditioned responses to external and internal cues, and an ambivalent or fluctuating attitude to the behaviour are common to disordered eaters and problem drinkers.

There are also similarities in certain of the treatment approaches. Cognitive interventions to improve motivation and to prevent or shorten relapses are shared lines of treatment. Patients with either disorder are encouraged to find alternative forms of relaxation and recreation. The commonalities of features and therapy facilitate a joint treatment plan for patients with the two conditions.

Personality disorders

The causal and temporal relationships between substance use and other psychiatric disorders are particularly intertwined for disorders of personality.

Behaviour and emotional features of a disordered personality appear *de novo* or are magnified by alcohol or drug usage. The substance-induced features remit in abstinence.

Two genetic variants of alcoholism have been suggested (Cloninger, 1987; see Chapter 6). Type I has a late onset and is modified by environment. Type II is of early onset, is unmodified by environmental factors, and is further characterised by antisocial behaviour with novelty seeking and limited concern for harm avoidance. This genetic model is not generally accepted but the concept of Type II alcoholism holds a resemblance to that of antisocial personality complicated by alcohol misuse (Schuckit & Irwin, 1989). A study of monozygotic twins who were reared apart has pointed to a genetic linkage between substance misuse and antisocial conduct (Grove *et al*, 1990). On the other hand there are several reports to indicate that alcoholism, primary affective disorder and antisocial personality are genetically disparate (Schuckit, 1985).

The conceptual difficulties are enhanced by the difficulties in reaching a satisfactory classification and description of personality disorders. The taxonomy has changed widely, from the categories of Kurt Schneider in German psychiatry (Mayer-Gross *et al*, 1954) to those of DSM–III–R. Criteria for the delimitation of the presently acknowledged forms have been sharpened but require further precision. The current categories, particularly that of borderline personality, are viewed with some doubt as unduly influenced by psychiatric preconceptions.

It may be agreed that personality difficulties predispose to substance misuse. Follow-up studies of attenders at child psychiatric centres indicate a higher than expected prevalence of alcohol and drug misuse in adult life; many of the substance misusers were treated for personality disorders as minors and as young adults (Ostman, 1991; Larsen, 1991). Anomalies of personality lead to the appearance of alcohol or drug misuse at relatively early ages and adversely effect outcome.

Behavioural and relationship features make treatment more arduous but not impossible. Treatment is facilitated by exploring emotional reasons for substance use such as feelings of isolation, suspicion, tension, anger, boredom or depression. The usual counselling techniques for substance misuse should include extra emphasis on alternative means than alcohol or drug intake for the alleviation of inner distress.

Further aspects of comorbidity

During the middle decades of the 20th century it was uncommon to find the coexistence in patients of a primary psychiatric disorder and substance misuse. Since that period the general increase of alcohol and drug misuse has made the combination more frequent. Moreover, the change from asylum care of the severely mentally ill to management outside hospital has left patients free to obtain a variety of psychoactive preparations. Alcohol and other substances are taken as self-medication in competition with prescribed medicaments.

The prevalence of alcohol misuse as well as smoking is increased among schizophrenic patients. Such patients may drink to relieve symptoms such as anxiety, dysphoria and insomnia or, in rare cases, psychotic symptoms (Noordsy *et al*, 1991). The Swedish adoption studies have suggested a familial link, presumably of genetic origin, between Type II alcoholism and somatoform disorders (Bohman *et al*, 1984). Increased alcohol use, in the short term, is a well recognised feature of post-traumatic stress disorder, and there is controversy as to whether or not alcoholism may arise as a long-term sequela.

The interactions between prescribed and unprescribed substances are affected by metabolic processes. A compound may promote, through hepatic enzyme induction, the metabolic inactivation of another preparation. Alternatively a substance can reduce metabolism of another drug by competition for a shared inactivating enzyme. The latter mechanism has been important when alcohol and barbiturates were taken together; alcohol utilises the microsomal enzyme oxidising system that is also needed to inactivate barbiturates, with sometimes a lethal outcome. The effects of

---

**Box 9.3   ICD-10 categories coding for disorders due
to psychoactive substance use**

F10–F19 Mental and behavioural disorders due to psychoactive
substance use:
- F10.-   Alcohol
- F11.-   Opioids
- F12.-   Cannabinoids
- F13.-   Sedatives and hypnotics
- F14.-   Cocaine
- F15.-   Other stimulants, including caffeine
- F16.-   Hallucinogens
- F17.-   Tobacco
- F18.-   Volatile solvents
- F19.-   Multiple drug use and use of other psychoactive
  substances

A fourth character broadly discriminates between disorders:
- F1x.0   Acute intoxication
- F1x.1   Harmful use
- F1x.2   Dependence syndrome
- F1x.3   Withdrawal state
- F1x.4   Withdrawal state with delirium
- F1x.5   Psychotic disorder
- F1x.6   Amnesic syndrome
- F1x.7   Residual and late-onset psychotic disorder
- F1x.8   Other mental and behavioural disorders
- F1x.9   Unspecified mental and behavioural disorders

A fifth character allows more precise delimitation of the type of
disorder, e.g. the combination .72 refers to residual affective disorder.
A longstanding depressive state induced by cocaine misuse could
therefore receive coding as F14.72.

---

prescribed and non-prescribed drugs are also enhanced by the slowing of
hepatic metabolism from alcoholic liver disease or among drug injectors from
viral hepatitis.

Schizophrenic patients in particular are additionally disadvantaged if
they misuse substances (Price, 1991). They are at extra risk of recurrences
both of their psychotic illness and of substance consumption. There are
organisational and sometimes financial barriers to their treatment which lead
to poor collaboration between therapeutic agencies. The practice of appointing
a case manager who has overall responsibility for a particular patient assists
therapy. Determined follow-up and support are necessary to alleviate the
difficulties that spring from the combination of disorders.

Classification

The taxonomy of the conditions induced by alcohol and drugs, as with other aspects of psychiatry and medicine, is never static. Investigatory findings and altered ways of considering medical disorders initiate changes in nosology. Classification in psychiatry is especially though often unwittingly responsive to the broader conceptual changes of the community. Additionally patients adapt symptomatology to blend with movements in the expectation and requirements of society and of their doctors. The changing pattern of symptoms in turn alters taxonomic perspectives.

The 10th Revision of the *International Classification of Diseases* (ICD-10) attempts to minimise the weakness of formal taxonomy for psychiatric disorders (World Health Organization, 1992). The contents were devised as acceptable across cultural and national boundaries. The psychiatric categories take account of changes envisaged within the classification series described by successive issues of the *Diagnostic and Statistical Manual* of the American Psychiatric Association. The broad structure of ICD-10 is expected to endure across a couple of decades.

The ICD-10 classification of psychiatric syndromes associated with alcohol and drug misuse is shown in Box 9.3.

References

Akai, J. & Akai, K. (1989) Neuropathological study of the nucleus basalis of Meynert in alcoholic dementia. *Japanese Journal on Alcohol and Drug Dependence*, **24**, 80–88.

Anthony, J. C., Tien, A. Y. & Petronis, K. R. (1988) Epidemiological evidence on cocaine use and panic attacks. *American Journal of Epidemiology*, **129**, 543–549.

Arendt, T., Bigl, V., Arendt, A., *et al* (1983) Loss of neurons in the nucleus basalis of Meynert in Alzheimer's disease, paralysis agitans and Korsakoff's disease. *Acta Neuropathologica*, **61**, 101–108.

Baines, M., Bligh, J. G. & Madden, J. S. (1988) Tissue thiamine levels of hospitalised alcoholics before and after oral or parenteral vitamins. *Alcohol and Alcoholism*, **23**, 49–52.

Bell, D. S. (1965) Comparison of amphetamine psychosis and schizophrenia. *British Journal of Psychiatry*, **111**, 701–707.

Bergman, H. (1991) Cognitive impairment and alcohol abuse. *Current Opinion in Psychiatry*, **4**, 424–428.

Berlyne, N. (1972) Confabulation. *British Journal of Psychiatry*, **120**, 31–39.

Berrios, G. F. (1989) Non-cognitive symptoms and the diagnosis of dementia. Historical and clinical aspects. *British Journal of Psychiatry*, **154** (suppl. 4), 11–16.

Besson, J. A. O. (1990) Magnetic resonance imaging and its implications in neuro-psychiatry. *British Journal of Psychiatry*, **157** (suppl. 9), 25–37.

Bleuler, E. P. (1916) *Textbook of Psychiatry* (trans. A. A. Brill 1924; reprinted 1951), pp. 312–313. New York: Dover Publications.

Bohman, M., Cloninger, C. R., Von-Knorring, A. L., *et al* (1984) An adoption study of somatoform disorders. III. Cross-fostering analysis and genetic relationship to alcoholism and criminality. *Archives of General Psychiatry*, **41**, 872–878.

Brower, K. T., Blow, F. C. & Beresford, T. P. (1988) Forms of cocaine and psychiatric symptoms. *Lancet*, *i*, 50.

Brown, R. G. & Marsden, C. D. (1988) 'Subcortical dementia': the neuropsychological evidence. *Neuroscience*, **25**, 363–387.

Cala, L. A., Jones, B., Burns, P., *et al* (1983) Results of computerized tomography, psychometric testing and dietary studies in social drinkers, with emphasis on reversibility after abstinence. *Medical Journal of Australia*, **2**, 264–269.

Carney, M. W. P. & Bacelle, L. (1984) Psychosis after cannabis abuse. *British Medical Journal*, **288**, 1047.

Charness, M. E. & DeLaPaz, R. L. (1987) Mamillary body atrophy in Wernicke's encephalopathy: antemortem identification using magnetic resonance imaging. *Annals of Neurology*, **22**, 595–600.

Chaudry, H. R., Moss, H. B., Bashir, A., *et al* (1991) Cannabis psychosis following bhang. *British Journal of Addiction*, **86**, 1075–1081.

Chopra, G. S. & Smith, J. W. (1974) Psychotic reactions following cannabis use in East Indians. *Archives of General Psychiatry*, **30**, 24–27.

Cloninger, C. R. (1987) Neurogenetic adaptive mechanisms in alcoholism. *Science*, **236**, 410–416.

Connell, P. H. (1958) *Amphetamine Psychosis*. Maudsley Monograph No. 5. London: Oxford University Press.

Cutting, J. (1978*a*) A re-appraisal of alcoholic psychoses. *Psychological Medicine*, **8**, 285–295.

—— (1978*b*) Specific psychological deficits in alcoholism. *British Journal of Psychiatry*, **133**, 119–122.

Davidson, K. M. & Ritson, E. B. (1993) The relationship between alcohol dependence and depression. *Alcohol and Alcoholism*, **28**, 147–156.

De la Monte, S. M. (1988) Disproportionate atrophy of cerebral white matter in chronic alcoholics. *Archives of Neurology*, **45**, 990–992.

Edwards, J. G. (1982) The question of psychiatric morbidity. In *Report of the Expert Group on the Effects of Cannabis Use*. Advisory Council on the Misuse of Drugs. London: Home Office, 40–47.

Freed, E. X. (1978) Alcohol and mood: an updated review. *International Journal of the Addictions*, **13**, 172–200.

Gawin, F. H. (1988) Chronic neuropharmacology of cocaine: progress in pharmacotherapy. *Journal of Clinical Psychiatry*, **49** (suppl.), 11–16.

—— & Ellinwood, E. H. Jr. (1988) Cocaine and other stimulants: actions, abuse, and treatment. *New England Journal of Medicine*, **318**, 1173–1182.

George, G. T., Nutt, D. J., Dwyer, B. A., *et al* (1990) Alcoholism and panic disorder: is the comorbidity more than coincidence? *Acta Psychiatrica Scandinavica*, **81**, 97–107.

Ghodse, A. H. (1986) Cannabis psychosis. *British Journal of Addiction*, **81**, 473–478.

Glass, I. B. (1989*a*) Alcoholic hallucinosis: a psychiatric enigma–1. The development of an idea. *British Journal of Addiction*, **84**, 29–41.

—— (1989*b*) Alcoholic hallucinosis: a psychiatric enigma–2. Follow-up studies. *British Journal of Addiction*, **89**, 151–164.

Glatt, M. M. (1961) Drinking habits of English (middle class) alcoholics. *Acta Psychiatrica Scandinavica*, **37**, 88–113.

Golombok, S., Moodley, P. & Lader, M. (1988) Cognitive impairment in long-term benzodiazepine users. *Psychological Medicine*, **18**, 365-374.

Goldman, M. S., Williams, D. L. & Klisz, D. K. (1983) Reversibility of psychological functioning following alcohol abuse. Prolonged visuo-spatial dysfunction in older alcoholics. *Journal of Consulting and Clinical Psychology*, **51**, 370-378.

Grove, W. M., Eckert, E. D., Heston, L., *et al* (1990) Heritability of substance abuse and antisocial behaviour – a study of monozygotic twins reared apart. *Biological Psychiatry*, **27**, 1293-1304.

Guthrie, A. & Elliott, W. A. (1980) The nature and reversibility of cerebral impairment in alcoholism: treatment implications. *Quarterly Journal of Studies on Alcohol*, **38**, 1749-1760.

Hamm, J. E., Major, L. K. & Brown, G. L. (1979) The quantitative measurement of depression and anxiety in male alcoholics. *American Journal of Psychiatry*, **136**, 580-582.

Harper, C. G. (1988) Brain damage and alcohol abuse: where do we go from here? *British Journal of Addiction*, **83**, 613-615.

——, Kril, J. J. & Holloway, R. L. (1985) Brain shrinkage in chronic alcoholics: a pathological study. *British Medical Journal*, **290**, 501-504.

——, Giles, M. & Finlay-Jones, R. (1986) Clinical signs in the Wernicke-Korsakoff complex: a retrospective analysis of 131 cases diagnosed at necropsy. *Journal of Neurology, Neurosurgery, Necropsy and Psychiatry*, **49**, 341-345.

——, Kril, J. & Daly, J. (1987) Are we drinking our neurones away? *British Medical Journal*, **294**, 534-536.

—— & —— (1989) Patterns of neuronal loss in the cerebral cortex in chronic alcoholic patients. *Journal of the Neurological Sciences*, **92**, 81-89.

—— & —— (1990) Neuropathology of alcoholism. *Alcohol and Alcoholism*, **25**, 207-216.

Helzer, J. E., Canino, G. J., Yeh, E. K., *et al* (1990) Alcoholism: North America and Asia. *Archives of General Psychiatry*, **47**, 313-319.

Hunt, A. & Jones, R. T. (1980) Tolerance and disposition of tetrahydrocannabinol in man. *Journal of Pharmacology and Experimental Therapeutics*, **215**, 35-44.

Jacobson, R. R. (1988) Cerebral damage in alcohol dependence. *Current Opinion in Psychiatry*, **1**, 323-324.

——, Acker, C. & Lishman, W. A. (1990) Patterns of neuropsychological deficits in alcoholic Korsakoff's syndrome. *Psychological Medicine*, **20**, 321-334.

Janowsky, D. S. & Risch, C. (1979) Amphetamine psychosis and psychotic symptoms. *Psychopharmacology*, **65**, 73-77.

Jones, R. T., Benowitz, N. & Rackman, J. (1975) Clinical studies of cannabis tolerance and dependence. *Annals of the New York Academy of Sciences*, **282**, 221-239.

Kendler, K. S., Heath, A. C., Neale, M. C., *et al* (1993) Alcoholism and major depression in women: a twin study of the causes of comorbidity. *Archives of General Psychiatry*, **50**, 690-698.

King, M. B. (1989) Psychosocial status of 192 out-patients with HIV infection and AIDS. *British Journal of Psychiatry*, **154**, 237-242.

—— (1990) Psychological aspects of HIV infection and AIDS. What have we learned? *British Journal of Psychiatry*, **156**, 151-156.

Kleber, H. D. (1989) Treatment of drug dependence: what works. *International Review of Psychiatry*, **1**, 81-89.

Lader, M. & Morton, S. (1991) Benzodiazepine problems. *British Journal of Addiction*, **86**, 823–828.

Larsen, F. W. (1991) A 30-year follow-up study of a child psychiatric clientele. II. Psychiatric morbidity. *Acta Psychiatrica Scandinavica*, **84**, 65–71.

Lishman, W. A. (1981) Cerebral disorder in alcoholism: syndromes of impairment. *Brain*, **104**, 1–20.

—— (1990) Alcohol and the brain. *British Journal of Psychiatry*, **156**, 635–644.

McEntee, W. J. & Mair, R. G. (1990) The Korsakoff syndrome: a neurochemical perspective. *Trends in Neurosciences*, **13**, 340–344.

McGuire, P. & Fahy, T. (1991) Chronic paranoid psychosis after misuse of MDMA ('ecstasy'). *British Medical Journal*, **302**, 697.

Madden, J. S. (1984) *A Guide to Alcohol and Drug Dependence* (2nd edn), pp. 83–84. Bristol: Wright.

—— (1990) Effects of drugs of dependence. In *Substance Abuse and Dependence* (eds H. Ghodse & D. Maxwell), pp. 41–42. London: Macmillan.

Mayer-Gross, W., Slater, E. & Roth, M. (1954) *Clinical Psychiatry*, pp. 94–96. London: Cassell.

Mendelson, J. H. & Mello, N. K. (1979) One unanswered question about alcoholism. *British Journal of Addiction*, **74**, 11–14.

Menon, D. K., Sandford, R. N., Cassidy, M. J. D., *et al* (1991) Proton magnetic resonance spectroscopy in chronic renal failure. *Lancet*, *i*, 244–245.

Mullaney, J. A. & Trippett, C. J. (1979) Alcohol dependence and phobias: clinical description and relevance. *British Journal of Psychiatry*, **135**, 565–573.

Nakamura, M. M., Overall, J. E., Hollister, L. E., *et al* (1983) Factors affecting outcome of depressive symptoms in alcoholics. *Alcoholism: Clinical and Experimental Research*, **7**, 188–193.

Noordsy, D. L., Drake, R. E., Teague, G. B., *et al* (1991) Subjective experiences related to alcohol use among schizophrenics. *Journal of Nervous and Mental Disorders*, **179**, 410–414.

O'Carroll, R. E., Hayes, P. C., Ebmeier, K. P., *et al* (1991) Regional cerebral blood flow and cognitive functioning in patients with chronic liver disease. *Lancet*, **337**, 1250–1253.

O'Connell, R. A., Mayo, J. A., Flatow, L., *et al* (1991) Outcome of bipolar disorder on long-term treatment with lithium. *British Journal of Psychiatry*, **159**, 123–129.

O'Leary, M. R., Donovan, D. M., Chaney, E. F., *et al* (1979) Cognitive impairment and treatment outcome with alcoholics: preliminary findings. *Journal of Clinical Psychology*, **40**, 397–398.

O'Sullivan, K., Whillans, P., Daly, M., *et al* (1983) A comparison of alcoholics with and without coexisting affective disorder. *British Journal of Psychiatry*, **143**, 133–138.

Ostman, O. (1991) Child and adolescent psychiatric patients in adulthood. *Acta Psychiatrica Scandinavica*, **84**, 40–45.

Parker, E. S. & Noble, E. P. (1977) Alcohol consumption and cognitive function in social drinkers. *Journal of Studies on Alcohol*, **38**, 1224–1232.

Pettinati, H. M., Sogerman, A. A. & Maurer, H. M. (1982) Four year MMPI changes in abstinent and drinking alcoholics. *Alcoholism: Clinical and Experimental Research*, **6**, 481–494.

Peveler, R. & Fairburn, C. (1990) Eating disorders in women who abuse alcohol. *British Journal of Addiction*, **85**, 1633–1638.

Pietraszek, M. H., Urano, T., Sumioshi, K., *et al* (1991) Alcohol-induced depression: involvement of serotonin. *Alcohol and Alcoholism*, **26**, 155-159.

Price, J. (1985) The Wernicke-Korsakoff syndrome in Queensland, Australia: antecedents and prevention. *Alcohol and Alcoholism*, **20**, 233-242.

—— (1991) Substance abuse among the mentally ill. *Current Opinion in Psychiatry*, **4**, 419-423.

Regier, D. A., Farmer, M. E., Rae, D. S., *et al* (1990) Comorbidity of mental disorders with alcohol and other drug abuse: results from the Epidemiological Catchment Area (ECA) study. *Journal of the American Medical Association*, **264**, 2511-2518.

Ross, H. E., Glaser, F. B. & Germanson, T. (1988) The prevalence of psychiatric disorders in patients with alcohol and other drug problems. *Archives of General Psychiatry*, **45**, 1023-1031.

Sakol, M. S. & Power, K. G. (1988) The effects of long-term benzodiazepine treatment and graded withdrawal on psychometric performance. *Psychopharmacology*, **95**, 135-138.

Schneider, K. (1959) *Clinical Psychopathology* (trans. M. W. Hamilton). London: Grune & Stratton.

Schuckit, M. A. (1985) The clinical implications of primary diagnostic groups among alcoholics. *Archives of General Psychiatry*, **42**, 1043-1049.

—— (1986) Genetic and clinical implications of alcoholism and affective disorder. *American Journal of Psychiatry*, **143**, 140-147.

—— & Sweeney, S. (1987) Substance use and mental health problems among sons of alcoholics and controls. *Journal of Studies on Alcohol*, **14**, 139-158.

—— & Irwin, M. (1989) An analysis of the clinical relevance of Type 1 and Type 2 alcoholics. *British Journal of Addiction*, **84**, 869-876.

Shrestha, K., Rees, D. W., Rix, K. H. B., *et al* (1985) Sexual jealousy in alcoholics. *Acta Psychiatrica Scandinavica*, **72**, 283-290.

Stockwell, T. & Bolderston, H. (1987) Alcohol and phobias. *British Journal of Addiction*, **82**, 971-979.

Tamerin, J. S. & Mendelson, J. H. (1969) The psychodynamics of chronic inebriation; observations of alcoholics during the process of drinking in an experimental group setting. *American Journal of Psychiatry*, **125**, 886-889.

Thornicroft, G. (1990) Cannabis: is there epidemiological evidence for an association with psychosis? *British Journal of Psychiatry*, **157**, 25-33.

Treffert, D. A. (1978) Marijuana use in schizophrenia: a clear hazard. *American Journal of Psychiatry*, **135**, 1213-1215.

Tyndel, N. (1974) Psychiatric study of one thousand alcoholic patients. *Canadian Journal of Psychiatry*, **19**, 21-24.

Victor, M., Adams, R. D. & Collins, G. H. (1971) *The Wernicke-Korsakoff Syndrome*. Philadelphia: F. A. Davis.

——, —— & —— (1989) *The Wernicke-Korsakoff Syndrome and Related Neurological Disorders due to Alcoholism and Malnutrition* (2nd edn). Philadelphia: F. A. Davis.

Winokur, C., Rimmer, J. & Reich, T. (1971a) Alcoholism IV: is there more than one type of alcoholism? *British Journal of Psychiatry*, **118**, 525-531.

——, Cadoret, R., Durjab, J., *et al* (1971b) Depressive disease: a genetic study. *Archives of General Psychiatry*, **24**, 135-144.

World Health Organization (1992) The *Tenth Revision of the International Classification of Diseases and Related Health Problems (ICD-10)*. Geneva: WHO.

10 Medical aspects of drug and alcohol misuse

Timothy G. Dinan & Karen O'Flynn

Alcoholic liver disease ● Viral hepatitis ● Chronic pancreatitis ●
Neurological disorders ● Skin and skeletal complications ●
Alcohol and cardiovascular disease ● Alcohol and infection ●
Physical investigations in alcohol dependence ● HIV and
AIDS ● Substance misuse in pregnancy

Disorders of every bodily system have been associated with illicit drug use, and with alcohol misuse. The roles of genetic, nutritional and environmental factors still need elucidation for many of the conditions.

Neuropsychiatric complications are discussed in Chapter 9. This chapter aims to provide the clinician with a revision and update of some basic facts of physical medicine relevant to the psychiatry of substance misuse, giving space to the unfolding knowledge about human immune deficiency virus infection. Three areas sometimes exposed as gaps in the psychiatrist's knowledge are dealt with in slightly greater depth: liver diseases, pancreatitis, and substance misuse in pregnancy and childbirth.

Box 10.1   Non-neuropsychiatric alcohol-related disorders

Gastritis
Liver disorders
Pancreatitis
Cardiomyopathy: arrhythmias
Carcinoma: oropharynx, larynx, oesophagus, liver
Peripheral neuropathy
Cerebellar ataxia
Myopathy
Pseudo-Cushing's syndrome
Contributes to: osteoporosis, hypertension, stroke

Alcoholic liver disease

Aetiology

The peak incidence of alcoholic cirrhosis is between the ages of 40 and 55, although cases as young as 20–25 are seen. About 30% of patients attending alcohol treatment units in the UK will, however, have normal liver histology.

Drinking six units each day (three for women) for 10 years is sufficient to increase the risk of developing cirrhosis. It can occur over a shorter time with higher consumption. That women are more prone than men to the toxic effects of alcohol suggests a hormonal vulnerability. However, at a given dose per kg, women have a higher blood ethanol concentration than men, perhaps due to lower body water to weight ratio, or to a lower availability in the stomach lining of alcohol dehydrogenase.

Acetaldehyde produced by the breakdown of alcohol by alcohol dehydrogenase is implicated in cell damage. Genetic markers have been reported (see Chapter 6). An inherited variant of alcohol dehydrogenase appears to be associated with liver damage in excessive drinkers (Sherman *et al*, 1993).

A good diet does not prevent cirrhosis, while poor nutrition aggravates alcoholic liver damage. A further environmental factor is previous hepatitis virus infection. Some studies have found higher rates of markers of hepatitis B and C infection in alcoholics, although antibody assays for hepatitis C (HCV) infection may show false positive results in alcoholic hepatitis due to polyclonal hypergammaglobulinaemia, which reverses with abstinence.

Clinical and pathological features

There are four histological entities associated with alcohol abuse: fatty liver (fat droplets in hepatocytes) is reversible and benign; alcoholic hepatitis (degeneration of hepatocytes, inflammatory infiltration and 'Mallory's hyaline'), which can lead to liver failure with jaundice, hepatomegaly and severe coagulopathy; cirrhosis (widespread fibrosis connecting the portal triads and central veins and regenerative nodules leading to architectural disruption) is complicated by portal hypertension, ascites (which can be complicated by spontaneous bacterial peritonitis), hepatic encephalopathy or renal failure; finally, some patients with longstanding cirrhosis develop primary liver cancer. The stigmata of chronic liver disease are telangiectasia, palmar erythema, and hypogonadism and feminisation in men.

Clinical examination, blood tests and scanning cannot distinguish the stage of liver disorder. In fatty liver hepatic function is preserved, with modest elevation of serum transaminases and gamma GT. Alcoholic hepatitis is characterised by leucocytosis, elevated ALT and in severe cases by prolonged prothrombin time and renal failure. The most reliable indicators of poor

Table 10.1 Alcoholic liver disease

Type	Characteristic features
Fatty Liver	Fat droplets in parenchymal cells
Hepatitis	Degeneration and necrosis with neutrophilic infiltrates
Cirrhosis	Widespread fibrosis

hepatic function are a raised prothrombin time (which does not correct with vitamin K) and low serum albumin. Elevation of serum alpha fetoprotein concentration suggests primary liver cancer.

Abdominal ultrasound scanning is of little value but may be used to screen for hepatic cancer. Liver biopsy is done to confirm the diagnosis and stage of liver disease and to exclude other diseases – particularly haemachromatosis which usually presents in association with alcohol abuse and for which there is specific therapy.

When abnormal liver function tests improve with abstinence from alcohol, the diagnosis is obviously much clearer.

Prognosis

A majority of patients who abstain from alcohol following a diagnosis of alcoholic cirrhosis are alive at 5 years. The survival rate falls to about 50% at 5 years if alcohol consumption continues. Liver transplantation for alcoholic cirrhosis (occasionally with hepatoma) has been conducted with published series showing good outcome of the transplant, if the patients do not return to excessive drinking. Not all groups have insisted on a minimum of several months abstinence before transplantation. Selection, often with the assistance of psychiatrists, is usually based on acceptance of alcoholism by patient and family, commitment to abstinence and good social support (Lucey *et al*, 1992). (For a review of alcohol and liver damage see Sherman & Williams, 1994.)

Viral hepatitis

Hepatitis B virus is a DNA-containing virus belonging to the hepadna viruses. The DNA has been cloned and sequenced and a recombinant hepatitis B vaccine is available. It is estimated that there are about 280 million chronic hepatitis B carriers throughout the world. Especially high rates are seen in parts of Africa and Asia, where transmission is mainly at or soon after birth from mother to child (vertical transmission).

The majority of transmission in Western countries is either by sexual contact or the use of infected needles. Infection rates are about ten times higher in homosexual than in heterosexual populations. Infection levels among intravenous drug users are especially high.

The usual incubation period for hepatitis B varies from 8 to 24 weeks. Most patients with acute hepatitis B infection are completely asymptomatic although others develop a flu-like illness, with jaundice occurring in 10% of cases. About 5–10% of patients become chronic carriers of the virus after clinical acute hepatitis. Some patients present with or later develop hepatocellular carcinoma.

In the late incubation period titres of HB_S Ag rise. This marker tends to rise in parallel with serum alanine transferase (ALT). In the majority of cases HB$_S$ Ag is no longer detectable after 3 months. When it persists after 6 months it indicates the presence of a chronic carrier state and the likelihood of recovery at this stage is considerably reduced. HB$_E$ Ag indicates active viral replication and tends to disappear more rapidly than HB$_S$ Ag. Persistence of the HB$_E$ Ag, though less common than HB$_S$ Ag, indicates high infectivity. The majority of those patients who make a recovery from hepatitis B infection develop anti-HB$_S$ antibodies.

Individuals at high risk to hepatitis B infection should be given prophylactic vaccine. Apart from illicit drug users and homosexually active men and partners, those requiring haemodialysis or multiple blood transfusions as well as health care workers are at risk. Two types of vaccine are presently available, a chemically inactivated plasma derived vaccine and a recombinant yeast vaccine.

Delta hepatitis may be superimposed on hepatitis B. When this occurs it is characterised by enhanced clinical severity and the risk of chronic viral hepatitis is also considerably increased. The delta agent requires the presence of hepatitis B in order to replicate and attempts at eliminating the latter would also prove effective against the former.

A newly identified virus capable of causing chronic liver disease, hepatitis C, has been detected with a high seroprevalence among drug users – for example, in Glasgow, 65 %. Risk of sexual transmission appears very low, except perhaps among HIV patients. At present the scale of the infectious threat posed by these seropositive individuals is unknown.

Hepatic encephalopathy

Hepatic encephalopathy is a chronic organic condition with intermittent exacerbations. It is associated with impairment of consciousness which can vary from mild confusion to coma. Neurologically the condition is characterised by a flapping tremor which is demonstrated by asking the patient to outstretch the arms. Deterioration is associated with the development of both pyramidal and extrapyramidal signs. Wilson's disease in contrast is associated with choreoathetoid movements and is less prone to show dramatic fluctuation.

EEG changes are characteristic of hepatic encephalopathy. Slow waves become increasingly dominant as the condition progresses and later on classic triphasic waves are seen.

Treatment is complex and involves a rigid restriction of dietary protein, and sometimes the use of antibiotics to decrease ammonia formation in the gut. If the patient requires sedation, a benzodiazepine not requiring liver metabolism, such as oxazepam should be used. Overall, the prognosis depends on the extent of liver failure.

Chronic pancreatitis

This condition is defined as a chronic inflammatory disease of the pancreas characterised by irreversible morphological or functional changes in the pancreas, typically causing considerable pain. The prevalence of the condition varies from community to community and has undoubtedly been on the increase over the last quarter century with increases in alcohol consumption. Approximately four per 100,000 of the population are affected and there is a male to female ratio of 10:1.

Alcohol consumption is the main cause of chronic pancreatitis. It is estimated that alcohol is involved in the aetiology of up to 85% of cases. It is now generally accepted that the condition does not arise from repeated acute bouts of pancreatitis.

The principal presenting complaint in the majority of cases is recurring or chronic severe pain. Other features include weight loss, steatorrhoea, and diabetes mellitus. In late stages of the illness jaundice may occasionally result due to involvement of the common bile duct. Up to 50% of patients with chronic pancreatitis which is alcohol-induced, have chronic pain while the remainder have intermittent bouts. The pain is classically described as producing a 'jack-knife' posture as the patient assumes a stooped position. Classically nausea and vomiting begin several hours after the onset of abdominal pain and if persistent usually indicate the onset of ileus. Steatorrhoea occurs in around 30% of patients and the amount of fat in the stools frequently exceeds that found in other causes of steatorrhoea.

Box 10.2   Clinical features of chronic pancreatitis

'Jack-knife' pain
Nausea and vomiting
Weight loss
Steatorrhoea
Diabetes
Jaundice (in later stages)

The causes of the abdominal pain are obscure and are not related to duct abnormalities. Patients with completely normal ductal systems may have severe pain while patients with grossly abnormal pancreatic duct systems may be pain-free. Calcification of the pancreas is not the basis for the abdominal pain. The pain is probably related to pancreatic secretion, for as long as the pancreas is able to secrete in a normal way secretagogues such as alcohol may induce pain. In support of such a view is the fact that when exocrine secretion is dramatically reduced pain is usually an infrequent clinical problem. Prospective studies show that abdominal pain tends to decrease with time and this is probably due to increasing glandular atrophy.

When the triad of calcification, steatorrhoea and diabetes are present in a context of pancreatic calcification as viewed in abdominal films then a firm diagnosis of chronic pancreatitis can usually be made without further investigation. Serum amylase levels are usually unhelpful as some patients have an increase due to extra pancreatic sources while others have constantly normal serum amylase levels. Abnormal lipase levels may be more helpful. Stimulation meals to test exocrine pancreatic secretions are less commonly used than before. Ultrasound and CT scanning are the main diagnostic aids today. Endoscopic retrograde cholangio-pancreatography (ERCP) is important in assessing patients with persistent pain for surgical therapy.

The management of the condition involves the use of analgesics, oral pancreatic enzyme replacement and H_2 antagonists. Surgical procedures including pancreatic duct drainage or partial pancreatectomy are sometimes employed. Overall the prognosis is poor and seems to be worse in alcohol than in non-alcohol related chronic pancreatitis. When the alcoholic continues to drink the prognosis is especially poor. Smoking and the emergence of diabetes mellitus are also very unfavourable signs. Of special relevance to psychiatric practice is that suicide rates increase significantly with the emergence of chronic pancreatitis. This is probably related to the very severe pain. The long-term management of the patient with chronic pancreatitis is complex and requires adequate input from physician, general practitioner and psychiatrist alike.

Neurological disorders

Alcoholic cerebral atrophy, dementia and the Wernicke–Korsakoff syndrome are described in Chapter 9. The two other conditions which psychiatrists treating alcoholics see most commonly are peripheral neuropathy and cerebellar ataxia.

Peripheral neuropathy

This occurs in some 10% of very heavy drinkers, more frequently in Wernicke–Korsakoff syndrome. It is probably partly due to vitamin B1 deficiency.

A sensorimotor neuropathy, it begins as weakness with diminished reflexes, pain and numbness in the lower limbs. Walking downstairs may become particularly difficult as proprioception is lost. Foot drop may develop. Spread is proximal and symmetrical. A unilateral weakness and numbness in an upper limb will more likely be due to pressure, for example after an intoxicated patient has fallen asleep in an awkward position on the arm for 12 hours paralysing an ulnar nerve ('Saturday night palsy').

Histology in alcoholic neuropathy shows destruction of the myelin sheath and axon.

This neuropathy improves with abstinence and thiamine, but worsens even with vitamin therapy if the patient continues to drink. Recovery is slow, and may not be complete. In severe cases the patient may need a wheelchair.

Cerebellar atrophy

This presents as gait ataxia, and nystagmus is rarely seen. The gait is wide-based, and the patient may look drunk as he walks. CT scan shows atrophy, which can be present before clinical signs.

The vermis and anterior lobe are primarily affected, with the granule cell layer showing greatest destruction. Treatment is abstinence from alcohol, and vitamin supplements. Once established the syndrome is largely irreversible.

Skin and skeletal complications

Skin

Psoriasis, which affects 2% of the North American and UK population, has been shown in studies in Scandinavia, USA and UK to be worsened by heavy alcohol consumption. Among men, a heavy drinker has double the chance of developing psoriasis than a lighter drinker. The incidence of psoriasis is also increased in AIDS. Anxiety, although a known precipitant of psoriasis and also more common in alcoholics, seems not to be the cause of the alcohol factor. The link is independent of liver disease. Treatment of psoriasis in heavy drinkers often proves unsuccessful until consumption is reduced.

Alcohol may play a part in the development of discoid eczema: the coin-shaped patches of eczema occurring particularly on the shins of middle-aged men and typically resistant to all but super-potent topical steroids. Rosacea, the common facial eruption of small acneform pustules often with prominent telangiectasia, is exacerbated by drinking. (See Higgins & du Vivier, 1994.)

Skin infection is probably the commonest single physical illness in injecting drug users. Staphylococcal or streptococcal cellulitis may develop at an injection site, and may lead to thrombophlebitis or an abscess. Chronic herpes is seen in more debilitated users.

Bone

Avascular necrosis is a recognised complication of alcoholism. Affecting especially the femoral head, the condition presents as pain and stiffness later accompanied by X-ray changes denoting patchy osteoporosis (Moniz, 1994).

There is a link between osteoporosis and excessive drinking. This may present as back pain when the vertebral column is affected and crush fractures occur. However, in post-menopausal women, it is now believed that moderate alcohol consumption may delay development of osteoporosis.

Healed rib fractures (due to past falls) seen on routine chest X-ray have been shown to be a marker for alcoholism.

Alcohol and cardiovascular disease

Alcoholic cardiomyopathy is a well accepted diagnosis, and usually presents as cardiac failure. Heavy drinking also increases the risk of cardiac arrhythmias whether or not heart disease is present (Koskinen & Kupari, 1992). Unexplained sudden death has been shown to be commoner in heavy drinkers, and prolongation of the QT interval on the electrocardiograph, which predicts sudden death in the coming months, is a correlate of heavy drinking. Variant angina may occur some hours after drinking a large amount of alcohol. A dose of 10–15 units (100–150 ml ethanol) can be shown to produce ST elevation on ECG in such patients.

Heavy drinking is associated with raised blood pressure, both ischaemic and haemorrhagic strokes and poor outcome in patients admitted with subarachnoid haemorrhage. At hypertension clinics, it has been shown in controlled studies that brief counselling about alcohol consumption results in reduced alcohol intake and commensurate reductions in blood pressure (Maheswaran *et al*, 1992).

Postoperative complications are three times as frequent in heavy drinkers, and impaired cardiac muscle and physiological stress response has been implicated. Impairment to the haemostatic system, for example platelet function, probably contributes (Tonnesen *et al*, 1992).

Light regular drinking (1–3 units per day, i.e. 10–30 g ethanol) is associated with a decreased risk of myocardial infarction (Marmot & Brunner, 1991). The U-shaped curve of risk of heart disease in relation to alcohol consumption, in which abstainers have a higher risk than light drinkers, has been shown to hold true after excluding those who are abstaining because they are already ill. One current suggestion for the mechanism for this apparent protective effect of alcohol is that alcohol reduces platelet aggregation. Regular consumers of alcohol tend to have higher serum levels of high density lipoprotein (HDL) and this has also been suggested as the mediator of the protective effect. However, light drinking is also associated with a group of favourable risk factors in terms of social class, smoking, body weight, blood pressure and exercise. The consensus in public health circles at the time of writing is that the public should not be encouraged to increase their drinking to protect against heart disease (Kemm, 1993; see Chapter 5).

Alcohol and infection

Although alcohol use, especially in excess, is generally viewed as immuno-suppressive, it is not clear that the documented alcohol-elicited changes in immune function (e.g. reduced polymorphonuclear leucocyte function) are of clinical significance. There is an increased incidence of bacterial infections among alcoholics, but nutritional deficiencies, liver cirrhosis, life-style, and hygiene are implicated. It has been found, however, that in the healthy general population a non-smoker will have a degree of resistance to the common cold virus if he drinks at least one alcoholic drink a day. This effect is not seen in smokers (Cohen *et al*, 1993).

Physical investigations in alcohol dependence

Serum gamma glutamyl transferase (GGT) will be raised in 60–70% of patients referred to psychiatrists with alcohol problems, and mean cell volume (MCV, which is higher in those who drink every day than in binge drinkers) in some 30%. In these patients, the raised MCV unless associated with physical signs or symptoms not related to drinking, or with anaemia, need not be investigated further. As with elevated liver enzyme levels, monitoring to observe a fall with abstinence (and rise with relapse) is all that is necessary. The GGT begins to fall with a 'half-life' of about 2 weeks immediately drinking ceases unless another cause of elevation is present. MCV falls more slowly, commensurate with the half-life of the red blood cell.

The MCV elevation is not contributed to by folate deficiency except in a few nutritionally compromised patients. There is a weak positive correlation between smoking and MCV.

The initial rise in GGT is due to enzyme induction, as with anticonvulsants and some other drugs. Obesity, perhaps due to fatty liver, is associated with mild elevations in GGT.

A raised serum bilirubin should alert the psychiatrist to more serious liver disease. And if there has been melaena, haematemesis or if the patient reports bleeding gums, a prothrombin time should be checked as well as the platelet count, since gastrointestinal haemorrhage is a noted and partly avoidable cause of death in alcoholics.

Serum potassium is often somewhat low at the beginning of severe alcohol withdrawal. It usually returns to normal spontaneously, although some physicians give potassium supplements for 2–3 days. Serum zinc and magnesium levels may also be temporarily low, though generally serum levels are not requested and the need for replacement therapy is not established.

Psychiatrists working with problem drinkers seldom need to order liver scans or refer for liver biopsy. However, if liver enlargement and abnormal liver function tests are not beginning to resolve within the first two weeks of abstinence, then a liver scan, a request for alpha-foetoprotein level (raised in hepatoma) or referral to a hepatologist are indicated.

Nausea, vomiting, abdominal pain and/or diarrhoea, all common in heavy drinkers and during alcohol withdrawal, should be investigated if the symptom persists into the second week of abstinence.

Carbohydrate deficient transferrin – CDT

Transferrin is a glycoprotein synthesised in the liver. Regular heavy drinking increases the proportion of transferrin in serum, which is deficient in one of its carbohydrate chains (Stibler, 1991). Most liver disorders, unless alcohol-related, do not show an excess of the carbohydrate-deficient form (CDT) (primary biliary cirrhosis is a rare exception). CDT levels return to normal within some 3 weeks after abstinence. Its specificity as a marker of heavy drinking exceeds that of GGT. It is seen as an expensive test (see Chapter 7).

HIV and AIDS

In mid-1981 reports began to appear in America of *Pneumocystis carinii* pneumonia (PCP) and Kaposi's sarcoma in young males whom it transpired were both homosexual and immunocompromised. The condition was dubbed acquired immunodeficiency syndrome (AIDS) and various theories were put forward as to its possible cause. By 1 May 1991, 359 271 cases of AIDS had been reported to the World Health Organization (WHO). Delays in reporting and under-reporting generally meant that these figures are underestimates; from 307 000 reported cases in December 1990 the true figure was estimated to be in the order of 1.3 million. The definition of AIDS announced by the Centers for Disease Control (CDC) in August 1991 includes anyone with human immunodeficiency virus (HIV) infection and a CD4 lymphocyte count of less than 200. It is thought that this definition will double the number of people with AIDS in the United States alone, where to date 120 000 have died from AIDS. How many individuals world-wide carry HIV is not known but it is estimated that there are at least 10 to 20 times more people infected with HIV at any one time than have AIDS.

Epidemiology

According to the World Health Organization (1991) it is likely that intravenous (i.v.) drug users will soon comprise the largest group of AIDS cases in Europe. The first 'hard' evidence for HIV infection among injecting drug users came from New York where three paediatric cases of AIDS were diagnosed in children born in 1977. All three were children of female i.v. drug users and had no other risk factors for AIDS. The first five cases in heterosexual adult injecting users occurred in 1980. Since then the number of cases in this population has increased rapidly with figures soaring world-wide. In New York alone there are approximately 100 000 injecting drug users who have already been exposed to the virus and an estimated 100 000 at high risk of becoming exposed. In Italy the 1981 figures showed a HIV positive rate of 1% among the i.v. drug using population; this figure was an alarming 76% 4 years later. The highest incidence in the UK was in Edinburgh, where in 1985 54% of injecting users were HIV positive. This rate has fallen to 20.4% (Bath *et al*, 1993).

Human immunodeficiency virus infection

HIV belongs to the lentivirus or slow virus class of retroviruses i.e. it can cause disease some years after infection. The virus has so far been isolated from semen, cervical secretions, cell free plasma, CSF, tears, saliva, urine and breast milk. As concentrations of the virus vary, HIV is not transmitted through all these secretions. Particularly infectious are semen, blood and possibly cervical secretions. The virus integrates into the host cell as a DNA provirus made by reverse transcriptase and persists in the host's DNA for the life of the cell. There may then be long periods of latency when although the viral DNA has been integrated it is not being transcribed into producing viral proteins. Certain factors can activate replication and lead to cell death and clinical effect. The integration of the HIV genome into the host cell is obviously a large obstacle to the development of any antiviral agent that may eradicate infection.

The most striking effects of HIV are on T cell mediated immunity. Early infection sees a rise in the number of CD8 cells after which lymphocyte numbers may be normal. At this stage however there may be a decreased response to a previously encountered antigen, possibly due to poor production of the cytokine, interleukin 2. Following a healthy period, a hallmark of disease progression is a fall in the CD 4 helper/inducer lymphocyte count. With full AIDS, the number of cytotoxic/suppressor CD8 lymphocytes also decreases.

Tests for detecting HIV infection first became available in 1985. Those most widely used are based on detecting antibody to HIV. Anti-HIV appears 3 weeks to 3 months after exposure to the virus although occasionally the interval may be longer. Once present the antibody is almost invariably detectable despite the effects of the virus on immune function and antibody response. It is general policy that a positive test result warrants repetition of the test. Further tests are being developed which concentrate on identifying the actual virus rather than the antibody. At present these tests are not very reliable.

The median time to development of AIDS is 10 years, that is, 50% will have the syndrome by that point. However, the course is extremely variable and symptoms of acute infection may appear 2-6 weeks after exposure to the virus.

The disease is staged using the CDC classification system (Table 10.2). The staging system is not intended to convey either prognosis or severity.

Factors influencing the rate of disease progression are not fully understood. Age and HLA type are important. Serial measurements of CD4 lymphocytes showing a fall below 200 predicts likelihood of developing AIDS. Herpes virus or cytomegalovirus (CMV) infection may increase the rate of progression by acting as cofactors stimulating HIV replication.

Table 10.2   CDC classification system for staging HIV infection

Stage I	Acute infection e.g. transient flu-like illness. May be unnoticed
Stage II	Period of latent infection
Stage III	Persistent lymphadenopathy at two or more extrainguinal sites
Stage IV	A: Constitutional symptoms e.g. diarrhoea, weight loss
	B: HIV-related dementia
	C1: Opportunistic infections as defined for AIDS
	C2: Other infections
	D: Cancers indicative of a defect in cell mediated immunity
	E: Disease not listed in other categories but which could be attributable to or complicated by HIV infection

Symptom overlap in drug users

In the medical care of drug users it must be recognised, but not exaggerated, that some symptoms of HIV infection resemble those connected with drug use. For example injection of foreign materials can lead to lymphadenopathy. However, good clinical practice can usually make the distinction, and care should be taken not to cause anxiety in the drug user or nursing staff by misdiagnosing HIV.

Symptoms of mild opiate withdrawal may resemble the lethargy, fatigue and excessive sweating of HIV infection. Pupillary dilatation and agitation will help diagnosis of a withdrawal state.

Involvement of the lung is very common in AIDS and accounts for almost half of the initial presentations. *Pneumocystis carinii* pneumonia (PCP) occurs in AIDS, although rarely in drug users with AIDS. Other respiratory infections commonly seen are cytomegaloviral (CMV) pneumonia, tuberculosis (TB) and conventional bacterial pneumonia. Non-infectious complications which can affect the lungs are Kaposi's sarcoma (rare in drug users) and interstitial lymphoid pneumonia. The shortness of breath, cough, and cyanosis found with PCP and TB may all be mimicked by drug-related bacterial pneumonia, endocarditis and chronic bronchitis.

Fever associated with HIV related PCP and TB needs to be distinguished from that due to injection abscesses, septicaemia, pneumonia and endocarditis.

Chronic herpes infection is not uncommon in the drug using population where poor diet is a factor and it is closely mimicked by the nasal ulceration seen in the cocaine abuser. Oral hairy leukoplakia and oral candidiasis in the HIV population give rise to the complaint of a sore mouth seen due to the poor diet in many drug users. Diarrhoea is a common symptom in patients with chronic HIV infection with and without other manifestations of AIDS and often no cause can be found. This is a particularly important symptom in regard to the drug using population as non-specific diarrhoea persisting for over one month would imply stage IV A infection. Diarrhoea however is a feature of opiate withdrawal. HIV-related causes of diarrhoea include cryptosporidium, herpes, CMV and mycobacterial infections as well as neoplasias, although tumour involvement of the bowel with Kaposi's is extremely uncommon in the heterosexual drug using population. Weight loss may occur as part of a general wasting syndrome and accompanies most CDC IV A infections. It is also a consequence of the anorexic effect of amphetamines and cocaine. Atypical mycobacterial and cryptococcus infection are implicated in hepatitis in AIDS patients.

Although only around 10% of patients with AIDS present because of neurological problems, up to 75% have evidence of disease of the central nervous system at necropsy. Opportunistic infections such as cerebral toxoplasmosis, CMV and cryptococcus meningitis can give rise to confusion and fits or episodic loss of consciousness. Drug-related causes of these latter symptoms include drug overdose and withdrawal (alcohol, barbiturates and benzodiazepines) as well as cocaine-induced fits. Paralysis may be a symptom of CDC III/IVa infection or may be the result of nerve damage from injection.

Abscesses are obviously common in the immunocompromised population but may also be due to infected injection material or leakage from the injection site; particularly when injecting barbiturates and crushed tablets. The small blood spots or bruises of thrombocytopenia are quite similar to the small spots of septicaemia or endocarditis, or the bruising from leakage at an injection site or arterial injection. Formication associated with cocaine is not to be confused with the itch caused by the seborrhoeic dermatitis or various allergies encountered in the HIV population (Brettle *et al*, 1990).

AIDS/HIV and working with drug users

Studies in the United States and the UK indicate that over 60% of heterosexually acquired HIV is related to injection drug use. Expensive drug habits may lead to prostitution, with the further risk of heterosexual spread.

There are some issues in dealing with AIDS/HIV specific to drug users. The illegality of injectable substances together with the punitive attitude of society deter this group from contacting health services. Even when contact has been made the default rate is high and contact tends to be resumed only at times of crisis.

Injecting drug users should be counselled on the safe use of drugs and if injecting continues they should be offered clean equipment (see Chapter 3). The pattern of drug use varies not only geographically but by the individual according to the supply and substance available. Inhalation or swallowing of drugs is obviously preferable for health reasons to injection. Continued injecting has been reported by some, but not all, to increase the rate of decline of the T4 lymphocytes. Injection of impure substances stimulates the immune system and thereby increases HIV multiplication. If complete withdrawal from opiates is not possible then an oral non-injectable opiate substitute, methadone or dihydrocodeine, is recommended. When the patient cannot budget several day's supply, this should be issued daily. As yet there is no reliable information of the effects of cannabis or cocaine on HIV.

Where injection is continuing the availability of clean equipment assumes paramount importance. The drug using community is itself aware of this fact. In 1984, a group of users in Amsterdam calling themselves 'junkiebond' started a needle and syringe exchange programme which later received health authority finances. Surveys of needle and syringe exchanges in the UK showed that 54% had less than 2 miles to travel to the nearest centre, 33% had not received treatment before and 66% were not in current treatment. Results showed that sharing of needles was reduced. However, the centres did not attract young or female users and only 53% attended more than twice. Despite the shortcomings of these programmes, the situation is preferable to that of no state aid which leaves the injecting community open to exploitation as in New York where clean 'kits' are sold on the black market at exorbitant prices. Exchange programmes also serve to put drug users in contact with methadone substitution programmes, a further example of harm reduction policies.

Further information on counselling and self-help organisations is to be found in Chapter 11.

Treatment

Once diagnosed HIV positive, treatment of this population is extremely difficult. The issues of compliance and default rates compound the difficulties found with other HIV positive populations. Obviously there is not at present an effective treatment for HIV/AIDS although zidovudine has been shown to increase the survival time and decrease the morbidity of AIDS patients. This drug is given 6–12 hourly to those with symptoms or a CD4 lymphocyte count of less than 200. However there are problems with it that are especially relevant to the drug user. As about 70% of the drug is metabolised via liver glucuronidation, there are likely to be several drug interactions. A higher dose is required if opiates are being taken. There is no evidence of reaction with benzodiazepines, cannabis or alcohol. Cocaine users are rare in study groups and so the effects of this are as yet unknown. Attendance is as always an issue in those currently using drugs. In these instances a 12 hourly dose is acceptable. If i.v. administration is needed, a central line may be required as venous access is likely to be difficult. Compliance can be monitored as adequate amounts of the drug cause a raised MCV.

As a drug acting on DNA, its use in pregnancy causes concern, though a survey by Sparling *et al* (1992) did not find evidence of harm.

Its use in asymptomatic HIV positive patients is controversial. Only some studies have found that it delays onset of AIDS, and its cost in terms of unwanted effects and finance is thought by many not to justify its use (Oddone *et al*, 1993).

The psychiatrist has a role in counselling HIV patients and their relatives. A detailed account of this is outside the scope of this text but it is essential to stress that testing HIV positive does not in itself imply illness. Due to the long incubation period of the virus, the patient may remain healthy for some time. It is again important to emphasise that it is possible to live with a HIV positive person without becoming infected. These two points are particularly important when dealing with relatives of HIV patients. Guidelines on safe sex are necessary and discussions should where possible include the partner. Supportive counselling is also often sought when the patient becomes ill.

When a HIV positive patient is admitted to the ward, basic precautions against infection of staff or patients should be taken. While extreme caution is required when dealing with blood or other body fluids, usual contact made in day-to-day living e.g. cups etc., does not transmit the virus. Laboratory specimens should be clearly labelled as HIV positive and give only the patient's hospital number to preserve confidentiality.

The problem of HIV infection has had a massive impact on society world-wide and the consequences are only becoming apparent. Apart from the health care, preventative measures and education required to deal with HIV in the general population, the extent of the epidemic will largely depend on the ability to revise both thinking and policies in relation to drug users.

Substance misuse in pregnancy

Although suspected since earliest times, it is only since the descriptions of the neonatal abstinence and foetal alcohol syndromes in the early 1970s that the teratogenic effects of recreational drugs have come to the fore. In the last 10 to 15 years the use of alcohol as well as other, less socially acceptable drugs by women of childbearing age has greatly increased and so therefore has the problem of drug use in pregnancy. Whatever the effects drug misuse has upon the foetus, its effects are likely to make themselves felt upon the developing child in a variety of ways, not least through the unstable home environment and possible neglect arising from maternal addiction.

For any given drug there is a threshold level at which foetal malformations will occur. Apart from the genetic susceptibility of the foetus to the effects of the drug, the route of administration and pharmacokinetics of the drug are important in determining that threshold level. Drugs taken orally may undergo extensive first pass metabolism in the liver. The drug may be metabolised to an ionised form which will enhance urinary excretion and decrease the ability to cross the placenta, or to a unionised form which increases the ability to cross. Intravenous, intramuscular or inhalational administration means that the drug does not undergo first pass metabolism and may cross the placenta directly from the site of administration. All drugs can cross the placenta to some extent, particularly if taken in large quantities over a long period of time. However other factors such as lipid solubility, extent of protein binding and molecular weight play an important role in determining the extent to which they do so. Although the placenta can metabolise drugs, the low levels of glucuronyl transferases which it contains result in a failure to terminate the biological effect of drugs. Drugs taken during the first 8 to 12 weeks of pregnancy have the most severe effects on embryonic development.

Alcohol

The foetal alcohol syndrome (FAS) is a term coined by Jones *et al* (1973) who reported that "eight unrelated children of three different ethnic groups, all born to mothers who were chronic alcoholics, have a similar pattern of craniofacial, limb and cardiovascular defects associated with prenatal-onset growth deficiency and developmental delay". This syndrome is now well established and its diagnosis is based on the presence of (1) prenatal and/or postnatal growth retardation, (2) central nervous system involvement which often includes developmental delays and intellectual impairment and (3) a characteristic facies which at its most severe includes microcephaly, thin upper lip, small palpebral fissures, flat maxillary area and poorly developed philtrum. Virtually all infants with FAS have very low birthweights for gestational age and in contrast to opiate exposed infants who are small for gestational age, those with FAS do not exhibit catch up growth. The facial features are due to midfacial hypoplasia. The small palpebral fissures are often due to microophthalmia. Other malformations such as strabismus, ptosis and malformations of the external ear have also been noted. Mild to moderate mental retardation is reported frequently with average IQ scores in the mid 60s, although the range is quite wide. (Reviewed in Clarren & Smith, 1978.) Lesser degrees of abnormality are also reported in offspring of alcoholic mothers. In the absence of facial dysmorphism, hyperactivity, sleep disturbance, abnormal language development and poor motor skills may be observed. These children are thought to display foetal alcohol effects (FAE) although genetic and social factors inevitably contribute.

As FAS is not seen in all offspring of chronic alcoholic mothers and occasionally occurs in infants of moderate drinkers, the aetiology of the syndrome is clearly not a simple alcohol dose–response relationship. Twin studies have shown the prime importance of differences in foetal susceptibility to the dysmorphogenic effects of alcohol in the expression of FAS. The issue of what amount of alcohol is 'safe' in pregnancy has long been debated. There is some evidence to suggest that 'light' drinking does not harm the foetus (Knupfer, 1991). Definitions of light drinking vary but lie somewhere in the order of no more than 4 units of alcohol not more often than three times a month.

Perinatal addiction

There are two important aspects of perinatal addiction, obstetric and neonatal. The long-standing problem of opiate and heroin addiction has recently been compounded by the issue of polydrug abuse. The psychiatrist must give time to take a good drug history, but it is impossible to know the concentration of active ingredient present in street drugs, what adulterants have been used and what effects they are likely to have on mother or child. Pregnant addicts generally receive poor antenatal care and their lifestyle renders them susceptible to a variety of medical complications such as anaemia, poor dental hygiene and hepatitis. Obstetric complications such as chorioamnionitis, pre-eclampsia and/or eclampsia may be related to poor prenatal care. Different qualities of drugs ingested along with fluxes in substance availability lead to periods of intermittent narcotic withdrawal. Between 18 and 50% of heroin addicts experience premature rupture of membranes – uterine irritability associated with periods of withdrawal is thought to be a possible factor. It is generally thought that when the mother is experiencing withdrawal phenomena the foetus is also experiencing some symptoms. The placenta of heroin-exposed infants often shows meconium stained histiocytes, indicative of episodes of foetal distress. First trimester abortion, abruptio placentae, intrauterine death and abnormal presentations are all more common in substance abusers than in the general population although the reasons remain largely unclear.

Prenatal care of the pregnant addict is difficult and there are several possible approaches. Allowing the addiction pattern to remain unaltered is obviously associated with higher risks of maternal and foetal complications and so is not recommended. Acute withdrawal is more stressful on the foetus than on the mother leading to raised adrenaline and noradrenaline levels in the amniotic fluid. Some clinics advocate slow detoxification. However, this may also be deleterious to the foetus and is not generally effective unless the social and psychological aspects of addiction are considered as well. Since the surge of enthusiasm that followed the reports of clinical trials of methadone in pregnant addicts in 1969, caution has been exercised. The benefits of methadone substitution lie in the avoidance of cyclic craving which is damaging to the foetus, elimination of the possible effects of adulterants found in street drugs and decreased maternal complications. Low dose methadone maintenance may lessen the severity of neonatal withdrawal. The dose of methadone in pregnancy is a difficult issue. Initial, low dose, methadone maintenance programmes were successful in that the more consistent medical and nutritional care resulted in improved pregnancy outcome. However the high doses of methadone used in order to produce a 'methadone blockade' led to a longer and more severe withdrawal period for the neonate. Thus although the dose of methadone should be kept as low as possible, it must at the same time be high enough to preclude abuse of other drugs.

The second aspect of perinatal addiction is neonatal withdrawal. Finnegan *et al* (1975) described the neonatal abstinence syndrome, the signs of which mimicked aspects of an adult withdrawing from narcotics. The syndrome includes a high-pitched cry, tremors, sweats, rapid respirations, sleeplessness, convulsions, gastrointestinal upset, lacrimation and excoriation of the extremities. Symptoms of withdrawal are usually present at birth but may not become evident for 3 or 4 days. With some non-opiate drugs such as benzodiazepines, onset of withdrawal may be as late as 10 to 14 days after birth. Neurological effects due to intrauterine opiate exposure have been reported with an abnormal Moro reaction at 7 to 8 months of age.

Withdrawal from non-opiate substances does not produce a syndrome of the same severity as that induced by narcotic withdrawal. Abstinence syndromes have been described in infants who have been exposed to phenobarbitone, diazepam and chlordiazepoxide *in utero*. These infants usually exhibit poor feeding, crying, restlessness and neurological impairment.

Therapy for neonatal withdrawal should as far as possible be non-pharmacological in order to keep hospitalisation to a minimum. Conservative measures such as using a pacifier and giving frequent small feeds are beneficial. Excessive weight loss, fever unrelated to infection or seizures warrant the use of pharmacotherapy. Drugs used for neonates withdrawing from narcotics are chlorpromazine, paregoric (anhydrous morphine 0.4 mg/ml), diazepam and phenobarbitone. There is little research on treatment of withdrawal from non-opiate drugs.

Follow-up of these infants should be at weekly intervals until there is a definite improvement and monthly examinations until six months of age are recommended, and at increasing intervals thereafter. Some of these children may be cognitively impaired. Problems specific to infants of narcotic abusing mothers are decreased growth (usually catch up by 12 months), poor development (comparable to that of controls by two years), increased risk of sudden infant death syndrome (particularly in children of cocaine using women) and high risk of child abuse.

Cannabinoids

One of the first properties claimed for marijuana in European medicine was the ability to increase uterine contractions during labour and thereby hasten the birth process. This property has been proven in several studies, where marijuana users showed an increased incidence of precipitate labour as compared to controls. An inverse dose–response relationship between marijuana usage and gestational age has also been reported with no difference in the infant's weight when compared to infants of a similar gestational age born to non-users.

Study of the effects of marijuana in pregnancy is greatly hindered by the correlation between marijuana use and alcohol misuse. Thus there have been reports of correlation between infants with FAS features and prenatal exposure to marijuana which are difficult to substantiate. There do however seem to be some minor physical anomalies resulting from heavy maternal use in the form of an unusually wide separation of the eyes. Primate work has shown an association between marijuana exposure and visual functioning. In humans, a decreased response to a light shone directly into the eyes has been reported in 46% of infants of marijuana using mothers and it has been suggested

Referral from:

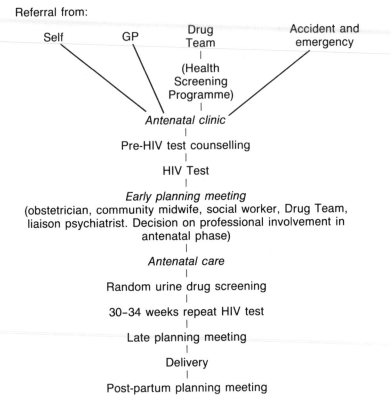

Fig. 10.1 Providing services to the pregnant drug misuser.

that maturation of the visual system is delayed as a result of drug exposure (Greenland *et al*, 1983).

Although increased tremors and startles are evident in neonates prenatally exposed to marijuana, there is no actual withdrawal syndrome and these infants are readily consoled. There does not seem to be any neurological or cognitive deficit in these children at two years of age although the issue is not yet clear. Much work remains to be done on this widely used substance and its effects in pregnancy.

Providing a service to the pregnant drug addict

Because of the suspicion with which many drug users regard authority figures, it is easy for the pregnant drug user to slip through the net of regular antenatal care. It is important that in the network there is a coordinating health worker, perhaps a drug dependence team member, who with a non-censorious attitude can bridge the mother's defensiveness and hostility and convince her that the services have one objective, namely the well being of her and her baby.

Early in the pregnancy a meeting should be convened of the GP, an antenatal team worker, the social worker, the community midwife and a member of the drug dependence team. Counselling about the importance of having an early HIV test may be indicated. A positive test might lead to the need for counselling regarding continuation of the pregnancy. Further meetings should be convened near to and after delivery and include the paediatrician, to discuss the social as well as medical needs of the mother and baby (Riley, 1987) (Fig. 10.1).

References

Bath, G. E., Burns, S., Davies, A. G., *et al* (1993) Injecting drug users in Edinburgh. *British Medical Journal*, **306**, 1414.

Brettle, R., Farrell, M. & Strang, J. (1990) Clinical features in drug takers. In *Aids and Drug Misuse* (eds J. Strang & G. V. Stimson), pp. 38–53. London: Routledge.

Clarren, S. K. & Smith, D. W. (1978) The foetal alcohol syndrome. *New England Journal of Medicine*, **298**, 1063–1067.

Cohen, S., Tyrrell, D. A. J., Russell, M. A. H., *et al* (1993) Smoking, alcohol consumption, and susceptibility to the common cold. *American Journal of Public Health*, **83**, 1277–1283.

Finnegan, L. P., Connaughton, J. F., Kron, J., *et al* (1975) Neonatal abstinence syndrome: assessment and management. In *Perinatal Addiction* (ed. R. W. Harbison), pp. 141–158. New York: Spectrum.

Greenland, S., Staish, K., Brown, N., *et al* (1983) Effects of marijuana on human pregnancy, labour and delivery. *Neurobehavioural Toxicology and Teratology*, **4**, 447–450.

Higgins, E. M. & du Vivier, A. W. P. (1994) Cutaneous disease and alcohol misuse. *British Medical Bulletin*, **50**, 85–98.

Kemm, J. (1993) Alcohol and heart disease: implications of the U-shaped curve. *British Medical Journal*, **307**, 1373–1374.

Jones, K. L., Smith, D. W., Ulleland, C. N., *et al* (1973) Pattern of malformation in offspring of chronic alcoholic mothers. *Lancet*, *i*, 1267–1301.

Knupfer, G. (1991) Abstaining for foetal health: the fiction that even light drinking is dangerous. *British Journal of Addiction*, **86**, 1063–1074.

Koskinen, P. & Kupari, M. (1992) Alcohol and cardiac arrythmias. *British Medical Journal*, **304**, 1394–1395.

Lucey, M. R., Merion, R. M. & Henley, K. S. (1992) Selection for and outcome of liver transplantation in alcoholic liver disease. *Gastroenterology*, **102**, 1736–1741.

Maheswaran, R., Beevers, B. & Beevers, D. G. (1992) Effectiveness of advice to reduce alcohol consumption in hypertensive patients. *Hypertension*, **19**, 79–84.

Marmot, M. & Brunner, E. (1991) Alcohol and cardiovascular disease: the status of the U-shaped curve. *British Medical Journal*, **303**, 565–568.

Moniz, C. (1994) Alcohol and bone. *British Medical Bulletin*, **50**, 67–75.

Oddone, E. Z., Cowper, P., Hamilton, J. D., *et al* (1993) Cost effectiveness analysis of early zidovudine treatment of HIV infected patients. *British Medical Journal*, **307**, 1322–1325.

Riley, D. (1987) The management of the pregnant drug addict. *Psychiatric Bulletin*, **11**, 362-365.

Sherman, D. I. N. & Williams, R. (1994) Liver damage: mechanisms and management. *British Medical Bulletin*, **50**, 122-126.

—— , Ward, R. J., Warren-Perry, M., *et al* (1993) Association of restriction fragment length polymorphism in alcoholic dehydrogenase 2 gene with alcohol induced liver disease. *British Medical Journal*, **307**, 1388-1390.

Sparling, R. S., Stratton, P., O'Sullivan, M. J., *et al* (1992) A survey of zidovudine use in pregnant women with human immuno-deficiency virus infection. *New England Journal of Medicine*, **326**, 857-861.

Stibler, H. (1991) Carbohydrate-deficient transferrin in serum: a new marker of potentially harmful alcohol consumption reviewed. *Clinical Chemistry*, **37**, 2029-2037.

Tonnesen, H., Petersen, K. R., Hojgaard, L., *et al* (1992) Postoperative morbidity among symptom-free alcohol misusers. *Lancet*, **304**, 334-337.

World Health Organization Statistics (1991) *AIDS*, **5**, 785-790.

11 Organising treatment services for drug and alcohol misusers

Sujata Unnithan, Bruce Ritson & John Strang

Specific issues for substance misuse services ● From estimating prevalence to estimating need ● Aims of care ● Alcohol misusers ● Drug misusers ● Future developments

---

Specific issues for substance misuse services

Separate or together, the relationship between drug and alcohol services varies greatly from one town to the next. Their organisation also varies, with service development and delivery being entirely separate in one district, while in the neighbouring district planning and delivery are fully integrated. The decision to develop drug and alcohol services as separate or together is usually driven by opportunity or by pragmatism.

There are certainly common issues across the substance misuse spectrum. The people being served are often disadvantaged, stigmatised, and frequently poor consumers of health care – to the aggravation of their own disadvantage. They do, however, make disproportional demands on health services. Additionally general practitioners and other generic care providers are often reluctant to become involved in providing care to this needy population, and hold prejudiced views about the group, so that only the most extreme or stereotypical case is identified. It is this very response from generic care providers (such as the general psychiatrist and general practitioner) which is all important: for every specialist doctor in addiction there are more than 10 general psychiatrists and more than 100 general practitioners in the UK. It is with the numerous patients who are not 'clear cases' (i.e. where the extent of pathology is, as yet, much less) that the greatest benefits are to be achieved in reducing overall harm (Fig. 11.1; see Chapter 5).

Why should the general psychiatrist and general practitioner be reluctant to provide care to this group? Apart from obvious considerations of fatigue with the existing clinical caseload and the burden of additional responsibility, research has shown that there are three particular areas of anxiety or uncertainty in practitioners:

(1) role adequacy (having the necessary information and skills in order to identify and respond appropriately)
(2) role legitimacy (the extent to which management of such problems is felt to fall within their responsibilities)
(3) role support (the confidence in the existence and adequacy of help and advice when it might be needed).

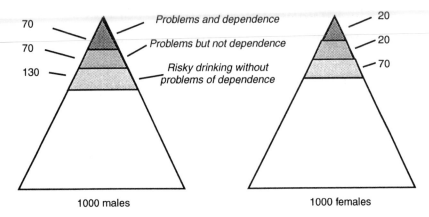

Fig. 11.1 Numbers of alcohol misusers in a typical general practice of 2000 patients.

As a result of these three anxieties, many practitioners experience 'role insecurity' with regard to working with the problem drinker or drug misuser.

Many of those who sustain harm from their drug or alcohol use will not be in contact with any service at all. Especially if drug use is illegal, socially proscribed or stigmatised (as with alcohol misuse in women for example) the population in need of help will remain partly hidden. Any consideration of the needs of the community must extend into these hidden populations where the profile of needs and the prevalence of comorbidities may differ substantially from those seen in the more visible parts of the drug and alcohol using population. Twenty years ago a survey in south London revealed that, of established problem drinkers, less than 20% were in contact with any treatment (Edwards *et al*, 1973).

From estimating prevalence to estimating need

As Rush (1990) observes, the main algorithm used to plan services has been 'demand based'; plans for future services have been based on past utilisations. Therefore, previous discrepancies in the services have a tendency to be repeated. In contrast, the 'system based' model projects what 'should be' provided, rather than repeating existing patterns, and thus can include consideration of the latest research data.

Whichever model is used, three basic questions need to be addressed for planning both alcohol and drug services: the conditions amenable to treatment, the treatment services existing and the predicted volume of service required. The first of these can be seen as an essential to any estimate of need. Presentation of drug and alcohol misusers to treatment may be via many portals of entry. As with a condition such as diabetes, the drug or alcohol misuser may present via a variety of sub-categories. Within the drug using population, the problem drug taker may present as: the dependent user, the intoxicated user, the user in withdrawal, the drug user with psychiatric or physical comorbidity and the drug user at an early stage in his drug using career (see Chapter 3). Other special sub-groups exist, e.g. the pregnant alcohol or drug misuser, those presenting via the criminal justice system and the homeless drug or alcohol misuser. In addition, slightly different presentations may exist in different ethnic groups.

The lack of uniformity of services in each region or district may be a result of the geographical distribution of drug misuse, or a reflection of entrepreneurial interest of key service developers. Central funding initiatives have distributed funds through the Regional Health Authorities and District Health Authorities but the majority of expansion has occurred at the district level.

Aims of care

Services should be locally accessible and approachable. Drug users must find that treatment at any drug treatment service will be confidential, despite the overlap with antenatal care or sexually transmitted disease clinics. The aims of treatment as outlined by the Advisory Council on Misuse of Drugs (1982) are the prevention of drug use and harm reduction. This dual function was felt to be best placed at a local level. The organisation of health care delivery in England during the 1980s permitted a layered response, commencing in the community, but it remains to be seen how this will develop with the new purchaser/provider relationship in the NHS.

For the alcohol misuser, a similar emphasis is placed on responding to the individual in the community, commencing with health education in alcohol awareness. Where patients contact services, a variety of aims of care need to be available. These may vary from advice regarding sensible drinking for some through a spectrum of services to residential care, and in-patient detoxification with a goal of complete abstinence where alcohol misuse is in a dependent form, or where there are physical complications.

Alcohol misusers

Estimation of prevalence, and cost to society

In England and Wales 7% of women and 11% of men are estimated to be drinking over 'safe limits' (see Chapter 5). The cost to society of alcohol misuse was estimated in the 1980s at £2 billion per year (Maynard, 1989). The average untreated alcohol dependent patient has been estimated to cost 100 times as much to general health care as a non-alcohol dependent patient (Holder, 1987).

Levels of response

Level 1. Health education

It has proved difficult to demonstrate that education is a significant way of affecting alcohol consumption. However, at the present time there is an increased emphasis on community based education and health promotion by health authorities, local community health councils, and school and work based alcohol awareness schemes. Friends and family arguably have the greatest influence of all levels of society in aiding change in a substance misuser.

Level 2. Police, lawyers, courts

As the police are often in contact with the problems caused by excessive drinking, they should know about local treatment options. Increased alcohol awareness and increased knowledge of local voluntary services may help police to divert the habitual drunkenness offender from the legal system towards social work or medical help. However, unlike some developed countries, Britain has been slow in enabling its cities to create detoxification centres for people intoxicated in public. There the drunk person can be cared for safely, sparing the courts and the police time. However, it has been difficult to demonstrate that such centres have an impact on the long-term rehabilitation of alcoholics.

Lawyers and courts are also in a position to influence outcome when recidivist drunkenness offenders and drink-driving offenders reach the legal system: diversion to counselling or treatment can be an adjunct or an alternative to sentencing.

In the UK, drivers who lose their licence under the drink-drive laws are termed 'high risk offenders' if they have driven at or above two and a half times the legal limit (i.e. with a blood alcohol concentration of 200 mg% or over), or have refused the breath or alcohol test, or have had two or more drink-drive convictions in 10 years. The Driving and Vehicle Licencing Agency advises them that they will be required to undergo a medical examination with blood tests before their licence is returned and that in the meantime they might consider availing themselves of the alcohol problems services.

Level 3. (i) Social services

With the opportunity of contact with many population groups, the social services are in a position to recognise, assess, counsel and, if necessary, refer on problem drinkers. Statutory social services encounter alcohol-related problems via child care issues. The social worker sometimes needs to find a place of safety for the child of a parent incapable through intoxication of providing proper care. Child abuse sometimes reveals an alcohol problem in a parent, other relative or child minder.

Those helping the homeless and the young need to be aware of alcohol problems.

(ii) Probation officers

The role of the probation services includes the continuing education of the individuals with alcohol-related offences and monitoring of these types of offenders. Alcohol education projects for young offenders, and drinking drivers have been established in some areas although their efficacy in preventing further offending still needs to be demonstrated.

(iii) General practitioners and primary health care team

Primary health care services are managed in England and Wales by the Family Health Services Authority (FHSA). Encouragement and funding for training for general practitioners in their ancillary staff requires facilitation from this level.

The general practitioner, being in the front line, has opportunities for early intervention. Simple advice regarding drinking has been shown to be effective. Wallace *et al* (1988) found that 47% of those patients who had received advice and were offered brief follow-up interviews by their GPs were able to achieve a reduction in alcohol consumption compared to 25% of those patients who had not received this advice. A similar study by Anderson & Scott (1992) has shown a greater reduction in the numbers of 'at risk drinkers' in those patients who received advice than in a control group.

In patients referred by a GP to a specialist service, those offered follow-up by the specialist did not do significantly better over six months than those returned to the care of their GP (the GP being given advice and support on appropriate treatment), although the sample examined by Drummond *et al* (1990) may possibly not have been large enough to show an extra efficacy of specialist treatment if that had been small.

Box 11.1   Levels of community response to alcohol and drug misuse

Family, friends, self-help groups, health education
Employers, police, priest, courts, publicans/bar staff
Non-specialised: primary health care, general hospital, social work
Specialised: statutory, voluntary, private
   Also have educational/training role

(iv) The accident and emergency department

Recognition of alcohol-related problems, advice about drinking and diversion to appropriate treatment services are important aspects of the service provided for excessive drinkers by the casualty department. Two-thirds of male admissions to accident and emergency departments with head injuries, for example, were found to have drunk the equivalent of six pints of beer or more (Murray, 1977) and in males admitted to an acute orthopaedic ward 19% had had an accident attributable to alcohol of whom 76% were classifiable as problem drinkers (Chick *et al*, 1991).

(v) General hospitals

Screening of admissions to medical wards reveals that 15 to 20% have a current or recent alcohol-related problem, or are drinking at hazardous levels (males 50 units per week, females 35 units per week). Hospital doctors should enquire about alcohol intake and alcohol-related problems including dependent symptoms. The liaison psychiatrist can increase awareness and knowledge both about early identification and toward improving management of the patient who presents repeatedly with alcohol-related problems. Counselling on medical wards (Chick *et al*, 1985) and in out-patient departments has a significant beneficial effect on subsequent drinking (Babor & Grant, 1992).

Antenatal services can also be a point of contact for patients otherwise unlikely to present for treatment. The process of seeking help in female drinkers is different from that in men (Thom, 1986) and pregnancy may be an opportunity for identification. It has been shown to be a time when women drinking excessively can be effectively counselled about their alcohol consumption.

General psychiatric services see approximately 75% of the alcohol misusers seen by psychiatrists. While somewhat more thorough than their counterparts in general hospitals, admitting psychiatrists still fail to record alcohol consumption in a significant proportion of case notes.

Level 4. (i) Community alcohol teams

Less than one in ten individuals with alcohol-related problems are in contact with a specialist agency. The community alcohol team, established in some districts, provides alcohol education, basic treatment, and one-to-one counselling. It serves as a bridge between the community and specialist unit in support of the idea advocated by the Advisory Committee on Alcoholism (Department of Health and Social Services and Scottish Office, 1977), suggesting community treatment with specialist consultant support. Typically the team may consist of a social worker, psychologist and community psychiatric nurse with the psychiatrist offering consultation. A particularly useful role is to advise the general practitioner on detoxification at home.

Few districts, however, have a community alcohol team. This may be related to the difficulty in committing the variety of specialist resources to the team, and the uncertainty about the best methods of organisation (Clement, 1987). Stockwell & Clement (1987) in a review of existing community alcohol teams, sounded a cautionary note. Although community alcohol teams make specialist services more accessible, are quick at responding, and good at engaging patients, they are not cheap and also increase demand on central services as a result of their function.

(ii) Specialist alcohol treatment units

Ettore (1985) in a survey of alcohol treatment units, found there to be 30 alcohol treatment units in the UK although at least one has since been closed. The alcohol treatment units provide facilities for in-patient and out-patient detoxification, liaison with rehabilitation and often introduction of patients to Alcoholics Anonymous. Currently, most districts have a designated consultant for alcohol treatment services. Since implementation of alcohol treatment units in the 1960s however, the emphasis on treatment has shifted from an in-patient to out-patient setting, research having shown out-patient and day-patient treatment to be as effective as intensive in-patient treatment (Edwards & Guthrie, 1967; McCrady *et al*, 1986; see Chapter 7). However, in-patient facilities still exist in the original format, particularly for the heavily dependent, the homeless and those with severe psychiatric comorbidity, such as a suicide risk, and also for those with severe physical problems including dual dependency on other drugs.

(iii) Specialist voluntary agencies and self-help groups

Self-help in the form of Alcoholics Anonymous (and for the families, AlAnon) is easily accessible to the population (see Chapter 7). Examination of the effectiveness of AA has shown that those who have actively participated fared better than those less active (Emrick, 1987). Abstinence was enjoyed for several years by 50%, and 60% improved to an extent. A recent survey of members attending Alcoholics Anonymous (AA general survey, 1991) showed a third to be female, compared to a fifth in 1972, and the highest percentage of members to be in the 41–50 age group. Thirty-one per cent had received counselling or treatment before AA, 16% since joining AA and 28% of doctors had presented AA as a programme of treatment.

The UK has a wide range of voluntary organisations offering counselling and advice to problem drinkers and their families. Often they have a shop front. Acquarius, the Alcohol Recovery Project, the Alcohol Advice Centres, and in Scotland the Councils on Alcohol, see thousands of clients every year. They tend to have joint health and social service funding as well as raising their own funds by donations. Counselling is often by lay people who have had a special training.

(iv) Private treatment

Following the pattern in the United States, the UK at present has some 25 private residential addiction treatment clinics. Curson (1991) has drawn attention to the paradox that as the residential component of alcoholism treatment clinics in the NHS has been scaled down, the private sector has increased its number of beds. Most of these clinics use the 12-step Hazelden or Minnesota model (see Chapter 7).

Drug misusers

Historical background

Until the 1960s, drug treatment services in the UK were almost exclusively medical and concerned with the management of middle-aged opiate addicts, from the middle class and with stable backgrounds. With the increased use of amphetamines, hallucinogens and the increased number of young drug users who were injecting heroin and cocaine, the Dangerous Drugs Act in 1967 set the scene for the creation of the specialist drug treatment clinics.

From 1968–1982 the specialist clinics were the automatic centres for referral, with little treatment occurring in other areas. During the same period, non-statutory rehabilitation houses developed, but maintained a specialist status. Since the early 1980s, however, the specialist services have played a different role in the management of drug users. Generalist services – in particular at the primary health care level – are encouraged to deal with the more straightforward drug users, with the use of triage to refer more complex cases to the specialist services.

Estimation of prevalence

An attempt to estimate the extent of the problem is fraught with difficulties (see Chapter 2). Even estimates of the prevalence and incidence figures of opiate use and dependence in the UK are nebulous at the very least. The Home Office Addicts Index is the only official register of notified addicts. In addition, this notification is dependent on compliance of medical practitioners, which has already been shown to be erratic (Strang & Shah, 1985). Other national data relating to Her Majesty's Customs and Excise seizures give some indication of the amounts of drugs entering the UK, although not those available in the street setting. Little information is available regarding the Regional, District or City levels of drug misuse. Community studies, however, have suggested the extent of opiate misuse to be five times that of the Home Office Addicts Index figures (see Chapter 2). From this, it is possible to see the difficulties in estimating 'unmet' need. Future services may therefore have to be planned with estimates of 'in contact' populations, i.e. those attending treatment clinics, general practitioners, etc. and 'out of contact' populations, i.e. the hidden populations such as the homeless and those in the criminal justice system.

Estimated spending on drug misuse (Griffin, 1992) has suggested that explicit costs of drug misuse are lower than many other conditions (£315 million compared to £496 million on arthritis). However, the hidden population may add a further £100 million of costs to this original figure.

Levels of response

Level 1. Health education and self-help

The self-help approaches and purveyance of basic advice can be implemented at all levels of treatment response. Research has shown that the levels of injecting, for example, could be reduced after increased pubic awareness of the risk of HIV (Ghodse *et al*, 1987). In addition, self-detoxification by opiate addicts is not an uncommon occurrence (Gossop *et al*, 1991) although no structured study has yet been conducted in the UK. As part of general harm reduction policies, the facilities to obtain clean needles and syringes have also increased. Provision and/or exchange of needles and syringes has occurred at specially located bases or via the community pharmacist.

Level 2. Police and criminal justice system

Many drug misusers are detained in police custody because of offences related to drug use. Department of Health Guidelines (1991*b*) encourage early medical assessment and preemptive treatment of withdrawal, including short-term methadone prescription. The same functions are encouraged of prison doctors to allow for safe detoxification and aftercare.

Level 3. (i) General practitioner and primary health care team

Drug users often present to their general practitioners. A study in 1986 shows that one in five general practitioners had been contacted by patients with opiate related problems (Glanz & Taylor, 1986). At this level, the management of coexistent physical complications, the management of pregnant drug users, counselling and short-term withdrawal plans (Cohen *et al*, 1992) may all be instituted. Studies have shown simple counselling for alcohol misusers to be extremely effective, and it may be thought that a similar effect on drug users could occur. From this level, a two way bond for the community drug team can be formed.

(ii) Crisis intervention

Specialist drug crisis intervention schemes are rare. However, the presentation of many drug users is via the emergency services, such as accident and emergency, emergency psychiatric clinics and also often out of normal hospital hours. Presentation may be due to acute intoxication, withdrawal or associated comorbidities. Appropriate training and treatment of this type of presentation is required.

(iii) Care of associated comorbidities

Physical complications – A triad of approaches to physical complications is required. First, the prevention of frequently occurring associated physical complications includes: implementation of hepatitis B immunisation and needle and syringe provision. Second, harm reduction schemes should include the teaching of safe injecting and needle-and-syringe exchange schemes with appropriate monitoring (Stimson, 1991). Finally, the early treatment of drug misusers with physical complications also needs emphasis. Facilities for adequate HIV counselling and anonymous testing need further development. Although most drug users do not have registered general practitioners, one survey showed most preferred their treatment to be located there (Bennett & Wright, 1986).

Psychiatric complications – Appropriate management of the commoner psychiatric complications of drug misuse can be performed at the level 1 response or level 3 response. Where generic services are in contact with community drug teams, this early intervention can be facilitated. Indeed, integrated medical input appears to be associated with increased contact between patients and community drug teams (Strang *et al*, 1991).

Level 4. (i) District generic services/community drug team

District generic services and the community drug team can form a union to allow freedom for local general practitioners and community nurses to practise in the field with the knowledge that general psychiatric back-up is available. A recent study of the success of this team approach has been seen in the Lothian Region (Greenwood, 1992). Here, the principle of shared care between general practitioners and community drug team helped cope with the increase in drug users presenting for treatment. Other logistic advantages included: increased general practitioner training, normalisation of care for drug users, management of physical health problems and cost benefits. The concept of the visiting specialist in addictions can add further to the filtering system and, at this stage, long-term treatment plans including specialist aftercare can also be predetermined. The Community Drug Team can also act as an effective liaison for pregnancy services (Dawe *et al*, 1992).

Surprisingly little attention has been paid to the setting for drug withdrawal – either in-patient or community. In contrast with findings from the alcohol field, in-patient detoxification of heroin addicts is associated with much higher completion rates than community detoxification (Gossop *et al*, 1986).

(ii) Regional specialist services

As an adjunct to the provision of training and facilitation of community work the regional services can play a major role in the management of the complex drug user, where issues of maintenance prescriptions or injectable drugs, for example, arise.

(iii) Prescribing services

The four main models of prescribing are described in Chapter 3. Rapid withdrawal and medium term withdrawal can be easily instituted at level 3 of the treatment response. Maintenance prescription or maintenance to abstinence plans are more easily supervised at level 4.

(iv) Rehabilitation or aftercare

Types of rehabilitation and aftercare have been described in the previous chapter. Traditionally, these are specialist, involving residential programmes and are situated in the voluntary sector.

Future developments

Special needs

Some of the subcategories of individual-in-need may require slightly different treatment provision. The homeless problem drinker or drug user will require continuing residential support. Women, whose help-seeking behaviour differs from men place a greater burden on vigilance by workers in the field. Finally, the problem of drug use or problem drinking and related problems in ethnic communities is unclear, as are descriptions of their experience and expectations of treatment.

General policies

National guidance has been issued on policy and practice by advisory groups and by the Health Departments in the UK – for both drugs and alcohol. Local collaboration and implementation are then required to harness effectively the energies of the vast network of agencies. This co-ordination is required in order to promote the development of a logical and efficient treatment system.

The role of the specialist

This role could be illustrated by visualising the tip of an inverted pyramid. The base of the pyramid, the primary care services, addresses the majority of substance abuse related problems. According to the extent of generic collaboration and competence, the size of the specialist 'tip' may need to expand or contract.

In the UK, since the publication of the government white paper 'Working for patients' in 1989, greater emphasis has been placed on defining hospital services provided. To this end, there has been a greater onus placed on the psychiatrist to describe his or her role as 'provider'. Guidelines for the psychiatrist involved in the management of district drug or alcohol services have been suggested by the Substance Misuse Section of the Royal College of Psychiatrists. Four main clinical components were defined as being under the supervision of the psychiatrist – management of physical complications, counselling, management of withdrawal states and formulation of long-term treatment plans (see previous chapters for expansion of these themes).

In addition to providing senior medical input, the psychiatrist plays a major part of the institution of training for the multidisciplinary team which may comprise: trainee psychiatrists, social workers, specialist nurses and probation officers.

Finally, the psychiatrist is also now required to implement audit of existing services to improve the planning for future services.

The generic services

Enhancement of primary care facilities and increased generalist involvement are important (shown to be very effective in the management of the problem drinker, for example) in implementation of treatment services at a local level. Greater identification and intervention for drug users at the generic level was emphasised by the Advisory Council on Misuse of Drugs (1982). Expansion of district based services to 'capture' and 'retain' individuals into treatment has also been underlined (ACMD, 1988).

Specific targets

Alcohol

For the UK, *The Health of the Nation* (Department of Health, 1991*a*) has stated the aims of an alcohol policy: to reduce the proportion of men drinking more than 21 units of alcohol per week, and women drinking more than 14 units per week, by 30% by the year 2005. Other national targets should also include reducing affordability by increasing the price of alcohol and monitoring licensing laws to limit or control availability (Anderson, 1991).

Drugs

HIV/AIDS   The Department of Health (*Health of the Nation*, 1991) cites HIV and AIDS under the category of 'major cause of concern', describing it as 'the greatest new threat to public health this century'. Certainly, the spread of HIV infection among intravenous drug users can be rapid, resulting in high prevalence rates in certain populations (50% of intravenous drug users being HIV positive in Edinburgh, for example). New targets regarding injecting drug misusers have been stated in *The Health of the Nation*, 1992 document, where the government has proposed a target reduction from 20% of injecting drug misusers sharing injecting equipment in the four weeks prior to the survey point in 1990 to no more than 5% of drug misusers injecting by the year 2000.

Hepatitis B   The overwhelming publicity surrounding HIV has somewhat obfuscated hepatitis B prevalence in intravenous drug users. The reality is that hepatitis B prevalence and seroconversion is at a higher level than HIV (Farrell *et al*, 1990). The Department of Health (*Health of the Nation*, 1991) in recognising this has recommended those users 'captured in treatment' to be involved in active immunisation programmes.

Measures of outcome

There has recently been an endorsement of worthwhile goals other than abstinence. In view of this perspective and the increasing use of methadone maintenance, new outcome measures in drug misuse need to be identified. Access to treatment and rate of return to treatment after relapse needs assessment. Other measures of related behaviour, i.e. sexual behaviour in drug users, and its relation to HIV transmission, also needs examination. In the alcohol field also, measures of changed behaviour, rather than simply documenting abstinence or not, are becoming accepted outcome indicators.

Dual services

Traditionally, alcohol and drug services are managed separately. However, with increasing numbers of dually addicted patients – those dependent on alcohol and drugs – the concept of combined services needs further consideration. Arguments against combined services have been that aims of treatment are often different, i.e. some alcohol misusers return to controlled drinking rather than abstinence; the difference in age groups; and the legal versus illicit status of the substances. Raistrick (1988), however, has emphasised the overlap in manpower needs and treatment methods. In addition, both groups of patients have a high incidence of social problems. From a treatment perspective, relapse rates after treatment for both alcohol and drug misusers are similar and there is overlap in the training in preventive strategies that both require. Many patients reveal no reluctance to be involved in a combined service, feeling that the mix can be a positive influence on treatment.

General conclusions

For the UK, a clearer identification of the deficits in provision by further epidemiologically based studies is required. Integration of all levels of care – in particular general practitioners and primary health care – is needed. There should be increased provision of assessment and counselling services at local levels, with greater numbers of patients involved in community based detoxification programmes. Despite the move to community treatment some patients with special needs will require in-patient facilities. In line with this should be an increase in the number of specialists to manage such facilities and improve training programmes.

With the increasing emphasis on clinical audit, standardisation of monitoring systems may allow greater comparison of outcome between services. However, there is considerable debate about what outcome measures are appropriate. Reduction of harm associated with the drug/alcohol misuse, and better social, physical and emotional adjustment, will probably turn out to be more important than outcome measured only as abstinence from the drug.

References

Advisory Council on Misuse of Drugs (1982) *Report on Treatment and Rehabilitation.* London: HMSO.

—— (1988) *Report on AIDS and Drug Misuse*, part 1. London: HMSO.

Alcoholics Anonymous General Services (1991) *Survey of Alcoholics Anonymous in Great Britain.* York: AA General Services Office.

Anderson, P. (1991) Health of the Nation: responses. Alcohol as a key area. *British Medical Journal*, **303**, 766-769.

—— & Scott, E. (1992) The effect of general practitioners' advice to heavy drinking men. *British Journal of Addiction*, **87**, 891-900.

Babor, T. F. & Grant, M. (1992) Project on identification and management of alcohol-related problems. Report on Phase II: a randomised clinical trial of brief interventions in primary health care. Geneva: World Health Organization.

Bennett, T. & Wright, R. (1986) Opioid users' attitudes toward the use of NHS clinics, general practitioners and private doctors. *British Journal of Addiction*, **81**, 757-763.

Chick, J., Lloyd, G. & Crombie, E. (1985) Counselling problem drinkers in medical wards: a controlled study. *British Medical Journal*, **290**, 965-967.

——, Rund, D. & Gilbert, M. A. (1991) Orthopaedic trauma in men: the relative risk among drinkers and the prevalence of problem drinking in male orthopaedic admissions. *Annals of the Royal College of Surgeons of England*, **73**, 311-315.

Clement, S. (1987) The Salford experiment: an account of the community alcohol project. In: *Helping the Problem Drinker* (eds T. Stockwell & S. Clement). London: Croom Helm.

Cohen, J., Schamroth, A., Nazareth, I., *et al* (1992) Problem drug use in a central London general practice. *British Medical Journal*, **304**, 1158-1160.

Curson, D. A. (1991) Private treatment of alcohol and drug problems in Britain. *British Journal of Addiction*, **86**, 9-11.

Dawe, S., Gerada, C. & Strang, J. (1992) Establishment of a liaison service for pregnant opiate dependent women. *British Journal of Addiction*, **87**, 867-871.

Department of Health and Social Services and Welsh Office (1977) *Report of the Advisory Committee on Alcoholism. The Pattern and Range of Services for Problem Drinkers.* London: HMSO.

Department of Health (1991*a*) *The Health of the Nation.* London: HMSO.

—— (1991*b*) *Drug Misuse and Dependence - Guidelines on Clinical Management.* London: HMSO.

—— (1992) *The Health of the Nation.* London: HMSO.

Drummond, D. C., Thorn, B., Brown, C., *et al* (1990) Specialist versus general practitioner treatment of problem drinkers. *Lancet*, **336**, 915-918.

Edwards, G. & Guthrie, S. (1967) A controlled trial of inpatient and outpatient treatment of alcohol dependency. *Lancet*, *i*, 555-559.

———, Hawker, A., Hensman, C., *et al* (1973) Alcoholics known or unknown to agencies - epidemiological studies in a London suburb. *British Journal of Psychiatry*, **123**, 169-183.

Emrick, C. D. (1987) Alcoholics Anonymous: Affiliation processes and effectiveness of treatment. *Alcoholism: Clinical and Experimental Research*, **11**, 416-423.

Ettore, E. M. (1985) A study of alcoholism treatment units: some findings on units and staff. *Alcohol and Alcoholism*, **20**, 371-378.

Farrell, M., Battersby, M. & Strang, J. (1990) Screening for hepatitis B and vaccination of injecting drug users in NHS drug treatment services. *British Journal of Addiction*, **85**, 1657-1659.

Glanz, A. & Taylor, C. (1986) Findings of a national survey of the role of general practitioners in the treatment of opiate misuse: extent of contact with opiate misusers. *British Medical Journal*, **293**, 427-430.

Ghodse, A. H., Treganza, G. & Li, M. (1987) Effect of fear of AIDS on sharing of injecting equipment among drug abusers. *British Medical Journal*, **295**, 698-699.

Gossop, M., Johns, A. & Green, L. (1986) Opiate withdrawal: inpatient versus outpatient programmes and preferred versus random assignment to treatment. *British Medical Journal*, **293**, 103-104.

———, Battersby, M. & Strang, J. (1991) Self-detoxification by opiate addicts. *British Journal of Psychiatry*, **159**, 208-212.

Greenwood, J. (1992) Persuading general practitioners to prescribe - good husbandry or a recipe for chaos. *British Journal of Addiction*, **87**, 567-575.

Griffin, J. (1992) *Cost of Drug Misuse*. London: Office of Health Economics, HMSO.

Holder, H. D. (1987) Alcoholism treatment potential health care cost saving. *Medical Care*, **25**, 52-71.

McCrady, B. R., Longabaugh, E., Fink, E., *et al* (1986) Cost-effectiveness of alcoholism treatment in partial versus inpatient settings after brief inpatient treatment: 12 month outcomes. *Journal of Consulting and Clinical Psychology*, **54**, 708-713.

Maynard, A. (1989) The costs of addiction and the costs of control. In *Controlling Legal Addictions* (eds. D. Robinson, A. Maynard & R. Chester). London: Macmillan.

Murray, W. R. (1977) Head injuries and alcohol. In *Alcoholism: a New Knowledge and New Responses* (eds G. Edwards & M. Grant), pp. 228-233. London: Croom Helm.

Raistrick, D. (1988) The combined approach - still an important debate. *British Journal of Addiction*, **83**, 867-869.

Rush, B. (1990) A systems approach to estimating the required capacity of alcohol treatment services. *British Journal of Addiction*, **85**, 49-59.

Stimson, G. V. (1991) Risk reduction by drug users with regard to HIV infection. *International Review of Psychiatry*, **3**, 401-415.

Stockwell, T. & Clement, S. (1987) *Community Alcohol Teams. A Review of Studies Evaluating Their Effectiveness with Special Reference to the Experience of Other Community Teams*. London: DHSS, HMSO.

Strang, J. & Shah, A. (1985) Notification of addicts and the medical practitioner: an evaluation of the system. *British Journal of Psychiatry*, **147**, 195-198.

——, Donmall, M., Webster, A., *et al* (1991) Comparison between community drug teams with and without inbuilt medical input. *British Medical Journal*, **303**, 897.

Thom, B. (1986) Sex differences in help seeking for alcohol problems – I. The barriers to help seeking. *British Journal of Addiction*, **81**, 777–788.

Wallace, P., Cutler, S. & Haines, A. (1988) Randomised controlled trial of general practitioners' intervention in patients with excessive alcohol consumption. *British Medical Journal*, **297**, 663–668.

Index

Compiled by Linda English